ENDORSEMENTS

Todd Gates and Tom Schwind have given all of us a generous gift. This book is a guide to Godly parenting in an ungodly world. It is practical, optimistic, and even, at times, very entertaining! There is real substance throughout its pages– rich Bible study, seasoned pastoral advice, and plain common sense. Prospective parents, parents of all ages, youth workers, grandparents and great grandparents will all enjoy and benefit from this timely work!

Rev. Rob Schenck
President and Lead Missionary, Faith and Action, Washington, DC
Author of "Ten Words that Will Change America"

Parenting is one of the most challenging and rewarding endeavors in life. It is therefore incredulous that so many enter this journey with little or no training on how to model Christ's life with their children and to build into their character for a lifetime of significance and impact.

That is why I am so excited about "Heritage Parenting" by Tom Schwind and Todd Gates because they understand discipleship as the way of life as Jesus modeled it. All of us as followers of Christ are called to make disciples – and if we are parents, especially our families.

Their book gives an excellent overall view of discipleship as a process, as well as providing very practical how-to steps.

Thank you Tom and Todd for your vital contribution to raising up a new generation of Godly young men and women!

Chuck Price
Campus Crusade for Christ

Focus! Focus is a great word to use when describing this book. It easily brings parents, Sunday school teachers, pastors, youth workers, and missionaries a clear view of the importance of discipling our children. The focus is on the parent's responsibility to, from an early age, teach their children about faith in Jesus Christ. Too often parents leave this major responsibility to others rather than engaging in the leadership role themselves. This book will be a blessing to all who read and use it to raise up Godly children. I strongly suggest that this book become a text for Christian parenting classes in every church.

Rev. Dr. John D. Abbott, Jr.
Pastor of Prayer and Discipleship
Center United Methodist Church, Indianapolis, Indiana

Gates and Schwind hit the nail on the head by encouraging parents to disciple their children in faith through lifestyle living. They share in very practical ways on how we as parents can intentionally disciple and impact our children through our daily relationship with Jesus Christ. I pray that the mainline churches such as Episcopal and Anglican churches would be strategic in parents disciple[ing] their children. I strongly recommend using this book as a guide.

Bishop. Todd McGregor
Diocesan Bishop of Toliara
Episcopal Church of Madagascar

The book that will change the way you look at Christian parenting.

Heritage Parenting

A Parent's Guide to Intentionally Raising
Godly Children

Dr. R. Thomas Schwind
&
Rev. Todd Gates

Heritage Parenting

Copyright 2015 by
R. Thomas Schwind and R. Todd Gates
All Rights Reserved

Published by
SVM Media, Marysville, Ohio
A Division of SycamoreView Ministries, LLC

ISBN Number   978-0-9905280-0-5
Library of Congress Control Number- *2015903360*

God is at work telling a story of restoration and redemption through your family. Never buy into the myth that you need to become the "right" kind of parent before God can use you in your child's lives. Instead, learn to cooperate with whatever God desires to do in your heart today so your children will have a front-row seat to the grace and goodness of God.

Reggie Joiner

Table of Contents

Preface

-------from Tom Schwind-------

To Beth, Michael, Andrew and Wesley. This book is dedicated to you. Thank you for your love and patience through this writing process and in all of life. I thank God for our three boys, Michael, Andrew and Wesley. Without them, I would not have experienced the level of love God has for me. From that first day, twenty years ago, when Beth walked two miles in the rain and walked through my church office door saying, "we are having a baby," my life has never been the same. I am not deserving of the love and grace God has poured upon our family. My gratefulness overflows to God the father.

Beth, Happy Anniversary. (25 years) I am so thankful for your constant love, enduring friendship and Godly wisdom. Without your love and support this book would not have been possible.

Also, I would like to thank my parents. My mom, Cheryl Forsberg who has always supported me with her love and prayers and I would never have finished college without the encouragement of my step-dad, Ted Forsberg. My dad, Dick Schwind showed me a good work ethic in my formative years.

I want to thank my in-laws Bill and Lois Laupp for your love and support. I miss you both.

Also, I need to express a big thanks to my good friend and co-author, Todd Gates. Todd is a former college football star. Since I have known him, he has always protected me from my "blind side." I always have considered you as my brother. He has been critical in developing this book you see before you. Without his talents and perseverance this book would not have been written.

Wherever you are in this great adventure we call Christian parenting, let me be the first to encourage you to enjoy every minute of your children when they are young, and every day thereafter. What you invest into them now will pay a lifetime of dividends in the future. Not just for them, or you, but also for the world Christ died to save.

SOMETIMES IT SEEMS THAT WE ARE ILL EQUIPPED FOR THE JOB. We each have made many mistakes and will make many more. However, we can take comfort in knowing there is no perfect parent except God, our heavenly father. Be encouraged by the words of the apostle Peter's profound profession of God's redeeming power, *"Above all, love each other deeply, because love covers a multitude of sins" (1 Peter 4:8)*.

We know every child is different. What worked for your first child most likely will not have the same results on the second. Like you, your child is uniquely made. This book will give you principles and encouragement to help you disciple your child. Be creative and intentional and enjoy every stage of your child's life.

You have this book in your hands because you love God and you love your child. My prayer for you and your family is you will be obedient to God as He speaks to you about the importance of disciple[ing] your child. So relax and enjoy the adventure. You are investing in the future!

-----from Todd Gates----

Twenty some years ago I was walking out the door of University Hall at Asbury Seminary when I spotted a guy with a Bowling Green (Ohio) T-Shirt on. Since I got my Bachelor's degree in Education at Bowling Green State University, I greeted him. That moment started a lifelong friendship with a true brother in Christ. We have consulted each other in ministry throughout the years, and I have come to not only enjoy Tom but deeply respect him as a Pastor and a man of God.

I was honored when Tom approached me for some help on a special project. He asked me to do copyediting on his dissertation. After I had begun working on his project, I realized he was presenting a radical point of view I never fully considered. His paradigm-shifting doctoral work on Christian parenting begged to be shared with a wider audience. While his research was intended for academic review, the concepts, biblical insight and thoughtful analysis of his dissertation convinced me Christian parents desperately need to know this information. I have been truly blessed by my friendship and work with Tom.

Thank you to my parents, Robert and Nancy Gates for their support and encouragement throughout my ministry. To my late father for my creative problem solving skills and to Mom for instilling in me a love of reading. And to my Grandmother, Inez Scholl, who would be pleased beyond measure at the publication of this book. Also, my brother Bryan Gates for his continued encouragement over the years.

Honestly, it was a revelation for me. My amazing helpmate and wife of 26 years Ginny and I have 4 children. We worked very hard at our parenting, and I think we made mostly good choices along the way. When I read Tom's dissertation, I realized the fullness of a profound truth- that for a Christian, PARENTING IS DISCIPLESHIP. Ginny and I exposed our children to all things religious and, I pray, raised them to love God and His people. But I wonder, "how much would more their lives have been enriched had I seen that important truth when my children were little?"

As the parent of a child with a disability (Mitchel has severe autism), I have learned and come to feel privileged to disciple the unique individuals in our temporary care and help them incline their lives toward God. I need to thank Mitchel for that. A debt too great to describe here is due to my amazing wife, Ginny, for her unwavering confidence in me, my abilities and what God has been doing in my life. And a big dose of humble thanks to her for serving as the "pastor's wife" for nearly twenty years in my pastoral ministry. Done properly, it's the hardest job in the kingdom. Most of all, to her I want to express my undying gratitude; "only God knows the sacrifices you have made for Him, the Kingdom, our family and me."

Also, last but surely not least, a big thank you to each of my four unique individuals, Lucas, Mitchel, Clayton, and Chloe. I never knew the fullness of love until I met you.

A Word about our Word – Disciple[ing]

In writing this book, we ran into one of those unpredictable stumbling blocks. Honestly, you can't dream this up. Considering the book is about discipleship and helping our children become disciples you would think it would be easy to use a word to describe the active verb of "to disciple." Disciple, as you know, is a noun or object word. It is also a verb that describes the act of making a disciple. This works the same for the word "mentor." It is a person and the act that person performs, "Jim disciples Carl. Jim is discipling Steve."

Ok. Please, bear with us for some further grammar reminders. When the word "disciple' is used as a present participle, it becomes "discipling," as in "Mom is discipling Billy." Right?

Here is the crazy part. We noticed that the written word "discipling" was nearly always read as "disciplining," No matter how many times we read over it, how many times we laughed about it, when we were just reading it, in our mind we always heard the word, "disciplining." When we look at the sentences, "Mom is discipling Billy" is a far different meaning than "Mom is disciplining Billy."

Eventually, we came to the understanding that this would be a problem for our readers. We scoured the thesaurus and search engines and came up with zero words that we could use instead. So, after wracking our brains and praying over and over again, we gave up, turned it over to God and said, "we'll find something."

As we were doing final edits on the book Tom suddenly, out of nowhere, blurted out, "Let's put the 'ing' in parenthesis" and have it read "disciple(ing)." We realized the odd usage of these marks slow down our brain just long enough to realize the actual and intended word. After our moment of glee ended, we decided on brackets and agreed that we could include the perfect word, "discipling," in our book as disciple[ing]. We no longer needed to worry about people thinking that "Mom should punish Billy" instead of reading him a Bible story. And that's the tale behind the odd usage of disciple[ing] in this book.

Introduction

There is only one way to bring up a child in the way he should go and that is to travel that way yourself. Abraham Lincoln

The purpose of this book is to encourage parents to disciple their children in the life-style approach Jesus used with His disciples.

We will show that parents are God's first and best choice to disciple their children. Teachers, coaches, Sunday school teachers, youth group leaders have an important supportive role in the development of children. However, from a biblical perspective the primary influence on your children is…YOU. We will show you clearly how God sets out His plan from the Old Testament for the training of children as well as from the New Testament, and especially the Great Commission.

The church also has an important place in the disciple[ing] of our children, however it is a secondary and supportive role. Clearly, choice or circumstance keeps some parents away from their children. For them, the church can play a major role in filling the gap left by absent parents. However, parental influence is the first choice in God's kingdom.

This book addresses the issue of parents taking an active and initiating role in raising their children with the desired goal of developing them into lifelong, active disciples of Jesus Christ. As parents, we have a short and closing window to take an active role in disciple[ing] our children. Our prayer is that this book will help you make the most of your precious time together.

Now hear us clearly, we want to make a bold and universal statement–– Christian parents want to raise Godly children. Righteousness, Holiness, Christlikeness, it doesn't matter what you call it, Godly parents want Godly children. That's part of being in a mature relationship with God, wanting circumstances to be Godly. We want our world to be conformed to God's character and let God's justice rain down upon us. We want our homes to be havens of peace and comfort. We want our workplaces to be harmonious and prosperous. We want our relationships filled with camaraderie and loving-kindness.

We know that you care about these things or you wouldn't be reading this book. An important issue we wrestle with in our quest towards transformation is "what other area of my life would be better with God's presence in it?" As we work toward *"being transformed through the renewing of your minds," (Romans 12:2)* we can find that parenting fits that bill. Our intention is that this book will be a vessel God can use to bring the fullness of his grace into the lives of Christian families.

This book is not a program or workbook. It is a life changing affirmation and viewpoint based not on doing, but on being. It isn't about doing more things or adding to the busy schedule. Though we do offer ways to implement the point of view, this book tries to enable you to develop a state of mind. A worldview, if you will, through which we come to recognize the intrinsic, eternal value of parenting and its place in the kingdom of God.

This worldview centers on God and takes very seriously the command that Jesus gave to His followers. It is known to us as the Great Commission.

> *[18]Then Jesus came to them and said, "All authority in heaven and on earth has been given to me. [19]Therefore go and make disciples of all nations, baptizing them in the name of the Father and of the Son and of the Holy Spirit, [20]and teaching them to obey everything I have commanded you. And surely I am with you always, to the very end of the age." (Matthew 28:18-20)*

Forward

Our Triune God is relational by nature, so not surprisingly he created men and women in his likeness that might know him in a personal relationship and enjoy him forever. He performed the first marriage in the Garden of Eden, then told our forebearers to "be fruitful and multiply and fill the earth" (Gen 1:28). Here is the beginning of what we call the Great Commission. God wants the whole world to learn how much he loves us.

Adam and Eve did their part by starting an exponential population explosion, but because of their sin, they lost the opportunity to reproduce spiritual children. Their failure, however, does not negate the means by which God intended through faithful parenting to rise up a posterity for his glory.

From the beginning, the family became the center of religious instruction and ongoing discipleship. Lest we miss the power of a few kindred hearts knit together in love and obedience, God had the principle written in The Law of Moses (Deut. 6:4-9). Longer and more structured meetings outside the home also play a role in education, but learning takes place most naturally in the home-like relationship.

Jesus brings the model beautifully into focus in his selection of the twelve. Peter, James and John had an even closer association. While ministering to the multitudes, he develops close relationships with these followers. Together they learn what it means to seek first the Kingdom of Heaven, and to teach others to do the same. This way of life was finally bequeathed to the church in the Lord's last command: "Go and make disciples of all nations" (Matt 28:19). In effect, he told them to replicate in their lives what he had done with them.

His example brings the Great Commission into the diverse vocations of every Christian. It makes no difference whether one is clergy or laity, or what gift of the Spirit one may possess. We should not minimize special ministries, like preaching or healing, but discipling is a lifestyle, the priesthood of all believers. And it is no where more necessary than where we live every day.

After Pentecost, for a long time the Apostolic Church continued the discipling method of Jesus, meeting largely in homes for "teaching, fellowship, breaking of bread and prayer" (Acts 2:42). In varied ways, this pattern has come to the fore again and again throughout history, especially in periods of great revival.

I believe there is a yearning for this life renewing discipline today. Many persons in the church are tired of just going through routine impersonal programs. They want something more satisfying, more heart-warming – a loving relationship with God and fellow believers that overflows into society. Such joyful witness creates a mystery that may cause even previously disinterested worldlings to want the Gospel.

Many reasons can be given for the tragic predicament of the world today, and how to address the multiple issues demanding attention. The popular media makes this as obvious as it is disheartening. But however we may approach the problems in our fallen world, we must not overlook how the troubles began with irresponsible parenting and the breakdown of the family.

This book speaks to this crisis in a very timely, practical, and winsome way. With captivating simplicity, it describes how we can grow together and build up one another in the faith. Adding to the realism of the book, offering reasons for hope in the future, the process of discipleship is integrated into the foundational pillars upon which the Christian family rests.

What gives the book a ring of authenticity is the authors' own experiences in disciple making. They have traveled this road themselves, so can help us avoid some of the pitfalls on the journey. I can learn from these teachers, and confident that their wisdom can help us all grow in grace and knowledge, I commend it to you.

Dr. Robert Coleman
Distinguished Senior Professor of Evangelism and Discipleship
Gordon-Conwell Theological Seminary

Heritage Parenting

What is Heritage Parenting? In a relay race, runners must pass the baton to the next runner. The first runner passes the baton and so finishes their share of the race. The next runner carries on the baton until their portion comes to an end and they pass on the baton. The last runner crosses the finish line. Heritage Parenting recognizes the timeless nature of the Gospel and a parent's responsibility and joy of effectively transmitting the truth of the Good News on to their children through the mentoring pattern of Jesus Christ.

In spite of the rampant individualism in western society, Heritage Parents recognize the decisive nature of the Gospel. They realize that the Christian faith is a timeless truth to be passed on to their children, who will pass it on to their own children. As a Heritage Parent, you will have the joy of effectively passing on your faith to your children.

However, this passing of the faith does not happen in a vacuum. Real hindrances to this process exist. Statistics show that most young people drop out of the faith community, question or even lose the faith of their childhood. Some hindrances we cannot control, such as the nature of the worldly system. Some hindrances come out of our own ignorance of how faith is passed and disciples are made.

In the first section, we explore the common practices of passing on the faith and their ineffectiveness. Then we delve into the nature of making disciples, duplicating the pattern Jesus employed with the Twelve. After that, we equip you with knowledge about the nature of children and the processes of growing up to increase your communication and empathy. In the final section, we offer a general paradigm of Christian family, Biblical models of parenting, and principles you can apply to your own family within your own context.

Make no mistake. Heritage Parenting is NOT "Seven Steps to a Happy Family." We feel we cannot possibly tell you how to handle your personal situation. No book of parenting laws will cover every situation. However, we do believe that adopting the Biblical perspectives and principles found in this book will put you well on your way to effectively passing faith's baton to your child.

Our first prayer is this book will help you understand the importance of passing on God's heritage to your children. And since knowing and doing are sometimes disconnected, our second prayer is that this book will assist you in passing on a living faith, God's Heritage, to your children.

The Great Commission all comes down to "Heritage Parenting." The pattern that Jesus used to develop His disciples can be used to raise disciples in your own home. Your children are a gift to you, a heritage, if you will. They bless us in their childhood and they bless their community and world as they move out of our care. To implant the Gospel in them is to bless and evangelize the future.

Our Third Prayer hopes for you that when you have passed the baton, you will be able to say along with St. Paul, "… *I consider my life worth nothing to me; my only aim is to finish the race and complete the task the Lord Jesus has given me—the task of testifying to the good news of God's grace.*" (*Acts 20:24*)

Ps 127:3 Children are the heritage from the LORD, offspring a reward from him.

Ps 119:111-112 Your statutes are my heritage forever; they are the joy of my heart. My heart is set on keeping your decrees to the very end.

[Jesus] Who, being in very nature God,
   did not consider equality with God
   something to be used to his own advantage;
rather, he made himself nothing
    by taking the very nature of a servant,
    being made in human likeness.
And being found in appearance as a man,
    he humbled himself
    by becoming obedient to death—
     even death on a cross!
Therefore God exalted him to the highest place
    and gave him the name that is above every name,
that at the name of Jesus every knee should bow,
    in heaven and on earth and under the earth,
and every tongue acknowledge that Jesus Christ is Lord,
    to the glory of God the Father.

Philippians 2:6-11

Section 1

UNDERSTANDING THE ISSUES

SECTION 1 - UNDERSTANDING THE ISSUES

Chapter 1 – The World We Know

The typical parent spends less than one hour per week in meaningful interaction with each of his or her children.
Researcher George Barna

The world's many dangers make parenting a tricky business. No longer is it enough just to provide the physical needs of our offspring. Instead of the daily challenges faced by earlier generations, we often feel overwhelmed by our new parenting struggles. In real ways, we face obstacles unimaginable to earlier generations of Christians. The challenges and temptations confronting our children would boggle the imaginations of our ancestors.

Every type of sin and vice flaunts itself (and many can be found after a quick search on the Internet). Everywhere we see an invitation to covet and a multitude of opportunities to be separated from our money. We find many appeals to provide salvation through government, through a movement, through a product, through social acceptance, through many things. Our children can easily respond to the lure of other, "cooler" religious messages.

We have a multitude of opportunities to sin. Though we like to think of ourselves as more advanced than historical figures, we are not really, not in the "human department." Even a quick read of the Bible and historical documents shows that people have not changed. Those historical stories describe people behaving the same way folks do today. It's not exactly a stretch to say we see the same stories in the Bible as we do on TV. King David's little incident involving Bathsheba would make a juicy drama indeed. (*2 Samuel 11 & 12*)

The Bible still describes us accurately today because human nature, our character apart from grace, has not changed. Circumstances, technologies, and culture have dramatically changed but human hopes and dreams, faults and limitations have not. Likewise, the egocentric, rebellious heart of man has never altered. It was the same for Moses as in Jesus's day, and the story remains the same today. Through all the blessings and benefits we now enjoy, we are still as stubborn and stiff-necked, as self-centered as any generation that ever lived.

Hundreds of generations before us, faithful parents toiled tirelessly at keeping their children safe from harm. They wanted for their children the same things we want; blessing and happiness. Those parents worked hard to make sure their children were fed and clothed and taught an occupation. Children and grandchildren learned from their extended family who provided for each other. They warned them about the consequences of sin but never had to deal with the information society's massive opportunity for temptation.

No longer is praying for our daily sustenance enough. We live in a culture "rich in things and poor in soul", unsupportive of the practice of Christian faith, often hostile even to the mention of the name of Jesus. We live in an era where the church has become afraid to take a stand on Godly truth. Organizational development and church growth have taken the place of evangelism, and hollow optimism replaces the gospel in some pulpits.

Unsurprisingly, young adults leave the church in record numbers. Most young people seek purpose and answers for living their life. Studies show they would actually prefer to find answers through the beliefs of their parents. However, the world provides answers which seem simple and apparent enough - more power, more status, more money, more things. But the truth is, that the world's answers have never worked in the long term. They only *seem* to be the right answers: solutions to the questions posed by the world, in the world's terms and while using human philosophy. How do you get justice? Revenge. How do you receive blessing? Buy it. How do you deal with pain? Lawsuit.

Our children grow into adulthood in a society that fails to see the real issues like suffering, inferiority, and desire. Not to mention the reality of evil. So, in a real sense we try to teach our kids to be deeper, more complex, more global thinkers than society can recognize. It's not society's fault, what can you expect from leaders and followers who don't look to God and the wisdom of Holy Scripture for guidance? It's all a little more complicated for a Christian wanting to believe that, "The real trick for living is loving people and using things– not the other way around."

We want to teach our kids to do well, to be successful, to be joyful. Our heart's desire is for them to follow God's ways because He is the source of all wisdom. Since God authored the universe and every living thing therein, who could have better advice on how to deal with the problems of living? But we look around us and see a world geared toward providing ungodly wisdom and self-centered life solutions.

This Goliath of secular values comes to the battle lines armored in worldly wisdom, with the weapon of media, camouflaged in "relevant" churches and infiltrating our home with the thinly veiled idols of popular culture.

We anxiously ask ourselves, "How do I, a flawed sinner saved by grace, compete against the juggernaut of society?" This Goliath of secular values comes to the battle lines armored in worldly wisdom, with the weapon of media, camouflaged in "relevant" churches and infiltrating our home with the thinly veiled idols of popular culture. Often our children's peers have already been co-opted with those ungodly assumptions and mindset.

The prognosis seems bleak. Truly, society may have broken the faith: the church may have missed the boat; we parents may have even fallen short but the gospel of Jesus Christ cannot fail our children. So let's not despair, there is actually plenty of good news.

Section 1 – Understanding the Issues

APPLICATION

List two or three things that you learned or found interesting:

1

2

3

Reflection and Discussion Questions

1) What issues do your children deal with (or will deal with) that you didn't have to growing up?

2) What is an issue you had to deal with growing up that your parents didn't have to deal with?

3) What were your parent's issues growing up?

4) What do you think about this statement, "Our earth is degenerate these days; there are signs that the world is speedily coming to an end; bribery and corruption are common; children no longer obey their parents; and the end of the world is evidently approaching." - a message carved on an Assyrian stone tablet.[1]

5) What are your thoughts about the Assyrian quote? Do you think our culture is getting better, staying the same or heading south? Why? What are the implications as parents?

Chapter 2 – Parents: the Most Important Influence

> *Children have never been very good at listening to their elders, but they have never failed to imitate them.* James Baldwin

Who do you think has the most influence on your children's spiritual and religious life? Given all the press, all the hype, we think you'll be surprised to hear the answer. It may make you pause, even feel a little intimidated, but the truth is out there. Research shows parents still influence their children more than any other single factor!

Recent studies verify the wisdom of the Bible regarding nurturing and raising children. The Bible clearly shows parents being the ones God has given the privilege and responsibility of raising the next generation of Christians. We know the importance of our children to our families and to our hearts. If you ever cooed over a baby picture, you know we are wired to love our children. And yet, we rarely reflect on their eternal importance. Those precious children hold the key to the future of the gospel, and we have been given the holy privilege of leading them to become strong, effective disciples of Jesus Christ.

We have seen too many ridiculous surveys and pollsters pretending to measure up to the truth standards of scriptures. We observe that newscasters often cite surveys as if they were truth, or justification of certain positions on issues. Certainly, this means something in a democracy, but often they are little more than a high tech way of saying "see, everybody's doing it."

Scripture stands alone as the great rock of authority. However, we do accept the wise use of surveys when looking at people's attitudes. In our research here, we have included thoughtful studies from some great Christian thinkers to show a wider perspective and to encourage parents. We want to show you how important you are to your children. Even when feeling as if we have little impact on our children's spiritual life, nothing could be further from the truth.

Parents, you are far more influential in your children's spiritual development than you realize. Additionally, the fact that parents don't understand their importance can, itself, be detrimental to our children. Consider this from researcher George Barna:

> *...surveys point out that most parents underestimate the influence they can exert on their children. Consequently, they often neglect emphasis upon activities that would strengthen their relational bond with the children. Many parents, even those who are born again Christians, also overlook the need to foster a deeper connection between their children and God, or to enhance the child's worldview as a critical component of their decision-making skills.*[2]

Barna's research shows that most of us don't realize the power of parenting. Because of that, we often overlook opportunities to develop that influence further. Partly because parents bought into the mindset that we don't really matter, we don't clearly see the payoff in disciple[ing] our children. (Please see "A Word about our Word" on page vii of the front matter for why we use this particular spelling of discipling.) Even though a deep connection with God remains the most valuable inheritance we can pass on, our parental "low self-esteem" gets in the way.

The revealing book *Soul Searching: The Religious and Spiritual Lives of American Teenagers* [3] by Christian Smith and Melinda Lunquist Denton is based on one of the largest ever surveys taken in regards to teenagers in America. The National Study of Youth and Religion (NSYR), is a comprehensive survey of over 3,300 teenagers that included in-depth follow-up interviews with over 250 of the respondents.

It may be hard to believe but research shows most teens are quite content to follow in their parents footsteps and the vast majority are happy simply to accept the one religion in which they were raised.

The findings in this study are consistent with the other research we found. For example, two surprising and hopeful findings about teens jumped out at us, "Most are quite content to follow in their parents footsteps."[4] In like manner, we discovered "the vast majority are happy simply to accept the one religion in which they were raised."[5]

This important study exposes the deep desire kids have to learn from their parents and to connect with the values their parents consider important. Given all the hype about the rebellious nature of young people, this information could certainly come as a surprise. But this is only the beginning of the surprises.

Given all the pushback of youth, parents have been led to believe teenage rebellion is normal. However, this large study gives an equally gargantuan finding on the importance of the parents influence on their children's spiritual development. "Contrary to popular misguided cultural stereotypes and frequent parental misperceptions, we believe that **the evidence clearly shows that the single most important social influence on the religious and spiritual lives of adolescents is their parents.**"[6]

You should feel empowered now that you are beginning to unlearn the false lessons of our culture. Parents are important! YOU ARE CRITICAL to the spiritual future of your children. Regardless of what pop culture tells us, our kids not only need, but WANT, a common path to salvation. Both kids and parents can become confused by the media's messages of teenage rebellion but the reality is somewhat different. Teenagers separating themselves from their parent's identity is nothing new.

Bringing this subject even further into the light is more research by Princeton Seminary Professor Kenda Creasy Dean. As *Professor of Youth, Church and Culture*, she did extensive follow-up work with the teens from the original NSYR study we mentioned above. This extension of the research of Christian Smith (*Soul Searching*) is found in her book *Almost Christian: What The Faith Of Our Teenagers Is Telling The American Church*[7] goes into greater detail, spending more time with the same teenagers who were part of the original survey.

Dean's findings confirmed the importance of the parents teaching their children. In fact, second of the five major findings from her research is, **"Most U.S. teenagers mirror their parents' religious faith."**[8] Isn't that amazing? Parents interpret the things we see and hear so differently. We too often let the popular wisdom color our views and assume our children don't want to share our religious faith.

As parents, we need to grab hold and cling to the job of disciple[ing] our kids. Parenting rarely finds success in an overnight miracle and raising children in the faith similarly takes time. But that faith download takes on such importance when Dean writes, **"Parents matter most when it comes to the religious formation of their children**. While grandparents, other relatives, mentors and youth ministers are also influential, parents are by far the most important predictors of teenagers' religious lives."[9]

Later on in this book, we will explain in greater detail the important of the parent's faith to their children's faith. Just as a teacher cannot impart knowledge they don't have, neither can a parent pass on a faith they don't own. However, in our ministry we have discovered that even the least theologically astute parent who instills in their child a loving loyalty to God has presented them with a valuable treasure.

We sum up with another of Dean's findings, **"The best way to get most youth more involved in and serious about their faith communities is to get their parents more involved in and serious about their faith communities."**[10] Being in relationship with your child and being in love with God cannot help but to inspire the same growing faith in the hearts of your child.

APPLICATION

List two or three things that you learned or found interesting:

1

2

3

Reflection and Discussion Questions

1) What's something your parents used to say to you as a child that you promised yourself you'd never say, but now you catch yourself saying all the time?

2) Who has made the biggest impact on you? Explain.

3) What do you think about this statement, "Research shows parents still influence their children more than any other single factor!"

4) What was the most meaningful statistic or insight you gained from this chapter? Why?

5) Are you encouraged or discouraged from your findings?

6) Is it a good thing that your children will mirror your faith? What can you do to make this mirror clearer?

Chapter 3 – Fallen Away: Describing the Problem

The recognition of sin is the beginning of Salvation.

Martin Luther

When Brandon went off to college he quickly knew, "We're not in Kansas anymore, Toto." He found new acquaintances with different values and wildly different perspectives. He met and made friends with Dave. His quick wit and funny banter made Brandon feel at ease and comfortable. They enjoyed going to campus events together and like many young adults off at college they stayed up late having fun on Saturday night. Brandon had been used to getting up early and going to church with the family. Left to his own devices, he often slept in Sunday mornings. Not that he wanted to skip church; he simply didn't have the skill or motivation to find a new church and church family. And unlike the classroom, nobody was taking attendance.

As Brandon grew to interact with more people, he found many who did not share his worldview, some who were openly dismissive of the very existence of God. These people were often smart and successful. Brandon began to attend church only when he went home. He began to find activities with more immediate payoffs than Bible Study or Youth Group. His growing independence seems to conflict with a creed that teaches total dependence on God as the way, the truth, and the life.

Soon, Brandon, slips away from the faith of his family and becomes what many are calling the "DeChurched." He has come to talk about hypocrisy and empty ritual in the church. He hasn't necessarily given up on God, but the world in front of his face is the world he focuses on. Brandon even uses the phrase, "Spiritual but not religious." He says he wants to be a good person, but he just has priorities other than "religion."

Brandon is not alone in this. He and millions of young men and women like him have become the rule rather than the exception. This phenomenon can be noted from recent surveys showing that college-age students are leaving the church in droves. One study indicates that between 70% and 88% of Christian teens are leaving the church after their first year of college.[11] Many other studies confirm this disastrous trend. One chilling example is the *2002 Report of the Southern Baptist Council on Family Life*. Their research showed that 88 percent of children over age eighteen from evangelical homes leave the church. You don't need a report alone to prove that point. Ask a parent, they will confirm the reality of those studies.

Now, we need to deal with a difficult truth. Though sometimes hard to hear, the truth is a great blessing. Honesty may be painful but "the truth will set you free." We make this connection from love, knowing that you would not even be reading this book if you didn't love your children and deeply care about their future.

So, don't feel harshly judged when we say that the research leads us to conclude that parents have generally failed to pass on their faith to their children. Since children are not fully discipled, and parents remain God's first choice in the discipleship process of children, then it seems clear where the responsibility lies. Using our God given intelligence, Christian humility and our desire for our children's success we acknowledge that we parents *"have fallen short of the glory of God." (Romans 3:23)*

Instead of heaping guilt upon ourselves, we offer our failings to Christ. Instead of living in dread for our children, we turn to a God who says, "Fear not."

This is bitter medicine that must be taken. The first step to healing means admitting we have been disappointing in providing the fullness of what is needed. Instead of heaping guilt upon ourselves, we offer our failings to Christ. Instead of living in dread for our children, we turn to a God who says, "Fear not."

When we read these disastrous statistics on youth in the church, there seems good reason to accept the idea parents have fumbled the ball. Clearly, we don't parent in a vacuum. Powerful forces draw our eyes away from the prize, and **it is clear that we have been ill-informed and under-equipped to properly disciple our children**.

The good news we find here shows that as families and society lose our connection with God we fall away from Him. While this may seem "odd good news" this shows that getting back to Godly principles and obedience will transform our children and eventually our society. Truly, there is no better first place to look for the root of the problem, and its solution, than to look in the mirror. While attributed to different sources, this thought makes the point, "First, be the change you want to see in the world."

On our own, we cannot change society. However, with God's help we can change ourselves. That is the first step in changing the future for our children. It's a solid principle in system analysis to understand that changing one factor in a system influences everything that relates to it. If we can let God change us within our family system, we gain the ability to change everything else. So, our key to changing the trajectory of our children's lives is to change ourselves. Far from being condemning, we present this as positive and hopeful news!

In any quandary, the first step is always to identify the problem. Then we need to see how changes in our attitudes and actions can help bring about change. Admitting that we have not done all that we could do should not produce a guilt trip. Not at all. We don't want to simply shame parents into doing something different. However, covered by grace, that same guilt can be useful in leading us back to God. A time of holy reflection can be a powerful thing. We trust that when feeling badly about our failings, our heavenly father is ready to redeem and restore us.

Once covered by grace, both remorse and guilt can be a path to healing and useful in leading us back to God.

Our goal here is to frame the context of our concerns about the world at this moment. From first identifying the problem, through leaning on God for our strength, to changing ourselves, we can turn these problems into solutions through grace.

After extensive research, we find we strongly agree with Barna as he lays out the seven reasons why parents do not do well in disciple[ing] their children. We believe that George Barna's research reveals the truth about Christian parenting taken as a whole. When we look at the hard truth here, it might sound harsh. But remember the Lord said, *"If you hold to my teachings, you really are my disciples. Then you will know the truth and the truth will set you free." (John 8:31, 32)*

When we first read Barna's research, we were tempted toward lamentation. However, as in repentance that brings salvation, we need to change our way of thinking before we can change our actions. Below we read Barna's summary of his research.

> *The survey data indicate that parents generally rely upon their church to do all of the religious training their children will receive. Parents are not so much unwilling to provide more substantive training to their children as they are ill-equipped to do such work. According to the research, parents typically have no plan for the spiritual development of their children; do not consider it a priority, have little or no training in how to nurture a child's faith, have no related standards or goals that they are seeking to satisfy, and experience no accountability for their efforts.* [12]

Reading that paragraph can be an eye opener, or perhaps a swift kick in the head. But if you read that quote like we did the first time (that is, while focusing on our failings as parents) then you are missing the great news. After re-reading it, the most important takeaway for us is this, **"Parents are not so much unwilling…as they are ill-equipped."** Wow, THAT is good news. Surveys show that Christian parents do care deeply about our kids' spiritual upbringing. The problem is that we don't know what to do. We care about our kids, but lack tools to implement our loving intentions. Frankly, being motivated and lacking knowledge brings us a lot closer to a solution than knowledge and apathy.

So, let's take the motivation out of the equation. That's been settled. Now we can look at why we don't seem to be effective. The following seven lessons can be gleaned from the research. For better or worse, these lessons give us a powerful starting place to help our beloved children become the beneficiaries of faith. Here is where we go from raising children we desire to have faith to helping them become living disciples of Jesus Christ. Here are the seven ways parents generally fall short in raising our children into a living faith that permeates their life. This list is from George Barna's conclusions from his research.

Seven Reasons Parents Miss the Mark

Parents:

1) Generally rely upon their church to do all of the religious training their children will receive.

2) Are not so much unwilling to provide more substantive training to their children as they are ill-equipped to do such work.

3) Typically have no plan for the spiritual development of their children.

4) Do not consider spiritual growth a priority.

5) Have little or no training in how to nurture a child's faith.

6) Have no related standards or goals they are trying to reach.

7) Experience no accountability for their efforts. [13]

When we know what problems exist, we can begin to address them. It's a lot like when your car's "check engine" light first comes on. Once you notice the warning you can go about fixing the problem.

If you own a car, this has probably happened to you. Your important and very expensive possession makes a noise that sounds suspiciously broken. You realize that if you ignore the warning signs you're likely to end up by the side of the road (hopefully in an area with cell phone coverage). You take the malfunctioning auto to the mechanic who tests the car and cannot hear the noise. It's extra frustrating that you nursed it into the shop, and then the vehicle stopped making that noise. It quit screeching, squealing, grinding, humming, or rattling. Nothing. Besides being highly annoying, not knowing what is wrong makes it much harder to fix. Thank God, He has illuminated our family's warning light so we won't be stranded by life's roadside with no hope of rescue.

The research has been done, and we know what is wrong. Remember, these are based on surveys of a large group of people. They may or may not apply to you. However, we recommend you spend time in prayer and reflection before discarding any reasons out of hand. Rejecting good data because we don't like what it says is the same as lying to the doctor because we don't want to have a certain disease. The doctor needs the truth!

A word about "Solution Goals"

In the coming exploration of the reasons parents are often ineffective about raising a child with spiritual power, we will end each exploration with a "SOLUTION GOAL." The Solution Goal concludes the writing with a short statement of the direction we need to be traveling to overcome the obstacles. That statement intends only to wrap up the chapter about where parents have been with a brief declaration of where we're going.

Section 1 – Understanding the Issues

APPLICATION

List two or three things that you learned or found interesting:

1

2

3

Reflection and Discussion Questions

1) How have you been disillusioned by religion? (the church/Christians/ church leadership)

2) Do you know any "Brandons" who have fallen away from God?

3) What are your thoughts when you think about whether your children are willing to accept your God?

4) How is God comforting you with these words from page 12? "Instead of heaping guilt upon ourselves, we offer our failings to Christ. Instead of living in dread for our children, we turn to a God who says, 'Fear not.'"

Chapter 4 – You Don't Know What You Don't Know

"I've been saying it so long to you, you just wouldn't listen. Every time you said 'Farm Boy do this' you thought I was answering 'As you wish' but that's only because you were hearing wrong. 'I love you' was what it was, but you never heard."

William Goldman, The Princess Bride

For over a century, Mr. Charles Duell, has been maligned in the press and popular mythology. In what we now know is an urban legend, Duell was misquoted as stating, "Everything that can be invented, has been invented." The poor guy reaped such criticism since 1899 because he was then Commissioner of the U.S. Patent office. This rumor can surely damage your credibility when you run the invention recording office. However, this quote actually came from the humor magazine of the day, "Punch," and not from Mr. Duell's lips.

This phony credit became so believable because it seems like it could be true. In our lifetime, we have seen many astounding events and inventions. The Space Shuttle, the Human Genome project, the Internet: who could have foreseen these revolutionary inventions? Who knows what will be next? It seems absurd someone could say that everything possible has been invented. However, the problem comes about with our inability to predict the future advances in technology and human ingenuity. And why is that? *Because we don't know what we don't know.*

How could anyone make allowances for ideas beyond their frame of reference? Only prophets and a few gifted artists and scientists have that ability. How could anyone act on information they don't have. For example, say you saw the daily news and noticed the stock market report. If you knew what you didn't know about the stock market, you could make a lot of money. Same thing goes for Las Vegas. How about predicting movie sales or the next great product? Accurate predicting of the future could be very good for you.

The craziest thing happens when we gain knowledge; we suddenly realize the amount of things we don't know. Education opens our eyes to the many possibilities involved in our field of study (whether it is physics or families). Answering questions creates more questions. Interestingly, in Jesus's time, a rabbi would teach by asking (not answering) questions. In a weird way, learning makes you become smarter but feel dumber.

In this chapter and the next, we will be talking about the difficulties faithful families have because of things most parents don't know and have never been taught. How could we know, having never been taught? Is it your fault? Absolutely not! Can your family benefit by learning them? Truly yes!

Not Unwilling, Just Ill-Equipped

Lesson 1 - Parents are not so much unwilling to provide more substantive training to their children as they are ill-equipped to do such work.

We live in a culture under the authority of experts. Knowledge is so vast and specialized that certain people, highly trained in narrow fields and letters after their name, tell us what to think about nearly everything. (And celebrities seem to give us their opinion on everything else.) When somebody starts spouting off an opinion we don't like we might respond with, "Who made you an expert?"

We bow to authorities in many areas. Often we have no choice. And worse, many times the experts disagree. How many nights have we looked at the evening news consisting of dueling experts opining on the economy, business, government and everything else of interest. Want to know how to think about something? An expert will tell you. We have been trained to bow to the greater intellect, education, or degrees of an expert.

That is not all bad. Obviously, knowledge is a good thing. My doctor went to medical school and knows more about medicine than I do. Praise God. But still, medical mistakes cost the lives of thousands every year. It is my to duty to make informed decisions because the results impact me far more than the doctor.

One smart lady gave Todd's wife Ginny some sage advice about dealing with their son Mitchel's disability. Under pressure to buckle to an inappropriate treatment under a specialist, Ginny's friend told her, "**They may be the expert in their field but YOU are the expert on your child**." Isn't that true?

You are the expert on your family! You are the expert on your child!

You see, part of our church wide family discipleship problem exists because we have fallen for the "expert ideal." Naturally, parents look to the church to help develop our children spiritually. Our admiration of experts and our own low self-esteem about spiritual matters lead some parents to believe they are not qualified. Certainly, experts know more about their field but we can enlist their help without abandoning our duty.

YOU are the expert on your family, YOU are the expert on your child.

Let us be clear here. It is not that parents don't care; it's that they think they can't do the job. This book exists to tell you not only that you MUST be the primary influence on your child's spiritual growth but that you CAN be. Fulfilling your God-given role remains a parent's responsibility. You don't need to do it alone. It is often wise to bring in some additional consultation in the development of your child. Thankfully, God has given many good advisors to help you. However, He has given you the primary role of mentor to your children.

SOLUTION GOAL –

EQUIP YOURSELF WITH KNOWLEDGE

Untrained

Lesson 2 - Parents have little or no training in how to nurture a child's faith.

Steve stood by for the "rec" league softball game with a tight smile. He would try nearly anything and never let his lack of athletic ability interfere with his ability to have fun with his friends. Tonight he played as a substitute for a friend. Without enough players, it would have been a forfeit, so Steve agreed to stand in. "I hate to admit it," Steve lamented, "But I've never played softball or baseball. I've been to a lot of games, but I never had the opportunity to actually put a bat in my hands and try to hit a pitch. So, even though it's slow pitch softball, I'm a little nervous because I've never been taught how to bat." After striking out on three pitches, Steve came back to the bench with a grin. "Wow, that's a lot harder than it looks," he laughed. "Maybe somebody can teach me how to bat and I'll get some practice. I think I might be able to do this with some coaching."

Another reason parents do not actually disciple their children is they have little training in how to nurture a child's faith. Like Steve, many parents are already in the game when they suddenly realize they really don't know what they're doing. Again, parents want their kids to grow in faith but are ill-equipped. One of those reasons is that no one has taught them what works, how to play the game. It seems like a no-brainer, but teaching is harder than it looks. This is especially true when we have no confidence in the subject.

So, wanting to solve the problem (and continuing to avoid the blame game) we ask ourselves this question, "Why do most parents not have the training to nurture their child's faith?" We believe there are several reasons. First, many if not most local churches have not made this particular ministry a major focus. This is true regarding children but basic training at all levels is severely lacking all over God's kingdom. A lack of confidence in doctrine and a post-modern acceptance of all views as equally valid negates their importance in the minds of many Christians. Holding these views inevitably leads to a decline in both evangelism and discipleship.

21

The second reason is that most parents have not seen the process in action, so they can't help but be unaware of the importance of discipleship. It is difficult to replicate what we do not know. In one church, we know of a Sunday School class called the "New Seekers Sunday School Class." You would think this would be a group of youth or young adults. This was true when the class first formed, but now the group averages age 50-65. The parents of the "New Seekers" still attend the class they formed when they were younger. No organized class existed for the current young adults. They were too busy and focused on other things. They had never experienced intentional discipleship. And, like most people, they never conceived discipleship as the path to raising the next generation.

The third reason is parents fail to see the need to nurture a child's faith. Struggling parents ask, "Do we really need to add something else to our busy life?" Or they wonder, "Won't the Holy Spirit just give my child the gifts of the Spirit? Won't that be enough?" For most people, no immediate downloading of gifts occurs but a gradual "transforming of the mind" brings the power of Christ into their daily living. Miracles clearly happen, however, God usually works powerfully in the daily nurturing into the image of Christ.

SOLUTION GOAL –

GET ADDITIONAL TRAINING

Over-Reliance on Church

Lesson 3 - Parents generally rely upon their church to do all of the religious training their children will receive.

As pastors with over forty years of combined experience we have often witnessed parents who experience this same sentiment. When we went for our theological education we went to outstanding schools with highly learned professors. So, we agree that expert education touches lives. Both of us can tell you of professors like Dr. Robert Coleman, Dr. David Bauer, and Dr. Joseph Wang, brilliant men whose tutelage changed our lives. But as pastors who worked with many families, we can verify the power of a solid base given in a Christian home.

Parents often feel unhappy with their own level of theological understanding, sometimes with good reason. On occasion, the most Godly of parents do not have the vocabulary to talk about the complex theologies behind finding salvation and living a Christian life. Most parents turn our kids over to experts to teach our kids reading, history, and mathematics. We ask, "Why not Christianity, as well? After all, that is how our culture trains children. So, why not simply trust the experts?"

We call on parents to let Sunday School teachers and youth pastors be a supplement to their children's spiritual education and not the center of it.

We have much more to expand on this as the book rolls on, but let's keep in our mind that following Christ is relational. A parent experiencing the fullness of grace along with their family feels much more like Christ's church. The relational aspect touches kids more deeply than downloading facts about grace. Don't get us wrong, we give thanks to God for all the caring and knowledgeable Sunday school teachers. But, we call on parents to let Sunday School teachers and youth pastors be a supplement to their children's spiritual education and not the center of it.

Also significantly, children and youth ministry clearly serves a need for children whose parents remain unchurched or who have little interest in the spiritual upbringing of their children. It is disturbing how many parents choose to be left out of the child's spiritual training process. To those families we happily say, "Let the church teach your children. We will take good care of them and teach them lessons that will enrich their entire life."

We have witnessed countless parents coming back to church after their first child was born. It seems like God pushes people's reset button when children come into their lives. Without question, having the parents come back to church is a great thing. However, there is a tendency to think taking a child to church and/or children and youth ministry is enough in the spiritual nurturing of their children. After all, it is better than nothing, right? Absolutely true. **But we think that God has more for us and our children than "better than nothing."**

Certainly there is nothing wrong with picking a church because it has a strong youth group or children's ministry. But, are we asking questions to find out if they nurture adults too? Is this a church where God has called me to be? Is it a place to serve and be obedient to God? Parents must also look at the Biblical teaching and discipleship for adults so they too can grow, when looking for a home church.

SOLUTION GOAL –

INSTRUCT YOUR OWN CHILD

APPLICATION

List two or three things that you learned or found interesting:

1

2

3

Reflection and Discussion Questions

1) Where did you receive most of your understanding about God while growing up?

2) "You are the expert on your child!" What are your thoughts about this statement?

3) What specifically do you need to do to be better equipped for the wonderful adventure of Godly Parenting? (Good news!! We hope part of this answer includes studying this book.) You have already started by having this book in your hand, this is why this book was written.

4) In your life, what possible ways might exist for you to get training?

5) Have you begun to understand what you "don't know?"

Chapter 5 – If You Fail to Plan, You Plan to Fail

"It does not do to leave a live dragon out of your calculations, if you live near him."   J.R.R. Tolkien, The Hobbit

Early American wit, inventor, scientist and founding father, Benjamin Franklin, used to say, "If you fail to plan, you are planning to fail." This truism points out that few complex things in life happen by accident. When we want something, we can often have the object of our desire by setting a goal and working toward it. By determining our desired outcome, breaking the process down into "bite-sized" chunks and then accomplishing small tasks we can achieve that goal. Or as mouse and media mogul Walt Disney used to like to say, "Make our dreams come true." However, he didn't turn his cartoon mouse into an entertainment empire by wishing on a star.

Not only should you plan once you set your goal, you need to have a suitable goal. You need a doable goal. As Jesus said, *"Suppose one of you wants to build a tower. Won't you first sit down and estimate the cost to see if you have enough money to complete it?" (Matthew 14:28).* Though he was talking directly about the cost of following Him, Jesus points out the importance of knowing what you are getting into before you can make a wise choice. This type of planning allows you to have confidence in your goal.

In any case, be wise and responsible with your life by thinking things through properly. Jesus says to even think deeply about following Him and see if it will be worth it. (We can assure you it is!) Everything has a cost. Plan for it and be ready when it comes.

In this chapter, there will be four additional lessons that parents need to learn. These lessons revolve around another business notion that says, "Proper planning prevents poor performance." We see how the failure to plan, follow the plan, and gather support have put families on the defensive. We believe this truth can easily be explained by the fact that no one has taught parents that it is permissible to set family spiritual goals and then work toward them in your daily life.

Understanding you have the same permission to work toward God's spiritual riches will open up a new level of freedom for you and your family. Seeking to grow in faith and follow God in your daily family life is not only acceptable, it is your birthright as a child of God. Learning what many parents have done wrong will be a tremendous step in deciding what you will do right. Planning empowers blessing.

Not a Priority

Lesson 4 - Parents do not consider Spiritual Formation a priority.

Another major reason why parents don't disciple their children is parents do not consider it a priority. This makes sense, doesn't it, when we've seen well-meaning Christian parents pass off their spiritual responsibility completely to the church or to youth groups? "Somebody else is more qualified to do it, right?" But isn't this somewhat like feeding kids doughnuts and Pepsi for their meals while reasoning, "They can eat what they want at home, after all, they get a nutritious meal at school."

Most of us have never questioned the way faith passes to the younger generation. We take kids to church and let the church minister to them. "Isn't that how it's always been? It's just going to happen, right? I give my kids an education; they get a job. I give my kids food; they grow. We grow they grow; it's natural, right?" It's not that average parents think spiritual growth should be on the bottom of the priority list; it's that we seldom think of it at all. When parents do think about passing on our faith, we often simply think, "why worry about it?"

The real question we must honestly ask ourselves is this, "What is God's priority for parents?"

The real question we must ask is, "What is God's priority for parents?" Here is the crux of this discussion of this book. As we'll be discussing in depth later on in the book, God commands parents to be the major influence in the spiritual development of their children.

If parents live our lives separated from God's ways regarding the nurturing of our Christian offspring, what will be the end result?

Looking at the condition of children in our society forces us to see the devastation brought about by ignoring God. The plain and simple fact is that children (people) need God. The more God they get, the better life turns out.

Human beings usually try to take the path of least resistance. Whether traveling or goal seeking we try to maximize our results while minimizing our efforts. This characteristic has served humanity well as we developed the agricultural, medical, and building technologies serving our species. After all, "Necessity is the mother of invention."

We call this a great blessing until the "minimizing of efforts" becomes the goal itself. In our super-committed world, the all-too-common outlook regarding raising children means parents taking the path of least resistance. It is infinitely easier in the short run to let kids have their way and do what they want. (It is certainly quieter!) But that is not usually what's best for our children.

Tom tells the story about working in a grocery, "Shortly after I got out of college I took a job as the bagger at a grocery store. This was long before I had children of my own. Working the register in the candy canyon meant I got to see lots of parenting in action. I noticed two main techniques for dealing with children asking for the sweet treats lining both sides of the checkout line."

"On the one hand, a child asks for candy and the parents responds with a 'no', or a 'not now,' and the sugary delight never makes it into the child's hand. On the other hand, another child asks for the all-too-obvious sugary treat and the parent says, 'no' or 'not now.' At this point, that child begins to whine, or cry, or act up. The parent gets angrier, and the child gets whinier. Eventually, the child ends up with a mouthful of candy and the parent finishes the trip to the grocery with a bad mood. There are many variations on that theme, but it became clear to me that some families handled that situation better than others."

Our job as parents is to raise kids who have the most skills for having a successful life. Raising children with Christ allows us to give them a living relationship with the living God. That provides proven priority and direction and gives rise to an infinitely better life in the long term. Eternally better.

On the other hand, many parents seemingly allow the television, Internet, and "popular" culture to raise their children versus supervising it themselves. Hardly recognizing it, parents place their children in a physically, emotionally, and spiritually dangerous world with little or no supervision. This world runs amuck with contradictory and hurtful values.

This reminds us of the story about the nasty old uncle who visits the home. He sits in the living room telling dirty jokes, attacking the family's moral values and trying to get the kids to buy inappropriate and misleading products. At some point, we must decide to either make him behave or send him packing. That nasty old uncle could possibly go by the name of Secular Media but might equally be "The World."

Many parents simply do not understand the way a mindset of Secular Humanism infiltrates and indoctrinates the minds of their children. (This is the belief that God does not exist– or is irrelevant– and that any view of life, nature or morality, which contains reliance on God or the Bible, is false and detrimental to humanity.) Making no choice is a choice. So, when Christian parents want their child to *"be in the world but not of the world"* (John 15:19) and yet don't make spiritual nurture a priority they do make a choice for their child to potentially live without Christ. The statistics bear this out. Faith is both taught and caught but neither happens in a vacuum. If you want your child to receive salvation and grow up with all the promises of Christ, then He must be a priority in your home.

SOLUTION GOAL –

PRIORITIZE SPIRITUAL DEVELOPMENT

No Set Goals

Lesson 5 - Parents have no set standard or goals they are trying to reach.

We often see a steep learning curve when moving into a new community. Todd shares, "Once, when relocating to a new church in a rural area, one of the church members suggested investing in the then-new technology of an automobile GPS. The Global Positioning System device gave me directions to every home or business I wanted to go. The voice of my choice even warned me when and which way to turn. While I quickly found it helpful I also discovered it sure wasn't foolproof."

A new user will find one major drawback. You have to know where you want to go for the GPS to be of any use. On the other hand, if you don't care where you are going then a GPS simply wastes your time, effort and money. Likewise, to effectively nurture your child's spirituality you must intend on going somewhere specific. Deciding your destination in advance helps you get there!

What caring parent would not want their child in Heaven with them for eternity?

One reason many parents fall short mentoring their children is parents have no set standard or goal. They really have no idea of where they want to go. The issue of intentionality factors in here. Parents often have the best of intentions but don't make the effort. This is because they never discerned an ambition for where they would like their children to end up spiritually. This heartbreaking reality means many parents give little consideration to the end result of human spirituality. With Christ, tremendous blessings can fill any life, transform any existence to a higher level and prepare our children for eternity.

What parent would not want their child to be with them in eternity? This profound goal reaches deep into our hearts. We ask, "Can I do anything to assist my children to spend eternity with me in God's presence?" We can be God's vehicle for enriching their lives by helping them discover grace, receive salvation, discern their personal ministry and set the stage for life everlasting.

When we set goals, we prioritize our life to accomplish what we need to fulfill our goals. When looking at our child's relationship with God as a priority why would we let school activities or sporting events or anything else derail this critical goal? That goal gets laid upon us when we first take that sweet bundle to church. As our children grow in body and in Christ, parents must be an integral part of that spiritual nurturing process.

We both have seen parents perform important religious rites in an amazingly perfunctory way, robbing the ceremony of meaning and majesty. When serving as pastors we often saw parents send their kids through membership class during their seventh grade year. Membership was their only goal. Kids would come to class and complete the required activities. These parents would have their children join the church and attend the ceremony. These parents somehow felt they had completed their job in raising their children spiritually and checked it off their list. Spiritual growth can hardly flourish with that type of checklist mentality.

When we set spiritual and religious goals and work toward them, we create opportunities for the growth and development of our children. In doing that we find ourselves training them, nurturing them and feeding their spirit in a way that brings them closer to God. We trek to a great destination, and it only makes sense to load up our kids and set the GPS for Heaven.

SOLUTION GOAL –

SET SPIRITUAL GOALS

Lacking a Plan

Lesson 6 - Parents have no plan for the spiritual development of their children.

Another reason this problem exists is most parents have never considered planning for the spiritual development of their children. This research shows us the wisdom of the age-old adage— "If you fail to plan, you plan to fail." This statement remains just as valid when dealing with spiritual nurture. It's not that we don't want the best for our children, but some parents simply don't have the understanding to make it happen. As in Lesson 2, it's not that we parents don't desire for the best, most of us have never had the truth revealed to us. Still, parents hold the keys to our children's spiritual upbringing.

The hard fact is that, statistically speaking, many parents are not intentional and do not take an active role in their child's spiritual development. This deficit is in especially sharp contrast when compared to the time we spend planning our children's education, college and activities. We plan for these important parts of life. Parents seem to have more intentionality when seeking success in these areas. If you want to know what we mean, watch bleary-eyed parents bring young swimmers to 5 a.m. practice.

When we work toward our goals and make deliberate attempts to achieve them, we do so with "intention." This defines purposefully working toward a goal, knowing the final destination, selecting specific steps to get there and making our life choices fit those steps. We do not "go wherever the wind blows."

In a world of specialization and hyper-defined roles in the workplace, it's no wonder parents let the experts do it for us. We remember watching major league baseball in the early 1970s. The starting pitcher would begin the game with every intention of finishing all nine innings. Sometimes, with too many pitches thrown or the pitcher having an off night, a relief pitching "closer" would finish the game in the later innings. However, when watching a game today, you will see many specialized relief pitchers coming into the game. Relief pitchers enter the game for a specific batter, out, or situation. Now it's common to see seven to eight pitchers in a game when one or two would have been the norm a few decades ago.

In the same way, many parents get relievers to disciple their children. In our specialized world it's easy to think the teacher, youth pastor, coach or some other specialist is in better shape for this most important task. Many parents never experienced disciple[ing] in the home either – they were sent to Sunday school for spiritual education just the same as parents send their kids to school for math and other subjects. The parent's parents relied on specialists and so the parents go with what they know.

Why is that so? A great number of parents have never thoughtfully developed a plan to disciple their children. Usually because we don't know how to set appropriate spiritual goals. So, we want to keep reiterating, "It isn't your fault!" Most parents don't even realize that we should have expectations about our children growing in faith. That's why we wrote this book; there IS a better way to pass on your faith to your kids. It is OK to have spiritual expectations and goals that you work toward. Likely, this is why you have this book in your hand. You had a sense there was more. The Spirit has been whispering to you.

SOLUTION GOAL –

DEVELOP A SPIRITUAL GROWTH PLAN

Lack of Accountability

Lesson 7 - Parents experience no accountability for their efforts.

"Character is who you are when nobody is watching," held basketball coach John Wooden of UCLA. Wooden led his UCLA teams to 10 National Championships in 12 years. This included 7 NCAA championships in a row! As a coach, Wooden knew a few things about human nature. That includes the truth that even champions fall short at times. More importantly though, his quote shows how being part of a team or family can help us live above our personal weaknesses or insufficiencies through accountability. That "team concept" gives the meaning and purpose of gathering together as the church. We can all do better together! We support each other and help one another discover God's strength through God's grace.

Lack of accountability comes in as the seventh reason why parents do not do well following through in disciple[ing] their children. It doesn't necessarily take a village to raise a child, but it does take accountability on the parent's part to keep them engaged and encouraged. When the daily grind wears us down, we are tempted to forego our time with our children and our own spiritual building blocks. How wonderful would it be to have parents encouraging one another?

Far from nurturing lone wolves, the church encourages a herd mentality. It's no coincidence that the Bible regularly refers to God's people as sheep. And the enduring picture of Jesus the Good Shepherd warms us. Our true nature creates joy in knowing we belong.

As Scripture tells us, *"we who have different gifts are part of one body"(1 Corinthians 12:12).* Our togetherness, our family attitude, comes from the kingdom concept that different people come together as a super team, forming the Body of Christ. In fact, we can't all be everything, it's pretty well impossible. That's good because our Christian humility gives us room to give our ego a rest and be part of the team. By asking to be part of an accountability group or having an accountability pact with a friend, we can be stronger than we think. We encourage all parents to commit to prayer for each other's children. Together, we achieve goals that might otherwise overwhelm us. We can be strong when the team helps us. Praise God, we are never alone in the body of Christ.

SOLUTION GOAL –

FORM ACCOUNTABILITY GROUPS

NOTE: In the appendix of this book, (on page 253) we have created a group guide that can help parents and other Christians who work with children. In this group guide, you can work together practicing and reflecting on the process in which Jesus taught the Disciples, which we explore in Section 2. After completing that section on the Discipleship Process, we invite you to get a group of people willing to explore the teaching technique of Jesus and see how it can help you make the most of the information in this book.

APPLICATION

List two or three things that you learned or found interesting:

1

2

3

Reflection and Discussion Questions

1) Look over the seven problems for Christian parents in chapters 4 and 5 and prioritize them. Which ones apply to you strongly, somewhat, or not at all. Rate them on what you see as most important to you and your child or children at this point in your life. What ones are you ready to get started on right now? Who will help you with this? As you read through this book, keep in your mind that God will help you with the specifics.

2) Who is the best person or group that can keep you accountable as you raise your child?

3) How can they keep you accountable? Be specific. What would a prayer group for your children look like?

4) Can you give an example of a time someone held you accountable and it helped you? Even when you fought against it?

Chapter 6 – The Ripple Effect

"The one indispensable requirement for producing godly, mature Christians is godly, mature Christians."   Kevin DeYoung

Raising our children as powerful followers of Christ transforms both them and our communities. Today, every aspect of society is affected by the lack of Christians being discipled in their home. We have an insufficient number of Christians committed to living out the gospel walking our streets, our hospitals, our halls of justice, our businesses, our social programs. When we look closely, we see a culture quickly losing its Biblical mooring. Addiction, suicide, teenage pregnancy, violence, school dropout and general hopelessness seem to overwhelm our society. *All the world's wrongdoing seems to go unchecked. Unchecked, possibly, but not unnoticed.* **There exists a common thread in all factors that can be traced to a lack of parental attention to the spiritual needs of their children.** This is not the only factor but certainly an important one. Fortunately, in considering this factor we find we actually have a strong influence with our families and our children.

We strongly believe the largest aspect of this problem is an indifference to God's Great Commission:

> [18]*And Jesus came up and spoke to them, saying, "All authority has been given to Me in heaven and on earth.* [19]*"Go therefore and make disciples of all the nations, baptizing them in the name of the Father and the Son and the Holy Spirit,* [20]*teaching them to observe all that I commanded you; and lo, I am with you always, even to the end of the age."*
>
> *(Matthew 28:18-20) The Great Commission*

(We will be covering the Great Commission in depth during Section 4). God's love in action, known as the Great Commission, directs us to help others adopt and grow in faith. Without our personal obedience to the Great Commission as an expression of the

Great Commandment, "*Love one another as I have loved you,*" (John 15:12) the entire church falls short of being *"the salt and light of the earth"* (Matthew 5:16). Our culture, the ocean in which humankind swims is being polluted by sin and evil. All the wrongdoing seems to go unchecked. Unchecked, possibly for now, but not unnoticed.

You might also think of us as grapes in a vineyard, deeply influenced by our soil and environment. Humanity has a sin problem. Left unchecked the world will do what the world does- walk smugly away from God into the night. *"⁹The true light that gives light to everyone was coming into the world. ¹⁰He was in the world, and though the world was made through him, the world did not recognize him." (John 1:9 & 10)* They rebel because they don't know God and so they think selfishly. How could it be otherwise?

Sadly, the research shows that many folks in the church look at problems and solutions from a worldly point of view. Where is the Church in reference to this problem? The Church should rightfully be in the middle of this problem, on the front lines of battle. In fact, this crisis exists because most churches have little discipleship teaching, modeling or few examples. As a whole, the Church appears to be silent about this predicament. Most churches tend to focus on the easy-to-count indicators like membership, attendance, giving, programming and the like.

> *If we have one ambition as Christian parents, growing disciples of Jesus Christ must be our desire.*

Spiritual growth and maturity doesn't seem to be the passion or heartbeat of most churches. While harder to measure, these goals should beat in our Christian heart. These ideals must be a hallmark of our leadership and a focus of our collective faith walk! If we have one ambition as Christian parents, growing disciples of Jesus Christ must be our desire. Disobedience to God's way has negative results to the household of God, deeply affecting the community and our world.

An active church, intentional in the Great Commission works tirelessly through the greater church like yeast. Todd enjoys baking and observes, "Yeast (or leavening) provides the lightness and fluff to bread. Without yeast, the dense flour and water mix never gains its pleasing flavor and texture. The yeast folded throughout the flour and water gradually uplifts the mixture. Then, shaped and baked, the bread fills us with tasty and satisfying nutrition for living." In the same way, the yeast of discipleship leads to a spiritual depth influencing the whole church.

Every aspect of the church receives positive impact by a member's personal growth in Christ. When a church focuses on the Great Commission, it inspires the life of the children's ministry, youth ministry, young adult ministry and all ages. Yes, even the youth group is impacted because parents actively disciple their youth who, in turn, invest in the life of the youth group. As Barna states:

> *Most Christian churches evaluate success in terms of program attendance, child satisfaction and parental satisfaction, but do little to examine individual spiritual advancement. However, the ministries having the greatest success at seeing young people emerge into mature Christians, rather than contented church-goers, are those that facilitate a parent-church partnership focused on instilling specific spiritual beliefs and practices in a child's life from a very early age.* **Sadly, less than one out of every five churches has produced such a ministry.** [14] *(emphasis added)*

Characteristic of a major human failing, many parents take the path of least resistance when it comes to disciple[ing] their children. Christian parents want their children to share their faith. However, as we've found out, they do not plan and are not intentional about this most important task. We trust the applications of the material in this book will be used by God to impress upon parents the importance and impact they have on their children spiritually. As you explore what God says about parenting and discipleship, you will reject a passive approach to the spiritual nurture of your children. Our Prayer for you includes a network of mature Christian parents who will support and pray for each other.

APPLICATION

List two or three things that you learned or found interesting:

1

2

3

Reflection and Discussion Questions

1) Thinking about the yeast and bread illustration, how does that apply to your family or the other organizations you belong to.

2) "Our Prayer for you includes a network of mature Christian parents who will support and pray for each other (and children)." Who are these people in your life?

3) How often and how long will you meet?

4) How about having your children in the prayer time and pray for them while they are there?

5) Can you "love one another as I have loved you?" Why and why not?

Chapter 7 – The Challenge of Worldview

> *In recent years our culture has sent hostile signals about the job of parenting, even though few men and women will ever do anything more important than nurturing and raising the next generation of children.* James Dobson and Gary L. Bauer

Studies indicate that, in nearly every category, there is little difference between Christian parenting and secular parenting. This fact reveals something important about the state of the Church. Those of us IN side of the church share a worldview with the people OUT side of the church. This confusion can be a major setback if it means we are only paying lip service to God and His narrow path. The problem may lie with how we see and understand the world.

A worldview, in its most basic definition, is how we look at the world. This includes our basic assumptions about how the world works and what we should expect from life. We have formed our worldview so fully; we rarely even stop to consider it. This deeply engrained construct helps us to refrain from reinventing the world every day. For example, have you taught kids to tie their shoes? We've developed some good ways to teach this to our children. Remember the "rabbit ears" trick. At first it was difficult for them to get. Yet, every day we tie shoes, literally without thinking about it. At some point early in our lives, through repetition and success, shoe tying became a completely automatic activity.

Worldview creates the foundation of our thinking. It helps us navigate a tricky and increasingly complex world. By settling our thoughts on how things work, we can adapt to the situation and make quick decisions. We do that every day.

A few questions regarding our worldview.

> *What is the best form of government?*
> *Are all people equal?*
> *Is God involved in the world?*
> *In general, can people be trusted?*

Does hard work ensure success?
Does prayer work?
Does strong faith ensure success?
Should corporations have rights?
Is doing whatever I choose extremely important?
Are fulfilling social obligations important?
Can people get close to God?
Should creation be honored?
Is a strong central government a force for justice?
Are people basically good?
Is family most important?

The answers you make to these questions (and many, many, others) have mostly been previously decided. We start with our basic assumptions which become the launching spot for all decisions. Each of us already has a fully-formed worldview. A large part of our opinions, decisions and actions flow from our mental building blocks. We build our opinions or views in the present based on those intellectual components. That is why propaganda is so effective, subtly seducing us by influencing our worldview and leading us to draw predictable conclusions.

We've heard "never discuss religion and politics in public." These topics convey our worldview, our assumptions on how the world works. Since we live in an obviously flawed world, human views cannot fully capture God's truth. Religion and politics take a stab at it by containing prescriptions on how the world should work.

An outright challenge to our worldview often draws anger and instigates the distress we feel with change. We find it frustrating and even painful to relearn the foundational truths of our life. To do so, we literally must transform our minds. Interestingly, the Biblical Greek word for "repent" (metanoeo) means, "to change one's way of thinking." Repentance isn't just changing what we do but changing how we think and feel.

For this reason, as the years go by, individual conversion becomes less and less likely. Our heart hardens and our mind becomes set. (As a note, in this book we will often use worldview and mindset interchangeably.) Better to build a proper worldview from the start than to try to change one further down the road.

The challenge for the Church is recognizing, as Walt Kelly's lovable cartoon character Pogo said, "We have met the enemy and he is us" (a takeoff on the famous Oliver Hazzard Perry dispatch from the War of 1812's Battle of Lake Erie).

More and more of the worldview of professing Christians intertwines with the secular worldview. We largely see things the way they do and accept the conclusions they do. In this way, Christians are not living out the Gospel worldview. In many cases,

> *Many Christians were never taught the core truths that allow us to interpret the world with a Biblically based, uniquely Christian point of view.*

in the hearts and minds of Christians, the kingdom of God and the kingdom of self have become the same place. In Barna's research he elaborates,

> *Most of the people who claim to have a biblical worldview show little evidence of such a perspective in their core attitudes, behaviors and religious beliefs. The data show that churches can have a very significant impact on the worldview of people, but they must start with an intentional process introduced to people **at a very young age**. Waiting until someone is in their teens or young adult years misses the window of opportunity. Clearly, more churches need to invest resources in such training.[15] (emphasis added)*

How has this come to be? How did we lose our distinctive view of how the world works? How do we lose sight of the really important things in life? A large part of the problem comes from the fact that most of us were not discipled ourselves. Therefore, our children and grandchildren have not been discipled either. It is not parents' fault. Many Christians were never taught the core truths allowing us to interpret the world with a Biblically based, uniquely Christian point of view. In general usage, a disciple is a supporter and follower or pupil. Christian discipleship presumes that all people will follow a leader. We have a choice; we can follow the King of Heaven or the prince of this world. We have often been confused and in our day worldly power has seduced the church.

When Jesus was being tempted in the wilderness (Matthew 4), He received the opportunity by Satan to take secular power. Satan offered him the kingdoms of this world if He would fall on His knees and worship Satan. Most scholars believe that this was not a simple bribe attempt, but a temptation to use corruptible worldly power for good. This nearly irresistible temptation has brought many idealists to their knees in the intervening years. The bottom line reasoning of this fallacy is "I can achieve God's good with Satan's power."

Interestingly, this is a central premise to the Tolkien classic, "The Lord of the Rings." The ring of power Frodo carries can never be wielded without corrupting the user. This is why the pure-hearted Frodo was chosen for the task of destroying it.

As with all Jesus' temptations, Satan brings them to Christ's disciples. All Jesus had to do was worship Satan, the prince of this world. If worship means to love, revere and adore, then Jesus' temptation felt the same as ours do. Therefore a question needs to be asked, "Are we placing the values of the world above the mindset of God?"

Satan is good with this, with anything really as long as we aren't worshipping God. Parents must look closely and be aware of this situation. Are we following cultural trends as the primary factor in making decisions? Are we allowing the internet to inform us on what is normal? We may be part of a generation of parents following the world's path and thinking we are raising a culture full of spiritually healthy children. However, what if the results do not back up our expectation? Once again, George Barna has done the research and comes to a conclusion about raising worldly Christians.

> *For years we have reported research findings showing that born again adults think and behave very much like everyone else. It often seems that their faith makes very little difference in their life. This new study helps explain why that is:* **believers do not train their children to think or act any differently.** *When our kids are exposed to the same influences, without much supervision, and are*

generally not guided to interpret their circumstances and opportunities in light of biblical principles, it's no wonder that they grow up to be just as involved in gambling, adultery, divorce, cohabitation, excessive drinking and other unbiblical behaviors as everyone else. **What we build into a child's life prior to the age of 13 represents the moral and spiritual foundation that defines them as individuals and directs their choices for the remainder of their life.** *Garbage in, garbage out; there's no magic that suddenly changes the young person from what they were trained to be in their formative years into a model Christian once they get older.* [16] *(emphasis added)*

Sadly, the disconnect comes because many parents today absorb, partially or fully, the world's standard of parenting. But we often give lip service to God's standards. What is the difference between the two? The world's standard is based on an individualistic view of life.

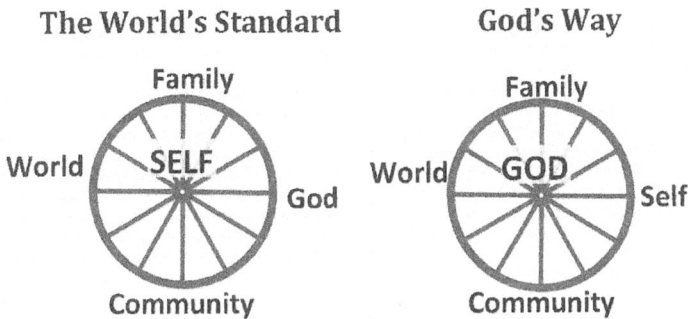

The World's Standard

Family
World — SELF — God
Community

God's Way

Family
World — GOD — Self
Community

In this diagram, we can see two wheels. All wheels need an axle to revolve around, as do all lives. In the first wheel, we see the world's standard showing the self as the axle around which everything revolves and God is just along for the ride. In the second wheel, God is the axle around which everything rotates. God is the center of life and living.

God's view of living finds its central focus on complete obedience to Him; a path apart from the world's standards. God's way means yielding the self to Him through prayer, through the Bible, Christian accountability and living a life in complete surrender to Him. Clearly, the world's view completely contrasts with God's view of servanthood and putting others first. We call God's view "Love." A Biblical Worldview gives us Jesus on the throne of one's life. In this way, all our intentions, inventions, intuitions and passions may revolve around God.

As you finish this Section, there may be a tendency toward anger or discouragement. That makes perfect sense because we are shining light on the worldview most of us have unknowingly adopted. We congratulate you for reading through this challenging section. We believe this demonstrates that you love God and love your children enough to honestly identify your needs and eagerly await the coming good news. So don't be downhearted. Remember, the Scripture teaches us, *"where sin abounds, grace abounds that much more." (Romans 5:20)*

Section 1 – Understanding the Issues

APPLICATION

List two or three things that you learned or found interesting:

1

2

3

Reflection and Discussion Questions

1) How would you describe your "worldview?"

2) Reflect on the wheel illustration you saw on page 45.

The World's Standard   **God's Way**

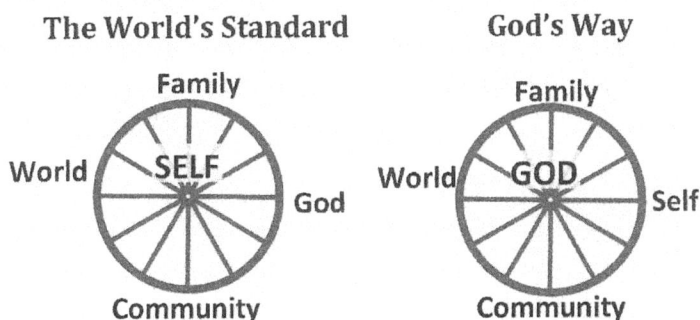

What is currently at the center of your wheel? If it is not God, do you want to change the center? If so, what is your first step? Next steps?

3) Reread the Barna quote on page 44 and discuss.

4) What ways do people show that God is at the center of their wheel? In what ways do they show God is not at the center of their wheel.

"...the love, respect, and confidence of my children was the sweetest reward I could receive for my efforts to be the woman I would have them copy."

Louisa May Alcott, "Little Women"

Section 2

THE DISCIPLESHIP PROCESS

SECTION 2 - THE DISCIPLESHIP PROCESS

Chapter 8 – Making Disciples

> *When you find your definitions in God, you find the very purpose for which you were created. Put your hand into God's hand, know His absolutes, demonstrate His love, present His truth, and the message of redemption and transformation will take hold.*
>
> *Ravi Zacharias*

Discipleship works in our lives as a process of transformation. Rightly understood (from our human viewpoint), discipleship covers everything from the first moment someone decided to share the Good News with us until the moment we go home to be with Jesus. God's grace worked on us even before then. From humble spiritual beginnings, we enter a course of development bringing us closer in relationship to our Lord. As the spiritual song "Amazing Grace" points out, "I once was lost but now am found, was blind but now I see." Like the little wriggling bug that undergoes a change from worm to butterfly, we go from one state of grace to another.

That little butterfly wasn't always so beautiful, but he always had butterfly potential. By the same grace of God through the work of God's people, a human life becomes a beautiful gift, a fragrant spiritual offering to God. Clearly, we participate in the process, but it is the Holy Spirit who transforms us into something better than we could ever be on our own.

We stress that the entire process is the work of God and an act of grace. Some draw an unnecessary distinction between evangelism and discipleship that says, "you hook 'em, God cleans 'em." They see a separation between what happens before and after the decision as separate events. Or, maybe, it is just easier to explain our lives Before Christ (BC) and After Christ (AC). As Scripture says, *"Therefore, if anyone is in Christ, he is a new creation; the old has gone, the new has come!" (2*

Corinthians 5:17) Regardless of our thoughts on evangelism and discipleship, the point **we would like to stress is God loves all people**. He works within circumstances so people can know him in a real and personal way. All Christians have a unique story of their transformation.

It is abundantly clear from our experience of ministry that some make a decision very early in their search for God and still grow slowly as spiritual infants in the church. Many years may separate their conversion and becoming mature Christian people.

Others may come from great backgrounds and/or have many spiritual qualities that need only God's transforming grace to make them spiritual titans. C.S. Lewis comes to mind as one who had many gifts for God to use. Lewis authored such famous works as "The Chronicles of Narnia" and "Mere Christianity." He brought with him a treasure of personal experiences and characteristics that blossomed richly upon his conversion. God transformed him from scholarly atheist to humble disciple of Jesus Christ. (If Lewis intrigues you, you can learn more about his transformation by reading his autobiographies "All My Road Before Me" and "Surprised By Joy.")

Honestly, we do not need to look at Discipleship as some mysterious process stolen away from Middle Age monasteries. The concept of changing hearts and minds certainly deserves respect. However, fear not. Becoming a disciple of Jesus Christ develops as a blossoming garden. You plant the seeds, water and nurture it while God performs the miracle.

In our ministries, we have noticed that planning around this process seems to generate more pushback than might be expected. It's weird because most of us believe we have a general understanding of discipleship. Moreover, that's mostly true at an abstract level. Most church folks don't fully understand simply because they've never been exposed to the nuts and bolts of creating disciples. They just don't have a good grasp of the significant details and processes. In some ways, we understand discipleship like we understand our computer. In general we know how it works but when it needs fixed, changed or improved…it becomes time to call in the I.T. tech.

Teaching discipleship is like the advice to "turn your problems over to God." Absolutely true! But how? Without someone to help you understand the way to stop and redirect your thoughts when you find yourself worrying, the need for continual self-encouragement, and the humble prayers necessary to release our own control, such "self-help" rarely works.

Probably, we Christians lack detailed knowledge about discipleship that we should have been given long ago. People just don't understand all it entails. "Sure, I want my kid (friend, neighbor, co-worker) to be blessed by knowing Christ but what do I do besides buy them a Bible and take them to church?" Both those things create a good start. However, there is more.

Another problem we have is, "not knowing what we don't know." Have you ever heard a scholar or wise Christian say, "The more I learn, the more I realize how much I don't know." We believe this section is going to open your eyes and allow you to ask the right questions. Once you recognize the process going on as a Christian grows into a mature faith, the better you will realize what you may lack (or what your child disciple lacks). Also, the better you will become at addressing the real issues.

Another reason we don't have a full appreciation for the beauty of discipleship may just be that Christians often accept the salvation experience as a one-time, complete-in-itself, personal experience. "Hey, that ol' rascal Bill came to the altar and got saved last week. He'll be changed now." Bill's heart may be changed, but his life may not yet be transformed.

Probably the biggest barrier to understanding Discipleship comes from failing to understand that Discipleship is a transformational process.

> [2] *Do not be conformed any longer to the pattern of this world, but be transformed by the renewing of your mind. Then you will be able to test and approve what God's will is—his good, pleasing and perfect will. (Romans 12:2)*

From personal experiences in our own ministries, we can both readily verify that God does work through immediate and revolutionary conversion. God uses any method He wants. After all, He is God.

One particular parishioner in Todd's ministry (we'll call him Carl) sat down on a curb with the intention of figuring a way to kill himself. He had several addictions, and with his life falling apart he sat there hurting and hopeless. As he sat there, Carl thought, "Well, people talk about God, perhaps He can save me from this pain. Since I'm left with nothing else, what could I lose?"

Then, Carl began to talk directly to God out of his inner desolation. "So, uh, God, I can't handle my life anymore. The pain I'm feeling, the pain I'm causing. God, people say you exist, but I don't know. It sounds too good to be true. If you exist and care, if you can take away my pain and change my life I'll be happy to serve you. Just show me some kind of sign so I can know you are real... If not, well, then I guess none of it matters anyway. Amen."

As Carl sat on the corner, the Lord spoke to him saying he was loved and that he would be delivered of his addictions. When Carl stood up from that curb, he was changed and never took another drink or used another narcotic again. From then on, he began to testify about God's love and life changing power. Carl will testify that God works through the miraculous. This does happen, even though change usually proceeds through a process and time.

We aren't looking at discipleship with fear and trepidation or overblown expectations. We see Discipleship as a transformational process, one that can be described - even charted. Understanding the process can help us set goals, select activities, even evaluate where our children (or others we mentor) stand in the midst of becoming a full-fledged disciple of Jesus Christ.

APPLICATION

List two or three things that you learned or found interesting:

1

2

3

Reflection and Discussion Questions

1) C.S Lewis had a radical experience of conversion at the age of 31. Writer J.R.R. Tolkien was a major personal influence on him and Lewis credits him with being a major factor in Lewis becoming a Christian. Who is a person that you are most surprised by either being a Christian with little parental support or is not a Christian with good parental support?

2) Who has come along side you to help you with your discipleship process?

3) Do you know a person in your life like Carl (mentioned on page 53)?

Chapter 9 – Understanding The Process

We may not be able to prepare the future for our children, but we can at least prepare our children for the future.
                                                        Franklin D. Roosevelt

We are deeply indebted to Dr. Robert Coleman who powerfully described this process of discipleship. His work forms the foundation of, not only this section, but our entire understanding of how human beings grow spiritually. Just like our physical life, we go through "stages" that can be acknowledged and described. We are fetuses, infants, then toddlers, then children, adolescents, youth, young adults, adults, middle aged and elderly. How a Christian Disciple becomes a Christian and moves forward in his walk with Christ can be understood through the eight steps below.

Jesus Practice of Discipleship

We look at the way and manner that Jesus made disciples through the lens of Dr. Robert Coleman's influential work "The Master Plan of Evangelism." (We recommend to you all of Dr. Coleman's insightful works including "Master Plan of Discipleship" and "Great Commission Lifestyle.") In his book, Coleman demonstrates how Jesus discipled the first Disciples. Jesus came not just changing the disciples, but also reaching out for the entire world. Jesus transformed the disciples to save their souls and give them abundant life, but also that they might reach others with the same blessings.

We could possibly say Jesus "primarily" discipled them to win the world, but it's more than that. Jesus did not USE or manipulate the disciples for his own ends! He brought them into the family… and then into the family business. As much as we want our children to join us in heaven, we also need to help prepare them for the fullness of being Christ's disciple. They become part of God's family business transforming the future.

55

Jesus came to save the entire world, not just a few. *"For God so loved the world that he gave his one and only Son, that whoever believes in him shall not perish but have eternal life."* *(John 3:16)* While Jesus spoke to the masses and ministered to individuals, he poured his life into the disciples. He performed His ministry to the many but discipled the few. Your own ministry may be in the church, in the workplace, in the community or the family. This ministry work reaches to the core of our life in Christ but disciple[ing] our children means connecting to them on an authentic and intimate level (This is not to suggest that we should be "buddies" with our children. We find that parenting strategy to be unhelpful on so many levels.) We must mentor our children and train them up in the way they should go.

It might be said that Jesus "primarily" discipled his followers to win the world, but it's more than that. Jesus did not use or manipulate the disciples for His own ends! He brought them into the family...and then into the family business.

When Jesus discipled his students, they worked closely and continually and became a tight-knit family. Jesus mentored the disciples, sometimes even addressing them as his children, *"The disciples were amazed at his words. But Jesus said again, "Children, how hard it is for the rich to enter the kingdom of God!"* *(Mark 10:24)* Even though the disciples were very different temperamentally (i.e. sons of thunder) and from many walks of life (from fishermen to tax collectors) Jesus brought them together as a family.

They talked together, traveled together and ministered together as part of Jesus' entourage. School was always in session, and the disciples saw Jesus in action on a daily basis. They, better than anyone, witnessed Jesus as he worked and played, ate and drank, laughed and joked, when he was authoritative and when he was submissive.

Coleman's Stages of Discipleship		
Stage	**Description**	**Biblical Example**
SELECTION	Using prayer and the leading of the Holy Spirit, the mentor selects a suitable disciple to instruct.	Matthew 4:18-22
ASSOCIATION	The mentor allows the disciple heavy participation in normal life with a premium on authenticity.	John 1:14
CONSECRATION	Through seeking God, the disciple discerns and accepts the devotion and dedication to following Christ.	1 Peter 2:9
IMPARTATION	Knowledge and acceptance that the Holy Spirit will be unconditionally received to guide the disciple.	1 Corinthians 2:11-12
DEMONSTRATION	Through exhibiting the authentic life of Christ, including challenges, the mentor creates a life model to follow.	Luke 11:1-4
DELEGATION	The mentor will give realistic and increasingly difficult assignments for the disciple's spiritual growth.	Mark 6:7-13
SUPERVISION	As participating in assignments, the disciple reports to the mentor who evaluates progress and adjusts the program.	Luke 9:10-11
REPRODUCTION	While growing into a mature Christian, the disciple eventually becomes a mentor and replicates the process.	Matthew 28:18-20

The disciples of Jesus committed themselves fully to the mentorship of Jesus. When reading the Scriptures, we see weakness and failings sometimes in the twelve, but we know they were doing the best they could. Not the best that could be done, just the best that an individual child of God could do. The example of Jesus and the disciples show the truth in the old preachers adage, "God doesn't call the qualified, He qualifies the called." And it shows. As illustrated by Dr. Coleman, "A few people so dedicated in time will shake the world for God. Victory is never won by the multitudes."[17]

A number of years ago, Dr. Tony Campolo spoke to the West Ohio Conference of the United Methodist Church. He asked the 2,500 clergy and laity gathered, "How many of you came to Christ through television or radio?" One person yelled out, and Dr. Campolo replied, "There you are, the one we've spent all that money on!" The point is that programs and media may plant a seed or water but can never make a disciple.

Jesus' plan was to gather a small group of people and invest his life into them. Just like you with your children, Jesus cared for them, supported them, He taught and re-taught them. Jesus hurt for them and ultimately bled for them. Mentoring a disciple is heart intensive but the only way to change lives is to pour yours into them. It can be hard work with little results at first, but time and perseverance allows the Holy Spirit to work from the inside out.

As mentors of our children, we parents must be committed to raising disciples. We don't need to be perfect at it; we should not be harsh about it. *And, fathers, do not provoke your children to anger, but bring them up in the discipline and instruction of the Lord. (Ephesians 6:4)* Dr. Coleman, in talking about the necessary commitment from a mentor to the disciple argues, "Jesus did not have the time nor the desire to scatter himself on those who wanted to make their own terms of discipleship."[18]

The disciple[ing] relationship finds its agenda set by the mentor and not the disciple. That is because a disciple will not, cannot, exceed the commitment of the mentor. Just as our leader should be the one we look toward to set the pace, we can either be committed or simply involved. The difference between involvement and commitment is like a ham and eggs breakfast. The chicken is involved and the pig is committed. Jesus calls us to be the pigs!

Clearly, Jesus looked for the ones who loved him. Did they know how much love they would have for Christ? When Peter denied Jesus three times, did he realize how much he would love Jesus later? He had no idea to what lengths he would eventually go to follow the Lord. Yet, in his growing pains, he still found acceptance by Jesus. The followers of Jesus were asked to give everything (even home and family). Jesus looked for and expected obedience because high stakes define the "salvation of the world."

Obedience is necessary to the monumental task at hand, but only grace makes long-term obedience possible. Dr. Coleman described the importance of discipleship to a Christian, "We have not been called to hold the fort, but to storm the heights. It is in this light that the final step in Jesus' strategy of evangelism can be understood."[19]

Obedience is necessary to the monumental task at hand, but only grace makes long-term obedience possible.

Just like physical life, a disciple starts with a selection and ends with reproduction. We will be looking at the steps of the process. We asked, "How is a disciple made?" We see the answer in Dr. Coleman's Steps of Discipleship. However, we must remember that the process of discipleship is more organic and fluid than a simple eight step chart can show us. We move from one area to another. If one moves too quickly, we may regress and fall back. "One step forward and two steps back" sometimes describes our progress as disciples.

If you've ever stuck with giving up a bad habit, you know it goes slowly. Parents, do you remember potty training? Rarely, do our kids start out getting it perfect. But, like the pattern of potty training, people grow spiritually and progress until they get it, and then they move beyond it. (We were tempted to using the shoe tying example again, but few things are as satisfying to a parent as when our kids get down the potty trick.)

So let us look at the steps of discipleship and keep in our mind that the boundaries between these phases of discipleship are transitional and not rigid. *More like crossing fields than fences, each new development will find the disciple walking from one area to another.* Eventually, we realize that the disciple has crossed from one realm to another, and when we do, it will be a celebration of the spiritual life.

APPLICATION

List two or three things that you learned or found interesting:

1

2

3

Reflection and Discussion Questions

1) For the remainder of the book Coleman's Stages of Discipleship will be expanded and expounded upon. Reread the table to get a better understanding of the flow. As you do think of an age appropriate activity you can do with your child.

2) Talk about this quote (from the discussion about transitioning between the stages): "More like crossing fields than fences, each new area will find the disciple walking from one area to another." What does this quote mean to you?

Chapter 10 – Selection

USING PRAYER AND THE LEADING OF THE HOLY SPIRIT,
THE MENTOR SELECTS A SUITABLE DISCIPLE TO INSTRUCT.

> *[12]One of those days Jesus went out to a mountainside to pray, and spent the night praying to God. [13]When morning came, he called his disciples to him and chose twelve of them, whom he also designated apostles. (Luke 6:12-13)*

Obviously, for a parent, selecting a disciple to mentor happens to be a pretty simple matter: the process of selection consists of finding your children. Granted, as parents we know that finding your offspring may be harder than it sounds. When they are little, they might be in a different room or hiding behind the sofa. Older kids might be running the neighborhood or, if you're rural, out in the woods or the barn. As teens they may be driving or out with their friends. Once they start walking, they start leaving. Despite all their mobility, these disciples have been selected for you.

We can learn a few things by looking at what Jesus looked for when he chose his disciples. Remember, Jesus looked at the twelve as both individuals and future leaders. He wasn't creating programming to reach the multitudes but molding role models and leaders. He wanted men that others would respect, imitate, and follow. Jesus concerned himself with their spiritual growth not only for their sake, but also for the advancement of the kingdom of God. Jesus needed leaders to lead the church after His return to Heaven.

The men Jesus selected clearly would not be chosen by today's church. None of them had an advanced degree nor substantial education. (Though Judas apparently knew how to use flimsy accounting methods.) It does not appear that they were men of wealth or position or high connection. **In many churches today, these guys would only have elicited a chuckle as their resumes were dumped into the trash can.** They had no worldly right to hold the position of student to the savior of the world. But they possessed, inside them, the most important quality of all - the willingness to be led by Jesus. They were common and ordinary men, but ones willing to be transformed by Jesus. As Dr. Coleman wrote, "One cannot transform a world except as individuals in the world are transformed, and individuals cannot be changed except as they are molded in the hands of the Master."[20]

The most important thing to know about Jesus' disciples is this, they were common ordinary men. But they were men who were willing to be transformed by Jesus.

We can keep this concept of selection in mind as we assess our children's progress and skills. We realize our children are talented in their own ways. So often, the world tells us gifted children go the furthest. Congratulations if your child meets the criteria for gifted, that is truly great (though this brings on another set of challenges). Much can be done for God's kingdom by those with amazing skills and talents. It's no accident that in our time talented musicians and athletes make a splash that few can. For example, Tim Tebow, the NFL quarterback, had youth football players around the country kneeling for a moment of thanksgiving after their touchdowns.

But the special are, by definition, NOT who make up most of the population. These "outliers" fall outside the statistical norm. However, God clearly works outside the statistical few and touches lives through the work of His unheralded children throughout the earth. The vast majority of us will never be great in the eyes of the world. However, it is through the quality of the love of millions of unnamed Christians that God changes the world.

So, do not despair if your child doesn't show any noticeable greatness (aside from mess making or missing mealtime). Jesus' disciples didn't show any aptitude for world changing until they had been through his hands-on course of study. Learning to follow Jesus allowed these common and simple apprentices to become some of the most important people in the history of the world. Never sell your child short but always consider what they can become in the hands of the master.

The Touch of the Master's Hand

'Twas battered and scarred,
And the auctioneer thought it
hardly worth his while
To waste his time on the old violin,
but he held it up with a smile.

"What am I bid, good people," he cried,
"Who starts the bidding for me?"
"One dollar, one dollar, Do I hear two?"
"Two dollars, who makes it three?"

"Three dollars once, three dollars twice,
going for three," But, No,
From the room far back a gray bearded man
Came forward and picked up the bow.

Then wiping the dust from the old violin
and tightening up the strings,
He played a melody, pure and sweet
As sweet as the angel sings.

The music ceased and the auctioneer
With a voice that was quiet and low,
Said, "What now am I bid for this old violin?"
As he held it aloft with its bow.

"One thousand, one thousand, Do I hear two?"
"Two thousand, Who makes it three?"
"Three thousand once, three thousand twice,
Going and gone," said he.

The audience cheered,
But some of them cried,
"We just don't understand."
"What changed its worth?"
Swift came the reply.
"The Touch of the Masters Hand."

And many a man with life out of tune
All battered with bourbon and gin
Is auctioned cheap to a thoughtless crowd
Much like that old violin.

A mess of pottage, a glass of wine,
A game and he travels on.
He is going once, he is going twice,
He is going and almost gone.

But the Master comes,
And the foolish crowd never can quite understand,
The worth of a soul and the change that is wrought
By the Touch of the Master's Hand.

Myra Brooks Welch

How beautiful to allow the Master to have His hand in the formation of our children. The willingness for Christian parents to allow God to mold their children allows the child to participate in God's great designs for humankind.

Parents, be aware the selection is actually yours. You select them not to be your child, but to be molded as Christ's disciple.

APPLICATION

List two or three things that you learned or found interesting:

1

2

3

Reflection and Discussion Questions

1) What is your response to knowing God selected you to be the mother/father of your children?

2) Why did God select you to be your children's parent?

3) Is it encouraging or discouraging to look at Jesus' disciples?

4) What do you think of this quote? "In many churches today, these guys would only have elicited a chuckle as their resumes were dumped into the trash can."

5) Read the poem, "The Touch of the Master's Hand." In what way does this encourage you to disciple your child?

Chapter 11 – Association

THE MENTOR ALLOWS THE DISCIPLE HEAVY PARTICIPATION IN
NORMAL LIFE WITH A PREMIUM ON AUTHENTICITY.

> *It's better to hang out with people better than you. Pick out
> associates whose behavior is better than yours and you'll drift in that
> direction.*   *Warren Buffett*

The next or second phase in the stages of discipleship is the
period of Association. Here we begin to see the connection between
the Mentor and Disciple begin to form. Association is the beginning
of relationship. This new interface sees the gradual influence of the
teacher spread to the student. Here one gathers in the characteristics
of another. It's actually the primary method for the transfer of values
from one person to another.

Jesus stayed with His disciples. He just let them follow Him and
be with Him. Jesus taught his disciples to grow close to himself.
School was always in session, and his curriculum was to reveal
himself to the disciples. Dr. Coleman writes, "In fact, this personal
appointment to be in constant
association with him was as
much a part of their ordination
commission as the authority to
evangelize. Indeed, it was for
the moment even more
important, for it was the
necessary preparation for the
other."[21]

The concept of
Association stands tall in the
process of transformation.

*It's true that, "you can't tell
anybody anything." Hearing
uses only a small portion of
our brains, but the more
ways we participate, the
greater our intake. The
greater our "buy-in," the
more the Holy Spirit can
interact with us.*

When you want change, it works far better being immersed in the
result than the problem. Ex Offender Re-entry program experts
know people coming out of prison have a difficult time changing
their lives when they go back to the same old neighborhood and

friends. Desiring a real change means living like you want to become. Finding meaningful re-entry into society means getting away from the people and situations that contributed to the criminal behavior. It means finding a new group of associates and opportunities.

Sometimes we wonder why it was so hard to get kids to adopt the ideas that you want them to have. As it turns out, the saying is true, "You can't tell anybody anything." The act of hearing uses only a small portion of our brains, but the more ways we participate, the greater our intake. The greater our buy-in, the more the Holy Spirit can interact with us.

> *Tell me, I'll forget,*
> *Show me, I'll remember,*
> *Involve me, I'll understand.*
> *Chinese proverb*

This saying may be at odds with the way most of us experienced school but still true nonetheless. Much of what passes as education consists of telling students facts and having them memorize and regurgitate them. Effective learning involves all of our senses and large portions of our brain. In this way, we do more than learn facts, we become transformed as the learning changes us.

Todd confesses to being partial to the "hands-on" approach. In his first job after college, he taught Distributive Education. Distributive Education, along with its student program DECA (Distributive Education Clubs of America) teaches business vocationally. Students learn principles of business in the classroom and apply them in the workplace. The student's employers offer regular feedback to help the teacher individualize instruction. This process helps them become better employees and trains them to run their own business.

Todd says, "I felt a real thrill when my students graduated from high school and started their own entrepreneurial business. Their "hands-on" training allowed them to leave high school - not just ready to study business, but to run their own business. I remember one particular young man, Tom, who grew up in a difficult home.

Upon graduation from my Distributive Education program (and high school), he began working the following Monday by opening his own business. It shows how much people can learn when you involve the whole person."

> *DECA enhances the preparation for college and careers by providing co-curricular programs that integrate into classroom instruction, applying learning in the context of business, connecting to business and the community and promoting competition.*
> *– From the Distributive Education Clubs of America website.*

This is Association: being part of the whole process. The disciple learns what works while beginning to understand why.

Association is also why your parents worried about you when they didn't like people you socialized with. In our "Midwest speak," one might say they "rub off" on you. This whole process of immersion leads us to become like our environment. As our brains change to accommodate our surroundings, we literally become our culture. For this reason, we recognize the importance of both the quantity and quality of family time.

Incarnation- The Ministry of Presence

> *And the Word became flesh and lived among us, and we have seen his glory, the glory as of a father's only son, full of grace and truth.*
> *(John 1:14)*

The other side of the discipleship coin shows the mentor. For example, pastors understand their ministry as one of incarnation or "the ministry of presence." When pastors sit by the bedside of the dying, join in celebrating a birth, take the youth on retreats or lead a mission trip, they participate in people's lives to bring Jesus to them. Pastors, like parents, don't just teach by talking about Jesus, the best ones teach by showing Jesus.

When we say that Jesus was God Incarnate, we are saying that the most divine Lord stepped out of heaven and walked with us. He became a man that he might dwell among us and minister to us. He came to transform us by associating with us, changing some of us and allowing those disciples to change others. Today, Christians exist as the product of the association of believers and the association of the Holy Spirit. One true thing we know about people, we become the product of our association.

The lessons Jesus used to mentor His disciples are a perfect fit for parents as they look at disciple[ing] their children. Dr. Coleman points out, "They were his spiritual children (Mark 10:24, John 13:33, 21:5) and the only way that a father can properly raise a family is to be with it."[22]

As we discussed early in this book, one of the reasons that we have issues in raising disciples is our deference to authority, especially information authorities. We have been conditioned to believe that experts have all the answers. Clearly, knowledge makes life easier but wisdom makes it better. Often, we trust in knowledge, when what we need is wisdom. Facts versus application. While giving children knowledge helps them grow, we ask "At what cost."

A focus on accumulating facts alone does not lead us into relationship. As pastors and educators we believe (along with many other educators) that the industrial model of mass education in use today neglects some pretty important areas of our kid's education. History has shown mass instruction to be less than optimal when used in the spiritual and moral realms of our children's lives.

It's hard to fathom another way when all we've know ourselves is school and grade level Sunday school. But, stuffing our kids with facts "downloaded" from experts creates a far less powerful model. Application is everything. How do we use these truths? How do we take them as our own? How do we become them? The answer, "is now, and ever shall be," for them to live in relationship with one who cares for them. So, to all the Sunday School teachers who watched us grow and taught us about God, we give thanks for you and your sacrifices. And we know most all of you will agree with this; Sunday School touches lives! But we need more.

Parents need to live out their faith while in relationship with their kids. As we've seen, subject matter experts hold a lot of information that kids need to know. Sometimes all this expertise gives parents information fatigue. What our kids need most of all, what impacts them more than anything else, is to be in relationship with a parent who desires to grow in Christ. Bottom line, Biblically, parents set the agenda for the family. Therefore, the most important human relationship that a child has must be the family bond of parent and child (mentor and disciple).

What our kids need most of all, what impacts them more than anything else, is to be in relationship with a parent who desires to grow in Christ.

So, what characteristic means the most in parenting a child in this special and spiritual relationship? We parents bring lots of gifts to the table. We have experience living life and that counts for something with a young person. Even though children think parents are out of touch, your life experience will mean a lot. You might not know the latest trends, but you do know the important and timeless things. You know life, you know God. As long as you have worked hard and earned your kids respect, you already have the needed strength, compassion, nurturing, authority, intelligence, and perseverance.

Authenticity

Every fruit of the Spirit: love, joy, peace, patience, kindness, goodness, faithfulness, gentleness, and self-control makes a valuable contribution to parenting. However, of all the virtues we could list, the most important to being in relationship with your child is…authenticity. By this, we mean being genuine and honest with your children. (Kids are super-human hypocrisy detectors and a sure way to lose the respect of our children is to preach something we don't practice.) Being authentic means to allow yourself to be human. Like all of us, you're going to shine some days and wear the tarnish on others. Being authentic allows our kids to see us as we are and how we respond to life as a Christian. What better training can a child have?

Now, when we take on the role of being authentic, it doesn't mean that kids have to know everything. By nature, kids learn many lessons from their surroundings. And frankly, like teaching algebra before arithmetic, kids have difficulty learn things out of order. Situations in life exist which children don't have the developmental framework to process. For example, is your neighbor having an affair? You don't need to bring it up with them. If they bring it up with YOU, that's a different story. (Be sure not to answer with more information than the child is asking for!) But be tender, knowing children need to learn the importance of sacred things, and how God holds them for our benefit.

Authenticity as a parent means living openly and honestly before your family. We pray and try to be authentic with God. We interact with a corrupt world and still try to be straight with ourselves. Sometimes we struggle but being honest with ourselves and our situation means we act rightly on the best available information.

The day kids realize that a parent isn't perfect, it is a tough day. But they will grow from it. From then on, why would we want to pretend that we are superheroes? Don't we have enough pressure from life? Why act as if we make zero mistakes, that we are more _____ (Fill in this blank yourself) than other people… than our kids? When children learn how Christian adults act, they will absorb the application of spiritual learning into their own lives. When they see how you deal with your own sins and faults, that example can help lead them in the paths of righteousness.

Dad and Justin are working in the back yard, digging up a flower bed. Their neighbor, Mr. Carlson, comes out and yells across the fence. Dad goes over and soon their conversation becomes heated. Justin can't hear but sees his father getting upset. Mr. Carlson, suddenly turns and walks into the house. Dad comes back over to Justin and starts working but is now in a foul mood. When Justin makes a mistake, Dad snaps at him but quickly recognizes he did it out of anger toward Mr. Carlson. Dad now has a choice:

A. "Do I say nothing because I'm the adult and I don't want Justin to think I do wrong things."

OR

B. "It's important to be honest, and I do feel bad about it. Do I apologize to Justin and tell him, 'Sometimes people say things out of their anger. I just did that and I am really sorry I did. Sometimes Dads say stupid things too. I'll try hard not to do that again. Will you forgive me?'"

When Dad chooses A, he sends the message that sometimes parents are unpredictable and can hurt your feelings when they want. When he chooses B, Dad sends the message that adults sometimes struggle with always doing the right thing, but when they mess up, it's important to admit your mistake and make it right.

In the Midwest, we say somebody "puts on airs." Don't be that person, acting like someone you're not with your kids. They know better, and you rob them of being in relationship with a real person. Knowing a real live person means much more than befriending a videogame character. Being a real, live person in relationship with a child goes so much further in creating a relationship with them (and is so much more fun).

This question of authenticity leads parents to pose the question, "How can I lead them to Christ if they think I'm broken or just wrong a lot?" A great question! Are your kids going to accept Christ for themselves and will they become perfect in love and all things? We hope so, but as we said earlier, transformation is a process. For most of us, letting kids see and understand our imperfections (as is age appropriate) and equally, our desire to overcome our frailties will help develop their faith walk.

APPLICATION

List two or three things that you learned or found interesting:

1

2

3

Reflection and Discussion Questions

1) Love is spelled T-I-M-E (Author unknown) How can you be more intentional and spend more love (time) with your children?

2) How could you start having a weekly or biweekly or monthly one on one intentional time with your child? Brainstorm some ideas and write them down. These planned and intentional times are EXTREMELY important to you and your children. Don't forget one on one time with your spouse also!

3) What does this quote mean to you? "The lessons Jesus used to mentor His disciples are a perfect fit for parents as they look at disciple[ing] their children."

Chapter 12 – Consecration

THROUGH SEEKING GOD, THE DISCIPLE DISCERNS AND ACCEPTS
THE DEVOTION AND DEDICATION TO FOLLOWING CHRIST.

> *If obedience is not rendered in the homes, we shall never have a
> whole city, country, principality, or kingdom well governed. For this
> order in the homes is the first rule; it is the source of all other rule
> and government.* Martin Luther

Another critical stage in the adventure of discipleship comes
when the disciple becomes aware of their special place in a bigger
story. They begin to accept the unique spot they hold in the ongoing
story of grace. When it happens, this young disciple becomes
consecrated or dedicated to the purposes of the Lord. That special
relationship of being set apart for God's work defines the act of
consecration. It is being devoted, hallowed, or even made holy.

To fully understand being consecrated, we have to recognize that
God works in all areas of life. God doesn't exist in the religious realm
of life only. God's grace underpins governments, businesses,
relationships and families. Is there any doubt that every part of life
could be made better with God's manifest presence? For a person, or
a child disciple, to become consecrated doesn't mean that they
necessarily need to become a pastor, missionary or another religious
vocation. These roles are clearly important, however, they do not
make up the only calling to serve God.

Since we each serve God in our own ways, the question for a
disciple becomes, "How can I bring God and His saving grace into
this situation?" Sadly, in this day and age, many people work in areas
where speaking about Christ can lead to difficulties. We know that
"God talk" is forbidden for schoolteachers and public employees.

One school bus driver we know was worried when a student
asked, "Hey, what is that book you were reading?" He replied, matter
of factly, "Oh, that's my Bible," and then was immediately overcome

with dread as having a Bible where the students could see it might cost him his job.

However, our bus driver friend adheres to the rules, yet brings God to work every day. Millions of people do that all over the world. They glorify God through the application of the Fruits of the Spirit, as well as interacting with people through a countenance of grace. *"But the fruit of the Spirit is love, joy, peace, forbearance, kindness, goodness, faithfulness, [23]gentleness and self-control. Against such things there is no law."* *(Galatians 5:22-23)* In this way, God's will for others can be done through Christ's disciples without a word being spoken. As St. Francis is reputed to have said, "Go, preach the gospel in all the world and if necessary, even use words."

Clearly, being consecrated meets a far greater definition than just a religious vocation. Consecration calls for enjoying a primary purpose in life, a focus that enlightens the other aspects of the disciple's personality. To be consecrated means having a reason for being. A terrific French saying describes this important concept. The simple phrase "**raison d'être**," translated as "reason for existence," describes the core or center of our being, the thing which informs everything else. Our raison d'être could be any number of things from pleasure to altruism. The best thing it could ever be is Christ.

Being Set Aside

We both agree, one of the great honors of being a pastor is the privilege of consecrating ceremonies. The church consecrates people and objects all the time. What is a church building if not a structure set aside for worship and ministry? Much art and architecture has been consecrated or set aside for God's work, for Holy purposes. Objects can be turned to God's purposes. For example, when the church got a new projector, they prayed over it and dedicated for ministry.

Todd shares that some of the most sacred moments of ministry came from consecrating people in ministry. "I'll never forget a particular mission trip I led. In the church, we prayed over the missioners and consecrated them for God's purpose, sending them to a third world nation to build a church. The Holy Spirit filled our hearts with the understanding of being sent by God to stack block and cement into a structure that would serve as a place of grace and healing among a group of desperately poor people."

Families can be part of this consecration when they bake cookies for a prison Kairos ministry weekend or fill a Christmas shoebox for Operation Christmas Child. When you pray over the cookies or shoeboxes (or any other work for God) you consecrate them for God's blessing to others. In many homes, a dinner time grace is a consecration of the meal for God's purposes.

Can there be a better use for something, or someone, than to bring God's love to a dark world? We doubt it.

Consecration means the setting apart of something for God's purposes. This word, literally, means to make holy, to sanctify. Jesus was set aside for a mission to earth. In John 10:36-38 the Lord Jesus shows the intentional purpose of His existence when He scolded his critics saying,

> "*[36]...do you say of Him, whom the Father sanctified and sent into the world, 'You are blaspheming,' because I said, 'I am the Son of God'? [37] "If I do not do the works of My Father, do not believe Me;[38] but if I do them, though you do not believe Me, believe the works, so that you may know and understand that the Father is in Me, and I in the Father."*
>
> *(John 10:36-38)*

In this passage, Jesus declares to his critics he was sanctified, devoted, set apart, or "consecrated." In this, He describes His presence as intentional. He didn't just show up, He was sent on a mission. "The Father sanctified and sent..." shows Jesus being consecrated or "set aside." **Since Jesus described himself as "set aside for God's use," we should be eager to see ourselves in the same light; the set-aside and sent people of God.**

Part of a Peculiar People

It will certainly help the young disciple to understand his or her place in life, their raison d'être, as part of something big. We are all (all of us) looking to belong to something bigger than ourselves. Until recently, humans have always understood themselves as part of something and not just an individual organism alone on the earth. We were part of a family, a tribe, a nation. We had purpose. For the Christian disciple, we understand the movement of God as something spanning the centuries and so a young disciple can understand the place they occupy in "The Family of God."

> *⁹But you are a chosen race, a royal priesthood, a holy nation, God's own people, in order that you may proclaim the mighty acts of him who called you out of darkness into his marvelous light.*
>
> *(1 Peter 2:9)*

Helping mentor your child disciple brings together the people of God, the Holy Spirit, and the church across the ages. Being set aside for God's purpose is to participate in a grand plan for the spread of grace within the human condition.

We can and should cling tightly to this notion that we are part of something momentous and powerful. Sadly, we have lost the impact of the radical nature of the gospel in human society. We see the violence, the hate, the deception and selfishness enough to realize the nature of the human condition. These things are as old as history. As far back as any human can see, back to the beginning of Genesis, we see rebellion against God and violence against people. Society is more subtle today but still organized around the militant principles of self-interest and exploitation. Click on your news site, see your local TV station, look at your place of employment.

Tom recently watched an interview with Billy Graham. The interviewer asked Dr. Graham if evil is worse now than ever before in human history. He replied, "Sin has always been in our nature but now we have 24 hour news to reveal it."

As Christians, we strive to replace the love of self with the love of Christ. We seek to see justice established among the nations and peace on earth, good will to all. This monumental goal is a tremendously powerful reason to live and serve. After all, Christ's mission was to die for love so that our mission can be to live for love.

We are part of God's bigger agenda. We belong to something larger than our pathetic little wants and desires. We are part of saving, not only our own soul but countless millions of other souls. Our mission means working with God to transform the world.

Shown in Obedience

We understand our place in the big plan of Christ's incarnation through our willingness to take part in it. **Being part of God's kingdom continues to be a participant activity not a spectator sport.** Understanding God's principles can be helpful but can never take the place of living them. Knowing facts about God, the Bible, and the history of the church can be enriching, but still never take the place of walking in relationship to God in Christ Jesus. Living the gospel transforms life in a way that head knowledge cannot do by itself.

For that reason, obedience is the call of all disciples. Some readers may have just cringed. That's because the word "obedience" has gone wildly out of favor. To suggest that someone be obedient sounds akin to suggesting they become robots, enslaved to puppet masters above them, cynically manipulated for their master's gain- essentially, becoming a slave.

The world holds no lack of people willing to use us to get what they want. Clearly that's true. However, we refrain from including God in that category. Yes, God wants us to do things we don't want to do or don't feel like doing. Just like when Mama swatted our hand away as we reached for the hot burner, she did right. Actions bring results, and the things we do will have consequences that God can foresee while we still have no clue.

Obedience is a trust issue. We may think, "If I give my decision making capability to someone else they will twist it and use me for their own good." This danger occurs regularly in life. However, that has more to do with the quality of the relationship than with the nature of obedience. Trusting God is a prerequisite to consecration.

Todd has a son in the Air Force. When Clay obeys his superior's commands, it's not because he is mindless but because he trusts his superiors. By joining, Clay made a decision to accept the leadership of the Air Force Chain of Command. He obeys orders unless the orders are illegal, in which case his superiors have violated the trust placed in them. As an Airman in the United States Air Force, he is not obligated to follow illegal orders.

Being consecrated as a disciple of Christ means to follow one path and "be on the same page" as the Lord. It means "being on the same team" and striving to be "all in" for Jesus.

In a similar way, following God, His commandments, precepts and statutes, brings blessings and not curses. God never gave an illegal or immoral command, so why hesitate? This brings us back to our sin nature. **It is our sin nature to obey our human desires; it is our grace nature to want the best for others. God calls us to live in the state of grace He has so freely given.**

Jesus isn't looking to join our personal agenda but waiting for us to follow His. Obedience shows the level of trust we place in God. We know full well that there will be difficulties and hard times but a disciple serves Christ knowing there will be both earthly and heavenly rewards too.

Being consecrated as a disciple of Christ means to follow one path and "be on the same page" as the Lord. It means "being on the same team" and striving to be "all in" for Jesus. Most of all, being consecrated means being devoted to Christ, intentionally serving Him and following Him wherever that path may lead. Far from becoming a slave, when a disciple obeys Christ, they become more free than they ever have been. Just as a church building serves its purpose, being a consecrated Christian means being set aside for the use and favor of Christ.

As parents, God calls us to consecrate ourselves to Him. As we draw closer to God, we help our children do the same. Could God have installed a greater motivation than having us lead our children? For us, this is a compelling factor for letting God have all of us.

ALL OF ME

All of me, not a part but all of me
All the heart and soul of me
Jesus I surrender
I believe, Lord, help my unbelief
On the altar now I lay all I am today
So use me, Lord, use me anywhere at all
Though my palace may be great or small
Let me fill it gladly
Take my life and let it be
Take my life be it poor or be it grand
Let me live by Your plan. Shape it with Your hand
As I am I come to Thee without one plea
Only that Thy saving blood was shed for me
All of me through the ages yet to be
I surrender Lord to Thee
I surrender all of me, I surrender all of me
All of me, I surrender all, all of me

Mosie Lister

APPLICATION

List two or three things that you learned or found interesting:

1

2

3

Reflection and Discussion Questions

1) "Consecration means the setting apart of something for God's Purpose." What types of things do you consecrate to God?

2) Parents, how important is it for you to consecrate yourself to God?

3) Is it possible to consecrate your children to God if you are not consecrated to God?

4) What is your biggest hindrance to consecrating yourself and family to God?

5) How can God help you to break this hindrance?

6) "Being part of God's kingdom continues to be a participant activity not a spectator sport." What is your opinion about this quote?

Chapter 13 – Impartation

KNOWLEDGE AND ACCEPTANCE THAT THE HOLY SPIRIT WILL
BE UNCONDITIONALLY RECEIVED TO GUIDE THE DISCIPLE.

> *[16] And I will pray the Father, and He will give you another Helper,
> that He may abide with you forever— [17] the Spirit of truth, whom
> the world cannot receive, because it neither sees Him nor knows
> Him; but you know Him, for He dwells with you and will be in
> you. (John 14:16-17)*

The presence of the Holy Spirit is absolutely necessary in the
process of making disciples. God, the Holy Spirit, needs to empower
both parent and child to understand and accept the knowledge that
doesn't come naturally. Impartation is the descent of the Holy Spirit
into the people and the process of a holy discipleship.

Only through the participation of God can we understand the
perspective of God. Right? Who could fully understand God from
their own experiences and knowledge? No one. God stands alone,
beyond our power to capture and harness Him through mere words.
The Bible makes God known to us through the writings of inspired
people. Words of our own could not begin to capture God's essence,
let alone God's plan for us. It is only through the Spirit of God that
we can begin to know God.

The Holy Spirit dwells or lives within us. Though we have the
Spirit of God, we cannot say that we ARE God, as some do. No, the
Lord has graciously given us a helper, a counselor, an advocate that
influences our heart and mind, *"But the Advocate, the Holy Spirit, whom
the Father will send in my name, will teach you all things and will remind you of
everything I have said to you." (John 14:26)* This helper opens to us the
wisdom and viewpoint of God.

Consider this, what could be more un-natural than loving our
enemies? It seems silly to hope goodness upon people we feel so
negatively toward. However, God calls us to do just that- love our
enemies. The Lord calls us to love far bigger than the world does,

"For if you love those who love you, what reward do you have? Do not even the tax collectors do the same?" (John 5:46)

The Spirit of God exists within the hearts and minds of those who love God and seek wholeheartedly to serve Him. The nature of the Spirit may be mysterious to our meager understanding. Nevertheless, we can be content with an incomplete understanding of how the Spirit acts within and upon us. When we have the spirit, we experience the Spirit but we do not control the Spirit. As Jesus taught, *"The wind blows where it chooses, and you hear the sound of it, but you do not know where it comes from or where it goes. So it is with everyone who is born of the Spirit." (John 3:8)*

So, how do we deal with a God who is both all-powerful and uncontrollable? This question plagues many people, but, truly, there is only one answer. We must submit to Him. As C.S. Lewis, says in "The Lion, the Witch and the Wardrobe" about Aslan the Lion (the Christ figure), "He is dangerous but he is good."

As parents mentoring our children, the question inevitably comes up, "OK, so the Holy Spirit is indispensable to the process of discipleship. Got it. Then how do we use the Holy Spirit to help train our children in the way they should go?"

The answer is stark. You cannot. You cannot do anything to the Spirit to make the Spirit do anything for you. He cannot be manipulated by us. There is only one way to deal with the Spirit. Invite Him in and follow where He leads.

It takes faith but we can trust God. The Spirit of God makes the wisdom of man look like nonsense. What God sees, what God wants, far exceeds the understanding of the world. As St. Paul put it, *"For the message about the cross is foolishness to those who are perishing, but to us who are being saved it is the power of God." (1 Corinthians 1:18)* The power, the wisdom of God is available to us only as we put ourselves forth to follow.

> *[11] For what man knows the things of a man except the spirit of the man which is in him? Even so no one knows the things of God except the Spirit of God. [12]Now we have received, not the spirit of*

the world, but the Spirit who is from God, that we might know the things that have been freely given to us by God.

(1 Corinthians 2:11-12)

There seems to be only one way to know the things of God and that is to know God. We move beyond the viewpoints, and the feelings, and the affronts of the worldly mind and grow into the mindset of God. Raising children in the ways of the Spirit must include the Spirit. We hear many people say today, "I am spiritual but not religious." However, to be "spiritual" one must have more than kindness, openness, or curiosity. You must have the Spirit of God dwelling within you.

You cannot do anything TO the Spirit to make the Spirit do anything FOR you. HE cannot be manipulated by us. There is only one way to deal with the Holy Spirit. Invite Him in and follow wear He leads!

As we mention earlier, a parent cannot pass on what they do not possess. Any process that depends on the Holy Spirit must include the Spirit abiding in the parent. Only then can the parent share the viewpoint of God on matters of faith, living and life eternal. With the Holy Spirit enlightening and or leading the parent, the child will receive the leading of God through the Spirit. **The Holy Spirit uses the conduit of the parent until that child is himself or herself, filled with God's Holy Spirit.**

As Christian parents, we must equally do what Jesus did for His disciples. We must give ourselves to them, for their benefit, for their grace, so that they may continue into the joyous life of Christ. As Dr. Coleman wrote, "Here is the great paradox of life, we must die to ourselves to live in Christ, and in that renunciation of ourselves, we must give ourselves away in service and devotion to our Lord."[23] We can rest assured that we are doing the right thing and leading the right way when we, as parents, accept and abide in the Lord's Spirit. We will know we are on the right path because the Spirit will let us know, *"The Spirit Himself bears witness with our spirit that we are children of God." (Romans 8:16)* The Spirit of God can be well trusted!

APPLICATION

List two or three things that you learned or found interesting:

1

2

3

Reflection and Discussion Questions

1) In John 14:26, Jesus said, "But the Counselor, the Holy Spirit, whom the Father will send in my name, will teach you all things and will remind you of everything I have said to you." What do you think when you realize the very presence of God (the Holy Spirit) is with you to help you disciple your child?

2) What type of response do you have when you hear, "I am spiritual but not religious." What does that really mean?

3) Can a person be "spiritual" without the presence of the Holy Spirit in their life?

4) Much has been spoken and written about the "Witness of the Spirit." "*The Spirit Himself bears witness with our spirit that we are children of God.*" *(Romans 8:16)* What benefits does one receive with "the witness of the Spirit?"

Chapter 14 – Demonstration

THROUGH EXHIBITING THE AUTHENTIC LIFE OF CHRIST, INCLUDING
CHALLENGES, THE MENTOR CREATES A LIFE MODEL TO FOLLOW.

Children need models more than they need critics.

Joseph Joubert

Demonstration is the heartbeat of our book on parenting and discipleship. Showing children how to live life as a Christian requires parents including the children in their own faith walk. This is a tremendous blessing for both parents and children. The principle of Demonstration means *showing* discipleship and comes from the honest-to-goodness truth that a child (anyone really) can learn only so much from directions. To activate learning in our life, humans need to see it, try it, evaluate it, re-try it and re-evaluate it (perhaps many times) before then implementing it. Somewhere along the line, depending on the lessons, the teacher, and our own capabilities, we find understanding and make it part of our own life.

Billy sits quietly in his fifth grade classroom paying attention to his experienced teacher. The teacher patiently explains to the students how long division works. She goes through several problems on the board. Billy raises his hand, and when called upon he tentatively states, "I don't understand that." What does Billy's teacher do next?

A. Says, "Billy, pay attention!" and then proceeds to do the same thing on the board with different numbers. When Billy doesn't get it right, she scolds him.

OR

B. Says, "OK, class," go ahead and try the problems in your book. I'll be by to see how you're doing in a minute." She then walks to Billy's desk and proceeds to let him watch her do a problem while she explains it. She then has Billy do a problem while he explains his work as he goes. She gently corrects his mistakes and eventually, together, they get Billy on track by doing long division together.

We hope that you appreciated the teacher in scenario B. That teacher wants Billy to gain the practical tools she teaches to him. She worked with him individually and helped him gain the skill through practice, figuring out where he went wrong and trying again until he mastered the needed skills. Thankfully, many classrooms feature such dedicated teachers.

With all the many aggravations found in modern life, we often lack the patience to live a life of demonstration with our children.

However, teacher B is far from universal in schools, colleges or on-the-job training. And sadly, too often, we parents act as the teacher in scenario A with our own children. We understand it, we told them and so we expect them to know it. With all the aggravations of modern life, we often lack the patience to live a life of demonstration with our children. How much better would it be if we would walk together with our kids teaching them the practical aspects of growing close to Christ and living His life among the people we know?

Let's consider that teaching scenario again as lived by a Christian parent.

Billy comes home from school and says to his mother. "Mommy, I'm worried about taking my math test at school. I think I understand after my teacher helped me, but I don't want to mess up and look stupid." Which scenario works better?

A. Mom turns from her work and says "Well, I understand that Billy, just ask God to help you do your best and to quit worrying." Then she returns to her work.

OR

B. Mom turns from her work and goes and sits next to Billy and says, "Well, I understand that Billy. You don't get to see it, but I worry about things too. Right now, I'm concerned about Grandma and her health. It makes me upset to think about her being really sick. I don't like how I feel when I worry. Do you get all nervous and maybe a little nauseous in your tummy, too? I thought so. Son, when

I start to worry about Grandma, or money, or even you I stop myself and ask a question. I ask myself, 'Self, have you done all you can do to take care of the things you can control?' When I can say yes, then I pray to the Lord."

"Remember how God told many people in the Bible to 'Fear Not.' Well, let's pray that God will deliver us from fear. I'll start praying, then when you're ready, you tell God what you're afraid will happen. Then I'll finish the prayer and ask God to give us the strength to trust Him in everything. Then, I'll say 'We give our worry to you God. Do with us what you feel best.' Then we will say 'Amen', and we'll trust God to watch over us. Then, whenever our mind starts to bring us worry we just tell ourselves, 'That's God's problem to care for,' and we'll find something else to think about. Are you ready to pray?" After they pray, Mom and Billy work through the math together.

When an appropriate opportunity presents itself to share our own walk with our children, we should interact with them over our choices and struggles.

The mom in scenario A clearly has the right answer. Turn it over to God and quit worrying. However, the mom in scenario B, who shared her own worries and prayed with her child was demonstrating the practical ways she lives as a Christian. She was being in relationship with both God and Billy and helping Billy to learn to walk with God.

Adults have things in their life that a child is not prepared to understand, mentally or emotionally. However, when an appropriate opportunity presents itself to share our own walk with our children, we should interact with them over our choices and struggles. **Take opportunities to make any event a teachable moment and a relational moment, for you and your family.**

> [1]*One day Jesus was praying in a certain place. When he finished, one of his disciples said to him, "Lord, teach us to pray, just as John taught his disciples."* [2]*He said to them," When you pray, say:*

"Father, hallowed be your name, our kingdom come, [3]Give us each day our daily bread.[4]Forgive us our sins, for we also forgive everyone who sins against us. And lead us not into temptation."'

(Luke 11:1-4)

Jesus demonstrated to his disciples how to live by living life with them. Look at Jesus' prayer life. He taught prayer by praying. As an observant Jew, he prayed in the common ways but He also communed with the Father in other personal ways as well. It must have seemed to His disciples that He was always praying. So when the disciples expressed interest in praying He took the opportunity to teach them. As we see above, they came to Him and asked, "How should we pray?" Why would they do that unless they saw Jesus praying and wanted to be part of that special moment? They wanted what Jesus

When an appropriate opportunity presents itself to share our own walk with our children, we should interact with them over our choices and struggles.

had. He didn't push them, he led them. They wanted His leadership.

In like manner, Jesus was constantly using Scriptures as teachable moments in the context of everyday life situations. The disciples eventually understood the importance of Scripture in their lives.

> *[23]Then he turned to his disciples and said privately, "Blessed are the eyes that see what you see. [24]For I tell you that many prophets and kings wanted to see what you see but did not see it, and to hear what you hear but did not hear it." (Luke 10:23-24)*

It was a real, honest-to-goodness privilege for the disciples to be with Jesus and see the amazing things they saw. As parents, we need to always keep in mind that everything a child learns is new and though many things seem mundane to us, to kids new discoveries can be amazing and powerful. Learning to be a human follower of Christ can be a treat or it can be a chore. We know that you want it to be a treat for your kids. So, grow deeper yourself and help your kids grow deeper to bless the whole family.

Jesus did not leave them on their own to pick it up. He was demonstrating real life to the disciples by acting within real life situations. This same "**life-style discipleship**" may be used by caring parents to teach their own children. Just think, going to the store can be a meaningful spiritual experience when done in the spotlight of Jesus and His life-style.

Imagine taking your child to the grocery store. Along the way, someone cuts you off in traffic. What do you say, how do you react?

The same "life-style" discipleship that Jesus used may be used by caring parents to teach their own children.

Curse or blessing? Can you hope that the person is simply selfish instead of rushing to the side of an injured child? Let's be real here, many if not most of the frustration in driving (and life) can be credited to our own self-centeredness. I want to be there NOW, I wanted to move into that spot. I want more space in traffic. Is a turn signal merely a cue to close with the car ahead of you so that car can't move in? Or can we be peaceful in traffic? It clearly can be done.

How about all the public annoyances at the grocery? The fact that products are often more expensive than we hoped. The checkout line slows to a crawl, and the cashier takes cranky to a completely new level. In spite of our struggles, how do we handle it? How do we explain it? In all these little moments of challenge, stepping back from our own selfishness can be a great lesson for kids. Dr. Coleman wrote, "People are looking for a demonstration, not an explanation."[24]

When it is all boiled down, those of us who are seeking to train people must be prepared to have them follow us, even as we follow Christ (I Cor. 11:1). We are the exhibit (Phil 3:17, I Thess 2:7, 8; 2 Tim 1:13). They will do those things which they hear and see in us (Phil 4:9). Given time, it is possible through this kind of leadership to impart our way of living to those who are constantly with us.[25]

Children live with us, they absorb us; especially if we choose to help them. When parents choose to make kids part of their life (and not just a parenting project we are responsible for) they find they can build an actual parent-child relationship. It is easier but far less profitable for our kids if we try to be their buddy or best friend. If you want to hear your child say they are your best friend, have it said by your adult child. They won't quit saying it when you refuse them something. When we make time to be family, we make time to help our kids mature, feel love, gain confidence, learn about life and catch our values.

APPLICATION

List two or three things that you learned or found interesting:

1

2

3

Reflection and Discussion Questions

1) "This is the heartbeat of our book on parenting and discipleship. Showing children how to live life as a Christian requires parents including the children in their faith walk." What are your initial thoughts?

2) What lasting lesson did you learn from your parents? How do you relate the story of Billy with your life? How can you be like the second example with your children?

3) What is your "take home" from Mom's reaction on pages 125-26?

4) List several ways you can be more intentional at home in demonstrating for your child.

5) What do your driving habits demonstrate to your children?

6) How important is it to have your children seeing you pray and read your Bible?

Chapter 15 – Delegation

THE MENTOR WILL GIVE REALISTIC AND INCREASINGLY DIFFICULT
ASSIGNMENTS FOR THE DISCIPLE'S SPIRITUAL GROWTH.

The way you delegate is that first you have to hire people that you really have confidence in. You won't truly let those people feel a sense of autonomy if you don't have confidence in them.

Robert Pozen

[7] And He summoned the twelve and began to send them out in pairs, and gave them authority over the unclean spirits; [8] and He instructed them that they should take nothing for their journey, except a mere staff—no bread, no bag, no money in their belt [9] but to wear sandals; and He added, "Do not put on two tunics." [10] And He said to them, Wherever you enter a house, stay there until you leave town. [11] "Any place that does not receive you or listen to you, as you go out from there, shake the dust off the soles of your feet for a testimony against them." [12] They went out and preached that men should repent. [13] And they were casting out many demons and were anointing with oil many sick people and healing them.

(Mark 6:7-13)

After a mentor spends their effort teaching, the time comes for the disciple to try it out on their own. It may be a small thing or a big event, but when disciples grow they will need to be given the opportunity to try out their wings. Learning usually comes in increments and skill sets, not all at once. Delegation shows the mentor or parent allowing the child disciple to perform the action themselves. It may be putting allowance in the offering plate, going to Bible study, leading a prayer or sharing the gospel. The facets of a faith walk are many and varied. The time will come when a parent must give their child an opportunity to perform.

When the time came, Jesus sent them out. He sent them on a specific mission. And, he refrained from giving them too much. The Lord tasked them, not to do everything but to do something specific. He gave them a well-defined project, instructed them about their tools and supplies, and even taught them the procedure to follow when they failed. The disciples received appropriate and helpful direction before their mission.

First, Jesus brought the group together for final instructions. He told them details of their mission and what they needed to accomplish. It seems highly unlikely that Jesus said, "Hey, y'all go out and evangelize. See you next week." No, Jesus set them up for success.

Jesus, as their mentor, also dispatched them 2 by 2 - using "the buddy system." Or as Todd's son in the Air Force says, "with their wingman." This mission partnership clearly shows Jesus thought about their personal safety and gave them their "buddy" for mutual support, decision-making and project execution. Going with a partner always works better.

The safety of strength in numbers cannot be underestimated. Sending them out in pairs also helped them look at problems and opportunities from different perspectives. We're sure that you can remember times when a fresh perspective helped you make good decisions. "Two heads are better than one," describes more than an illusionist's coin.

The Scripture also tells us that Jesus, "gave them authority over unclean spirits." While not clear exactly how this was done, we see the effect as they cast out demons and healed people. (Remember, all these things Jesus clearly demonstrated daily as the disciples watched.) He gave them the tools necessary to complete their mission. This practical tool, authority over unclean spirits, helped keep them safe, meet the goals of the mission and increased their confidence. Stop and think how much better you would feel about going out alone into a potentially hostile setting when Jesus himself gave you power over the forces of evil. Clearly, this helped ensure the best performance of the disciple's mission.

Another instruction that Jesus gave them was to "live off the land." Or rather, live in and with the community in which you are immersed. This is incarnational ministry at its finest. Any tools that would make them self-sufficient hindered their mission. This part of the mission meant they needed to be entwined with the local population. They were not to be outsiders among the people they shared with but become one of them– to live with and among them. In a culture that strongly valued hospitality, it was a calculated decision when Jesus told them to put themselves at the mercy of the community.

The Lord also told them to stay with one family. He cautioned them against flitting around or moving when they think they have found a better place. These things create jealousy or rivalry, which would damage their mission. He wanted them to "Find somebody to take you in and depend upon them. Allow them to introduce you to their circle of friends and neighbors." The disciples would pay their way by blessing their new friends with the message and purpose with which Jesus sent.

Failure is good. Failure is a good teacher. Failure is the one indispensable ingredient for growth and success.

In case Jesus' disciples were rejected, He gave them a ritual to perform allowing them closure and the ability to mentally move on. He taught them to, "shake the dust off the soles of your feet as a testimony against them." Novices will always experience setbacks and failures. Expect them to. Then give them a way to reset their thinking and make a clean break from their past failure. This lesson will make parents better mentors and, after all, isn't a clean break from the past one of the great gifts of grace?

> *Over, over,*
> *done and gone*
> *The past is over*
> *The new is on*

Rhyme to teach children to help them "shake the dust off their feet" and close the book on a failure.

Here, we feel compelled to examine the virtue of failure. Many times, we parents feel it is our duty to protect our children from failure. We think that we guard our children's fragile ego or their self-image when we protect them from failing. We seem to worry that failing will be more than our child can bear. On the other hand, sometimes parents might be overly worrying about how it makes them look. **Keeping your child from failure robs them of particularly important experiences of life.**

Failure is good. Failure is a good teacher. Failure is the indispensable ingredient for growth and success. Few people go through life without failing. And many successful people have failed badly in their life. In fact, a mentor who refuses to allow their student to fail under controlled circumstances leaves them utterly unprepared for the realities of living. As has been quoted to numerous people:

> *Success is getting up one more time than you've been knocked down.*
> *Oliver Goldsmith*

We, all of us, gain confidence through success and failure. Rare is the child, student, disciple who never knows failure. Therefore, an integral part of teaching happens to be dealing with challenges. A challenge, by definition, carries with it the risk of failure. Being challenged means that skills are put to the test. (We will discuss more about Child Development in Section 3 – Making the Connection.) This time of challenge leads us into the most productive, most growing times of life.

We grow when we stretch. We stretch when we move beyond our comfort zone. Most importantly, parents need to embrace the notion that we grow only when part of us leaves our comfort zone. So, with the wisdom of your experience as a safety net, allow your young disciple the opportunity to occasionally get knocked down! Then they can enjoy the victory of getting back up stronger than ever.

APPLICATION

List two or three things that you learned or found interesting:

1

2

3

Reflection and Discussion Questions

1) What was an exciting event or activity you remember as a child that your parents delegated to you? How did this make you feel?

2) What can you delegate to your children at this time? (age appropriate) How do you think they will feel about this new adventure?

3) What is your take on "failure as a good teacher?"

4) The authors loved this statement, "Success is getting up one more time than you've been knocked down." Do you agree or disagree? Give an example for your answer.

Chapter 16 – Supervision

WHILE PARTICIPATING IN ASSIGNMENTS, THE DISCIPLE REPORTS TO
THE MENTOR WHO EVALUATES PROGRESS AND ADJUSTS THE PROGRAM.

*I was very, very little - it was the first time I ever cooked on my own,
with my mother's supervision - and I made scrambled eggs. I felt so
accomplished, like magic!* Gail Simmons

In Supervision Phase, the mentor allows the student to perform
their delegated responsibility, evaluates their attempt and then gives
feedback. Supervision means a process of building expertise and
autonomy in the student or child disciple. This process will be
followed by a new delegation phase, which takes into account how
the student did the first time and how they responded to the
mentor's feedback. Then, the student gets another opportunity for
more growth, responsibility and freedom.

In aviation, budding pilots first spend time in the classroom
learning about the principles of flight. Next, they spend time flying in
the plane with an instructor coaching them. Then, and only then,
when the instructor becomes comfortable with the skill of the trainee
will they allow the student to "solo." This significant step comes only
when the certified instructor believes that the student can safely
perform all basic aviation skills. During their "solo flight," the
student must perform all activities alone for the first time. From
preflight check, takeoff, powered flight maneuvers to landing; each
task is executed by the student pilot because there is no instructor in
the plane.

Because of the many dangers involved in flying, this milestone
marks a major advance in a novice pilot's instruction. When a student
successfully solos, a ceremony of some sort usually follows. Often,
following old-time flying tradition, the tail of the solo pilot's shirt is
snipped off and displayed as a memento. Flying legend says that the
tradition goes back to the days when early flyers flew in open cockpit
planes with the student in front of the instructor. To direct the

student, the instructor would pull the students shirttail and yell over the wind into his ear. Losing your shirttail signified that you no longer needed the instructor. In flight schools across the country, you can often see shirttails with names and dates mounted on the walls.

This "solo" reminds us of a disciple growing in knowledge and ability. The same with a parent and child disciple, soloing does not end the instruction. In fact, a student pilot still needs much instruction before they can receive their pilot's license, rent a plane, and travel across country on their own. After the first solo they will need more help than ever, because the danger increases when they first leave the care of their instructor.

Jesus gave the twelve disciples clear projects to work on. Jesus trained them, and let the disciples observe him at work. At a certain point, there came a time in the ministry of the disciples where they needed to move forward and do the work themselves.

Jesus gave the twelve clear projects to work on. He trained them and let them observe Him at work. At a certain point, there came a time where they needed to move forward and do the work themselves.

Tom has enjoyed playing guitar for many years. As his three boys [Selection] grew up, they watched and listened to their daddy playing guitar [Association/Demonstration]. Tom enjoyed using the guitar to help himself worship God musically. He allowed his boys to be part of that and showed them how to worship God in a personal way, through the music they played.

Tom taught them their gifts and skills can be used for God's glory [Consecration]. In this way, through seeking God the Father, the Holy Spirit became part of the equation. One cannot truly worship without the Holy Spirit. Through allowing the Spirit to come into this act of devotion, it became worship set aside for God [Impartation].

Tom's oldest son, Michael, was about seven when Tom began teaching him to play guitar. A typical practice session would begin by showing Michael how to play a song [Demonstration]. Then for the rest of the week Michael would practice the song on his own [Delegation]. Throughout the week, Tom would listen to Michael play the song and check on the progress and give him input [Supervision]. Michael was a quick study and in no time he played with the praise team in his church.

At first, the guitar was so big and heavy Michael had to sit on a stool and have someone bring it to him to play. Years have flown by, and now Michael has led his own praise teams and is teaching others how to play guitar [Reproduction]. Reproduction is the last principle we have written about in this Section.

This guitar illustration demonstrates only one of endless examples of how Jesus' discipleship process can be imitated. It is a part of a lifestyle; this is why we wrote a lot about "life-style discipleship." Of course, Jesus didn't teach his disciples to play guitar. However, He used these same principles to disciple his twelve apostles.

Beginning with Selection and ending in Reproduction, Jesus made disciples who made disciples. This line of spiritual descendants reaches down through the ages to us today. We have the privilege of passing it on to the next generation. We always say, "since the Son of God used these methods, His followers would be wise to do the same."

APPLICATION

List two or three things that you learned or found interesting:

1

2

3

Reflection and Discussion Questions

1) What hobby or new skill do you need right now for someone to demonstrate, delegate and supervise? Why do you need another person to show you? What connections are similar to parenting/disciple[ing] your child?

2) Is there an activity you have given your children in the past and didn't follow-up on the process that, in hind sight, you wish you had rechecked? What was the event? What would you do differently?

Chapter 17 – Reproduction

WHILE GROWING INTO A MATURE CHRISTIAN, THE DISCIPLE EVENTUALLY
BECOMES A MENTOR AND REPLICATES THE PROCESS.

> *"No worldly pursuit compares to the joy of experiencing the change
> of one soul from death to life."*
>
> *Dillon Burroughs*

> [18] *And Jesus came up and spoke to them, saying, "All authority has
> been given to Me in heaven and on earth.* [19] *Go therefore and make
> disciples of all the nations, baptizing them in the name of the Father
> and the Son and the Holy Spirit,* [20] *teaching them to observe all
> that I commanded you; and lo, I am with you always, even to the
> end of the age." (Matthew 28:18-20)* THE GREAT COMMISSION

Every living thing reproduces in some way. In the natural world,
we find many different manners and methods of reproduction. The
same truth exists in the spiritual realm. Faith begets faith. If your
faith lives, it will reproduce.

As people who have had the privilege of leading many through
the sinners prayer, we can say this without qualification, "There are
few greater moments than being with a person when the Holy Spirit
humbles their heart and opens their eyes." *"Therefore, if anyone is in
Christ, the new creation has come: The old has gone, the new is here!" (2
Corinthians 5:17)*

Remember the joy of meeting your child for the first time. It
happens many different ways but brings a warmth and joy to us. If
you have ever described anything as a "miracle," one of those times
was probably at a birth or upon seeing a baby. Something about this
astounding event speaks to us about our Creator. In that wondrous
moment, we get a glimpse of the miracle of creation. Not just the
human variety of creation but the realization that everything, all of
creation, was birthed by the declaration of God. We parents, in some
mysterious way, through God's universal plan get to take part in that!

Just as we reach a level of maturity in our bodies, we can physically reproduce. In like manner, when we reach a level of spiritual maturity we will be able to spiritually reproduce. When our students, our children (our disciples of Christ) reach that level of maturity, they will be able to lead others to Christ. A mature disciple understands the nature of the Christian life and experience enough to share it with others. We're not talking simply about a formula of words but sharing the essence of Christ by example; by word and deed. And for those longing to hear it, the word of God is a healing medicine, a saving force that changes lives and restores the soul.

Clearly, helping another person (adult, youth, child) find God pleases the person finding God. Even more, a real Christian will be pleased to have helped others find a saving relationship with the Lord. The path of grace leads us there. A person filled with the Spirit cannot help sharing the Spirit with others. It isn't even a conscious decision but an overflow of grace. Have you ever seen an artesian well? The water coming up from underground flows on its own because of natural pressure. An artesian well needs no pump to bring the water up from the ground, the amount of water exceeds the well capacity and just pours out on its own.

God is also pleased.

> [8] *"Or what woman having ten silver coins, if she loses one of them, does not light a lamp, sweep the house, and search carefully until she finds it?* [9] *When she has found it, she calls together her friends and neighbors, saying, 'Rejoice with me, for I have found the coin that I had lost.'* [10] *Just so, I tell you, there is joy in the presence of the angels of God over one sinner who repents." Luke 15:8-10*

To fully realize the implications of the Reproduction phase, we must understand it as a command. Christ gives us the Great Commission as the work of our Christian walk (Matthew 28:19-20). He stated it to his disciple, not just for the twelve but for ALL of His disciples.

We, all Christians, must be part of the worldwide effort to bring the message of salvation through Christ to everyone. When we look at the text of the Great Commission, it becomes quite clear what Jesus wants. He wants us to GO MAKE DISCIPLES. We might be out preaching, or teaching, or baptizing but all of these activities serve one goal.

Some may be out speaking in cities and in communities and in foreign lands, sharing the word of God and the gospel of hope. Others may be teaching the word of God pertaining to the Christ, some may be teaching the words of Jesus about how to believe and act. Still others can be found in the churches and the rivers and creeks, and even the swimming pools baptizing people into the family of God. These activities powerfully impact the world. But the words of Jesus show that these activities have a specific purpose, without which they lose their importance.

A person filled with the Spirit cannot help sharing the Spirit with others. It isn't even a conscious decision but an overflow of grace.

The entire reason for this trilogy of ministry lies solely in their assigned purpose. These actions fit Jesus' goal to "make disciples." This is their *raison d'être*, their very reason for existence. Every activity we do to reach out and connect the gospel with others is living the Great Commission. C.S. Lewis, Oxford Scholar and author of "Mere Christianity," describes in that book that our common faith might be considered a "Good Infection."

> *Good things as well as bad, you know, are caught by a kind of infection. If you want to get warm you must stand near the fire: if you want to be wet you must get into the water. If you want joy, power, peace, eternal life, you must get close to, or even into, the thing that has them. They are not a sort of prizes which God could, if He chose, just hand out to anyone. They are a great fountain of energy and beauty spurting up at the very centre of reality. If you are close to it, the spray will wet you: if you are not, you will remain dry. Once a man is united to God, how could he not live forever? Once a man is separated from God, what can he do but wither and die?* [26]

It is our goal, our duty, our privilege to help people get close to God and help them receive all the beautiful benefits of being near. In many ways, one could view this as the purpose of our existence: To know God and to make Him known. What God is looking for are followers who will work with the Holy Spirit to create and nurture other followers. This is the duty and the purpose of our existence: to reproduce.

Parents, God has selected our children according to the plan God has for them. For better or worse, they are ours. As the days and years go by, we hope for children and grandchildren to give us joy, to share life with us as family, and to take our heritage into the future. As we raise them in Christ and teach them to become disciples, we will have the joy of watching them live out the role God has for them in the spread of the gospel. In this way, we gain spiritual sons and daughters, grandsons and granddaughters and descendants aplenty. In this very same way, we transform the world!

Jesus had as His mission, the salvation of the world. We believe parents can and should replicate the principles Jesus used with His disciples. This process will transform, not only the lives of our children, but the content of our entire world.

APPLICATION

List two or three things that you learned or found interesting:

1

2

3

Reflection and Discussion Questions

1) Describe your emotions the first time you saw your child/children at birth? What flooded your mind as you saw this bundle of joy? Did your mind flash to the future?

2) Read Matthew 28:18-20. This is known as the Great Commission. (In chapter 26 we will go into greater detail.) How does the Great Commission relate to parenting and discipleship? What does it have to do with reproduction?

3) In the Great Commission, is Jesus giving the disciples a suggestion or something stronger? Did this command only apply to the disciples?

"Parents are so busy with the physical rearing of children that they miss the glory of parenthood, just as the grandeur of the trees is lost when raking leaves."   Marcelene Cox

Section 3

MAKING THE CONNECTION

SECTION 3 - MAKING THE CONNECTION

Chapter 18 – Why Study Child Development?

If a child lives with criticism, he learns to condemn.
If a child lives in hostility, he learns to fight.
If a child lives with ridicule, he learns to be shy.
If a child lives with shame, he learns to feel guilty.
If a child lives with tolerance, he learns to be patient.
If a child lives with encouragement, he learns confidence.
If a child lives with praise, he learns to appreciate.
If a child lives with fairness, he learns justice.
If a child lives with security, he learns to have faith.
If a child lives with approval, he learns to like himself.
If a child lives with acceptance and friendship, he learns to find love
in the world.   Dorothy Nolte

As much as we desire perfect communication with our children, doing so is far harder that we think. When dad wrinkles his forehead with a puzzled expression, looks at Billy and teasingly says, "What planet are you from?" Dad's not far from the truth.

As if they actually come from a different planet, country, or culture, children experience the world FAR differently than adults do. The way they look at the world around them, the way they relate to other people, their goals and motivations may really surprise us. Understanding the ways our young disciples see the world will better help us parent them and "bring them up in the ways and instruction of the Lord." (Ephesians 6:4)

Learning about how children grow will help us communicate with them, teach them and connect with them. **However, probably the most helpful thing a parent will gain from learning about the ways children think and develop will be a growing sense of empathy. To be able to appreciate the world from your child's**

eyes means a greater ability to feel what they feel and know what they know.

Todd shares, "My single greatest "epic fail" as a parent occurred with my son Clay. I am ashamed of it to this day, and share it only because it might help you. Clay was a little guy about kindergarten age. Ginny and the other children were away for the evening. While home with Clay, I began trying to catch up on some "important" work (so important that I can't begin to remember what it was today). Clay kept interrupting, and my endurance grew thinner with each disruption."

"When I had finally reached the limit of my patience, I snapped, 'Clayton, Go Away.' The corners of his mouth turned down and his shoulders hung low as he said, 'Yes, daddy.' He slowly turned and left the room. 'Finally some peace and quiet for grown up stuff,' I muttered."

"A short time later, Clayton came into the kitchen where I had my work spread out on the table. He had his coat and his hat on. He also had a small bundle of things wrapped up in a bandana. I looked at him quizzically and he looked up at me with big moist eyes, and said, 'I'm going now but I want you to know that I love you.'"

"I cannot tell this story without tears running down my face, they are right now as I type these words. The meaning of his words ripped into my heart. He took my words literally and was preparing to leave home as if I'd sent him out into the world on his own."

"I knocked my papers to the floor as I grabbed him up, hugged him tightly while tearfully explaining that I just meant 'go in the other room for a while.' I cried, he was confused. This traumatic experience taught me to watch my words carefully with my children. I hope it taught Clay, "whatever stupid things my Dad may say, he always loves me.""

The important thing I wish I had understood at the time, we hope to pass on to you in this section. Children hear, see, and experience events differently than you do. Their normal development means that at differing ages they need us to translate life into terms, ways, and stories that they have the ability to comprehend. I desperately wish I had known that my five year-old boy didn't see the world in the same way I did.

In this stage of development, Clayton's thinking was very concrete and he could only hear the words exactly the way I said them. I said the words, "go" and "away." He heard that he should "Depart from this place." There is no nuance in a five-year old child's brain. He couldn't say to himself, "Surely, my father doesn't want me to leave home like a vagabond, he must mean something else."

I since learned that two to seven year-olds do not possess that ability to infer alternate meanings. We need to translate to them as if they speak a different language. **Even though their words are in English, the thoughts behind them are often far different than our thoughts.**

Knowing the way our children, our young disciples, think, change and judge will be amazingly helpful to our goal of raising Godly children. This section will help you learn to bridge the understanding gap with your children and reach them where they are. In a sense, you are becoming a missionary to your child. In comprehending and reaching into their world, you will reap the rewards of more effective teaching, clearer communication, an ability to predict their choices and a deeper sense of empathy with your young disciple.

Understanding the process of human development leads us to understand how children grow and think. This puts parents in the position to deal with children at their own development level. By working with them in the manner most meaningful to them, we maximize our efforts and their success. As a disciple[ing] parent, this truly helps us reach them to teach them.

Gone are the days we think of children as short adults. Neither do their grasping minds perform like a grownup intellect. It's not that they just have fewer experiences than we do. No, the child sees, feels, experiences and reacts differently than adults.

Miraculously, their little brains grow and change; literally transforming in cell structure as they mature physically and gain new experiences. As a child grows, brain cells called neurons make more connections based on how much they are used. Pathways used more frequently become larger and stronger. Like a rushing flood cutting new channels for the river, these connections makes difficult activities easier. Practice doesn't just make you better, it changes you.

Even simple movement contains great complexity. Consider how easily you stand and walk across the room. You don't even think about it, you simply decide, "Oh, I want that book." Then your body rises to its feet and you stride across the room and grab it. You don't even consider how. Now watch a toddler do it. Looks a little harder, doesn't it? Novice walkers... toddle. That is to say, they "walk with short, unsteady steps." Soon enough though, except in special cases, the toddler will become a walker, then a runner, and perhaps an athlete.

A child's brain makes connections far faster than adults do because the brain molds itself to new demands. Children find picking up a new skill far easier than even young adults do. Amazingly, miraculously, children grow into countless abilities they did not have at birth. This ability to adapt means we change, we grow, we overcome obstacles.

This great Psalm 23 describes us as the sheep of God's flock. We are part of His herd, part of a community, part of a people. American cinema aside, the lone wolf should not be admired but pitied.

If you know any children, this revelation should come as no surprise: Children grow up. Their body becomes larger, and their abilities develop. Even so, the inner development of a child means so much more than meets the eye. Tremendous changes take place in the body, the mind, and the personality of growing children. Our early years show the most dramatic change, but we change throughout life. Even in our later adult years, we change as experience and reflection lead to new perspective and greater wisdom.

Normal change happens in a planned sequence. Children become adults, in far more than shoe size, academic achievement or legal status. Their personality grows along with their social and moral aptitudes. Since these children are created in the Imago Dei (the image of God), we must look at them in all the fullness of their creation. Children (and adults, too) should be considered far greater than just a single human unit. God wants us to be in relationship with our families, the Kingdom and with Him.

Human beings clearly need to live in community. We are social beings. It's no mere coincidence that the Bible refers to us as sheep many times. One of the best-loved scriptures of all times, Psalm 23, describes us as sheep, beginning with *"The Lord is my Shepherd."* This great Psalm 23 describes us as the sheep of God's flock. We are part of His herd, part of a community, part of the Kingdom of God. American cinema aside, the lone wolf should not be admired but pitied.

Let's understand how our children grow as human beings and as disciples. In any undertaking, we cannot expect them to learn the right lessons in a class presented out of season. Faith is taught in a growth progression. Just as we cannot demand they learn the classical "Minuet in G" before "Hot Cross Buns," we need to first teach the foundations of faith. As we discuss in this book, parents disciple their child through modeling, instruction, application and more. (The discipleship process can be reviewed in Section 2 of this book.)

So, to gain an understanding of the ways in which our children grow and develop, we will explore Cognitive, Psychosocial and Moral Development (loosely intelligence, personality, and ethics). We will consider, "How did we adults get to where we are now? How did we see things when we were a certain age? In what ways do we process the information we receive at certain developmental levels? How does that help us understand our kids? How does it enable us to convey God's truth into their lives?"

We will also try to help you better answer the question, "how can I understand my young disciple?" This exploration is hardly an exhaustive study but merely a survey of the foundational works in these fields. Our aim is to acquaint you with the basic concepts and the vocabulary to discuss and consider these theories of human growth as you disciple your child into the Kingdom of God.

In this section of the book, we will learn about child development in our young disciples. We will be reviewing Jean Piaget's Stages of Cognitive Development, Erik Erikson's Stages of Psychosocial Development and Lawrence Kohlberg's Stages of Moral Development. These resources give us an understanding or model of how children change and grow. After all, growth is the point of this book. By having a basic understanding of the natural processes of growing, parents can help children develop in the direction children need, in the ways they need, and in the timing they need it.

By understanding how kids grow and learn, we help them exploit their strengths and mitigate their flaws. We will assist them to become the people God created them to be. Knowing this information doesn't excuse inappropriate or dangerous behavior. It does give us preparation for the challenges our kids will face in certain stages of life. As the Boy Scouts remind us, "be prepared."

In any undertaking, we cannot expect them to learn the right lessons in a class presented out of season.

We are fearfully and wonderfully made by God. God has created us as creatures who grow, learn, and expand our abilities. God has given us the ability to understand our world as parents and mentors. Therefore, we will be over-viewing the work of Piaget, Erikson, and Kohlberg to lay a foundation for understanding the needs of our young disciples.

The following four items are the basic assumptions that govern the essential principles of Child Development. Therefore, we can understand most kids, as well as comprehend the exceptions and special circumstances:

1) Childhood Development for the majority of children happens in regular progression and along regular rules.

2) Development happens at different rates for different children.

3) Development occurs in an orderly way for most children.

4) Development takes place gradually and not rapidly.

Think of development as a voyage we all must travel. We each start out weak and grow stronger. We start as children and become adults. We start out as disciples and become mentors. Our purpose becomes clear as God gives us our children. We must help them to learn the things they need to learn to travel through this life successfully.

Many important things vie for our attention and the few precious hours we have with our children. The very best thing you could ever teach your child is to have a relationship with God. It is critical to their future. Understanding how your children see, experience and understand their world will help them tremendously as you parent, but more importantly, as you disciple your children.

A confession of two fathers: By God's amazing grace, when our children were in these developmental stages our wives (who were both trained as teachers) had a good grasp of the information we discuss in this section. We strongly believe we would have been better fathers if we knew the basics of this material. Thank God, LOVE covers a multitude of sins. We urge you to both learn this information AND count on love.

APPLICATION

List two or three things that you learned or found interesting:

1

2

3

Reflection and Discussion Questions

1) What is the wackiest belief you held as a child?

2) When was the last time you intentionally tried to see the world through your children's perspective? What prompted you?

3) How did/would this help you be a better parent?

4) How would your child describe you to another person?

Chapter 19 – Cognitive Development

Each day of our lives we make deposits in the memory banks of our children.   *Charles R. Swindoll*

Cognitive Development describes the way people grow in intelligence. At the beginning, babies learn to decipher the sensations they get from their senses. From there, growing children begin to develop and use increasingly sophisticated mental tools such as the attention of working memory, comprehending/producing language, calculating, reasoning, problem solving, and decision making.

As we grow, we pick up knowledge in astounding ways. Educators at school or home will likely recognize the name of Jean Piaget (1896-1980), the Swiss Child Development Specialist. He is widely considered as the most significant Developmental Psychologist to date. Piaget led the way in developing our scientific understanding about how children's learning differs significantly from adult learning. Piaget's work forms the basis for our description of Cognitive Development.

Previous to Piaget, parents and scientists assumed child development simply flowed from an accumulation of knowledge. People thought the more facts children got, the more experiences they had, the more they matured. Clearly, experience contributes to maturity. However, Piaget's work points to the extreme complexity of cognitive development. Far from the simple gaining of knowledge, there appear to be at least four major Factors Influencing Development. These four processes go on continually and often simultaneously in the cognitive growth of your child.

<u>Maturation</u> starts with the instructions and processes written on our DNA at conception.

13 For you created my inmost being;
you knit me together in my mother's womb.
14 I praise you because I am fearfully and wonderfully made;
your works are wonderful,

I know that full well.
[15] My frame was not hidden from you
when I was made in the secret place. (Psalm 139:13-15)

As these processes unfold in the life of the child, God's gifts and graces show themselves as the child matures physically and mentally.

Activity in their environment provides new experiences for the raw material of learning. New experiences add to the growth and change involved in the child's upward trajectory. However, this does not account for the wildly divergent skills humans attain. Thinking, processing information and engaging in new experiences simply adds new "grist to the mill" of cognitive development.

Social Transmission shows in the cultural and social aspects of life. We learn from others directly and through our culture. Family, school and church all give new input and new motivations for us to consider. Without the experience, tradition and wisdom of society, every new person would have to reinvent fire. (Or build your own audio player from scratch.)

Equilibration describes how we use the things we know and incorporate them into our various understandings. When things "make sense" to us we are at equilibrium. When we reach a point where we have new information that doesn't "make sense," we search for a new understanding that incorporates everything new. What a shock it is to find that the nice accountant at work has embezzled funds and now the company we work for has to close. Or the smelly guy that sat in the park every day was a millionaire and left it all to the homeless shelter.

And, yet these paradoxes might cause us to think about new experiences in a different way. We may even have to completely change the way we think about everything. The perfect example is found in the sentiment, "I once was lost but now am found, was blind but now I see" (from the song *Amazing Grace* by John Newton).

As these four influences work simultaneously in the developing child, we see the child's thinking grow more complex and advance to a higher level. It's not just a simple linear transition, different phases or stages of development happen to normally growing people. As mentioned, we don't just get more complex because we gain new experiences. Children see the world in very different ways as they grow in brain development and, consequently, their thinking and understanding.

Piaget set out Four Stages of Cognitive Development (different from the Four Factors Influencing Development). In these various stages, we see vastly, distinctly different areas of a child's growth into adulthood. He defined them as the "Sensorimotor Stage," the "Preoperational Stage," the "Concrete Operational Stage," and the "Formal Operational Stage." We will discuss them in turn, as we look at the Cognitive Development of Chloe.

Piaget's Stages of Cognitive Development

Stage	Age	Characteristics	Developmental Changes
Sensorimotor Chloe infant	Birth to 2 years	Baby knows the world through physical sensations and the movement of the world around them.	Infants learn that objects still exist even when unseen (*Object Permanence*). They discover they are separate from the world around them. Their actions make cause and effect in the world around them.
Preoperational Chloe age 4	2 years to 7 years	Children begin to think symbolically using words and pictures to represent objects around them. They still can only see their own point of view.	Playing and pretending become important. While they are growing in use of language, they tend to be very concrete in their thinking. They are very egocentric and find it difficult to consider the perspective of others.
Concrete Operational Chloe age 8	7 years to 11 years	Older children begin to think logically but can do so only about concrete objects.	Thinking becomes more organized and logical. Understanding that similar things can appear differently (*Conservation*). Starts to begin discovering general principles from specific information- but only about concrete things (*inductive logic*).
Formal Operational Chloe age 14	11 years to 15 – 20 Years	Early teens or adolescents begin to think with simple abstractions and reason hypothetically about problems.	Emergence of truly abstract thought. Thinks about moral, ethical, social and political issues requiring theoretical and abstract reasoning. Starts reasoning from general principles and applies them to specific information and applications (*deductive logic*)

121

The Sensorimotor Stage

One game we play delights babies and grownups alike. The "Surprise Game" (closely related to "Peek-a-boo") always seems to tickle baby Chloe. Auntie or some other favored friend or relative holds a favorite object in the baby's gaze. Baby Chloe then finds it and smiles. Auntie plays within her view and then hides it or covers it up. When the object is gone, baby loses interest. It's not there. Out of sight, out of mind. Then Auntie makes it reappear while exclaiming, "Surprise!" When baby Chloe plays, she often squeals with delight, making the people around emit their own burst of laughter. Best done with great repetition; the game creates so much enjoyment we can hardly tell who enjoys the game more, baby or grown-up.

Like so much childhood play, lots of work happens during a silly game. Chloe, from birth to age two, lives in the **Sensorimotor** (senses and movement) stage of development. During this time, she learns the world has many rules. One example is happening in the "Surprise" game. Though seemingly obvious to adults, the basic skills of "Surprise" far exceeds Chloe's understanding.

As a longtime resident of planet earth, we know things continue to exist even when we don't see them. This brain skill, called **Object Permanence**, helps set the stage for Chloe to start thinking about other things as separate from oneself. To her, the object exists when it's seen and doesn't when unseen. End of story. However, we adults have learned to view the world and to consider the many unseen things as a regular part of life. Mom knows she can find her car in the driveway.

Through games like "Surprise", and a multitude of other experiences with movement and feelings, Chloe learns she is different from the other objects in her world. From birth to age two, she operates in this Sensorimotor stage. This begins to prepare Chloe for the budding development of her self-identity. Chloe starts understanding her own separate nature, that the objects she sees and feels have their own unique existence. She learns that they are separate entities. This understanding helps her develop the ability to relate her actions to changes in the world. (A game of drop the cookie, anyone?)

This tremendous growth sets the stage for Chloe's "Eureka" moments. She begins to understand that she can manipulate the world around her. She comes to realize when she acts she changes her world. She rubs mushy carrots on her face and sees how mommy reacts. She hits daddy with a block and watches what he does. She holds a stuffed animal close and feels warm and fuzzy. In this way, Chloe learns how the world works. She will eventually gain sufficient knowledge and ability to meet her own needs. It starts here while watching how the world works and how it feels. **In this stage, her parents are the mirror in which baby Chloe sees herself.**

Children in the Sensorimotor stage gain understanding of how things work. As they encounter new experiences, they develop new **schemas** of understanding as they gain new information and insights. (Schema is a word Piaget used to describe the various mental "schemes" or strategies we use to make sense of the world).

Assimilation occurs when a child sees a zebra as a horse with black and white stripes. Accommodation happens when she recognizes zebra as a unique animal.

Children create understanding of their world through two main ways, **assimilation** and **accommodation**. Assimilation happens when the child experiences a new event, and they place that information into one of their previously held schemas. For example, when Chloe sees a zebra she will see a funny looking horse with black and white stripes. Accommodation occurs, on the other hand, when she discovers the new event and modifies her schema, or perhaps creates an entirely new schema. At this point, Chloe adds zebra to her animal list as a separate creature.

When adults make these amazing jumps in understanding, it transforms how we see the world. We call it an epiphany or a

123

"moment of clarity." Little children like Chloe have these inspiring moments regularly. How exciting it must be to be a baby or toddler!

The Preoperational Stage

As the age of sensory exploration begins to wind down, Chloe moves from toddlerhood into the very beginnings of the **symbolic thought** adults use. This **Preoperational stage** begins around age 2 and progresses through the age of 7 or so. (In discussing developmental stages, all ages listed can only be approximate because children mature at different rates.) In this stage, baby Chloe moves into childhood and new influences come into the foreground of her attention. Chloe begins to use words and pictures to represent objects, "Ball, cat, chair." She begins to talk as she, gains the ability to name objects and actions she sees. "Daddy walk dog."

It's been said, "We spend a lot of time and energy in the early years teaching our kids to walk and talk. And the rest of their childhood trying to get them to sit down and be quiet." Turns out, they were going to do that anyway.

In Preoperation, children develop language and their basic symbolic ability to connect words with objects and then pictures. At this age, kids begin to use symbolism, which is evident in their playing and pretending. Preoperational children have a rich play life. Imagination and role-play become a regular part of the child's life. As proof of this, you can enjoy thousands of adorable internet videos of children pretending to be their dog or cat, mommy or daddy, a firefighter or a cowboy. In their make-believe, they may be a teacher, a superhero or even inanimate objects like a tree.

At this age of Preoperational thought, Chloe begins reading. She enjoys bright picture books with a few simple words on the page. Picture books abound, and kids who enjoy reading have a great many opportunities to do so. As you explore bookstores or websites, you find that children's books are separated into age groups. Sorting books this way intends to appeal to children through connecting books and readers of appropriate ability.

The success of this approach shows how children's capacity to enjoy a book change with their growth in abstract thought. "Redwall" chapter books will not interest a child who gets a thrill reading "Clifford, the Big Red Dog." You can also notice that the number of words goes up, and the number of pictures goes down as the age of the reader increases.

Another interesting characteristic of children in the Preoperational stage becomes clear when they try to describe things. Chloe is very **egocentric**, meaning she has not yet developed the ability to see things from another viewpoint. Perfectly naturally, at this stage she has a very difficult time seeing things from other people's perspective. She tends to think everyone thinks as she does, and believes even objects have feeling like hers. (It is common to see children punish a chair they run into because the chair must have been naughty or to feel badly for discarded objects.) As Chloe grows in her thinking ability, she will begin to experience a "de-centering" of her own viewpoint. Here we find the beginnings of empathy.

As she progresses through this Preoperational stage Chloe gains the beginning of language and has started symbolic thought- words and pictures can correspond to real objects. This will eventually lead to **abstract thinking**.

However, Chloe's thought world still lacks nuance. Yes or no, black or white, good or bad, this or that– she still looks at the world through the lens of these basic distinctions. Certainly, many cases exist for drawing hard lines throughout life. We do not advocate universal relativism for kids or grownups. But at this age, "Either/ Or" thinking holds Chloe's preoperational mind completely because she is not yet able to make such advanced distinctions.

As we will see later in our review of ethical thinking, Chloe's Preoperational view also possesses a kind of **Moral Realism**, which leads her to be very strict about right and wrong. This budding symbolic understanding allows her to focus on only one feature of a situation. To her, Billy broke the rules against eating before dinner. This is true to her even though mom gave him the apple because dinner was late.

Chloe will eventually begin to understand rules of behavior and the nuances. Starting out early, knowing that rules should be obeyed is a good skill for a Christian child. Remember though, in her tender years she will be very concrete, insisting everyone follow the rules but unable to understand the motivations, moral exceptions, and grace that make up morality.

The Concrete Operational Stage

As Chloe grows to around the age of seven, she progresses into the stage of **Concrete Operations**. Once again, there is no hard line between the Pre-Operation and Concrete Operation stages. In this stage, Chloe and other 7 to 11 year olds tentatively begin to enter the world of adult type thought (**Formal Operations**). She even starts to do some of the logical thinking that adults can do. However, she can only reason this way with events and examples right before her eyes. She can see the baseball rolled under the car and look there to find it. She will not find it if it rolled under the car and passed into the bushes. An adult would think to look in the bushes. This ability with concrete situations gives rise to the name of the developmental stage.

One of the skills Chloe will now develop involves a growing understanding the nature of objects. This concept of **Conservation** helps her recognize that sometimes things differ from how they appear. For example, Chloe now understands that a short, wide cup of milk holds the same amount as the tall thinner cup. Their relative appearance no longer fools her.

This reminds us of the old joke, "What weighs more, a ton of steel or a ton of feathers? ... Neither, both weigh a ton." Adults can usually work that out in their head rather quickly if they stop to think about it. We equate feathers with light and steel with heavy. So Concrete Operations kids have difficulty separating the concept of weight with their concrete picture of heavy and light objects. Early in Concrete Operations, children will still find their thinking dominated by the appearance of an object.

Chloe helps her dad work in the garage sometimes and learns a few shop skills. One of the talents she gained is how to use a screwdriver to put in and take out screws. One day, dad asks her to open up the paint can. While holding the screwdriver in her hand, Chloe finds it impossible to open the can. Then, she looks at the screwdriver's flat edge tip and sees the recessed lip of the paint can. Suddenly, she realizes how to pry the lid off the can. She tries it once, then again and eventually gets the lid off. Chloe used her blossoming Concrete Operations ability to solve a real-world problem. Her dad is pleased and so is she.

Chloe lacks the ability to go the next step yet. She doesn't yet have the ability to think through the dilemma, determine a problem-solving technique and then select a tool to accomplish the task. That is too advanced for *A child in the Concrete Operational Stage begins to add a simple type of logical thought to their mental pantry.* her now, but she is growing towards it. Such examples of adult-like thinking begins to happen in this stage of development but being able to manipulate abstract objects is still off in the future.

Another feature of the Concrete Operational Stage empowers the child with blossoming **Inductive Logic** and reasoning. Inductive Logic goes from understanding specific concrete examples to developing general rules about those examples. (Inductive = from specific to general.) The child who works in the garden will notice that plants not watered will begin to wilt. When watered they perk up. She will figure out water is good for plants.

Inductive reasoning helps us generalize. While not always correct, inductive reasoning is a useful skill. Going from what we know about one thing, we may be able to form a judgment about what we don't know. This is especially useful when predicting what will happen. "Last time I ate anchovies they made me sick. If I eat these anchovies, I will become sick again."

As Chloe grows in the Concrete Operational Stage, she shows the beginnings of the logical, reasonable mind of an adult. As Chloe's cognitive development proceeds, she develops more of this ability to make predictions about the world. It's amazing how far she has come in only a few short years. She began by being only able to sense what was around her. She now comes to understanding the world well enough to make good guesses about situations she has never seen, such as "All plants need water." Chloe and other concrete operations children have now set the stage for real grownup thinking. Her maturity and development of Concrete Operations now sets the stage for her ability to use abstractions and interact with the world in very adult ways.

Formal Operational Stage

The word "Formal" is used to describe adult-like operations, not because they wear a tuxedo, but because they concentrate on the thought process or form of thinking. These "Forms" can be used in our thinking without the need for specific examples. Chloe and other children around the age of 11 begin to gain the ability to disconnect form from content. She can manipulate imaginary objects in place of concrete ones. Object A is the biggest. Object B is smaller than A, while Object C is the smallest. Which object is medium sized? Being able to figure out such simple thought puzzles starts Chloe in the ability to consider hypothetical situations, opening a whole new world of complex thought to her.

Consider this. You just got an unpleasant letter from the IRS. You stand with the mail in your hand, a frown on your face. In the workings of your mind, you ponder the possibilities that could arise from the curtly worded letter. As you consider each scenario, you begin to formulate possible strategies for dealing with the problem and their possible consequences. You evaluate the various solutions, prioritize your action plan and then finally move to the filing cabinet to get your records.

Before you walked to get those files, all of this evaluating and strategizing and planning happened in your thoughts. All these mental gyrations occurred completely within your conscious mind.

Like walking across the room for a book, you took it for granted. It just seems to happen.

This miracle of abstract thought begins to take shape in the Formal Operations Stage of cognitive development. Thankfully, Chloe's world is far less complex than yours (though the media and the world bring more information at an earlier age than ever before). Around the age of 11 or so, Chloe begins to transition from needing concrete examples to consider, toward using symbols or abstractions. She begins to be able to think abstractly. As she grows into an older teen, she will soon be able to develop this skill well enough to consider moral, philosophical, ethical, social and political issues. These issues require some very complex manipulation of thought.

Chloe and children of this age begin to use **inferential reasoning**. They have the ability to answer this question...*If Billy is taller than Mary and Mary is taller than Carl, who is the tallest?* As obvious as it seems to you and me, your nine year old cannot answer that question. Their 12-year-old sibling can answer it because they are gaining the ability to think about events they didn't actually experience and make conclusions based on their ponderings.

As they grow in their formal operations, children will develop a new form of reasoning beyond **Inductive** (from specific to general). The new line of thought is called **Deductive Reasoning** (from general to specific). Deductive reasoning allows people to take general principles and apply them to specific situations. Piaget asked children the following question, *"If you had a third eye, where would you want it to be?"* Children in the Concrete Operational Stage (age 7-11) responded the best place would be in the middle of their forehead. Children old enough to be in the Formal Operation stage gave different responses such as, "on the hand because I could use it to see around corners." This creativity inherent in Formal Operations lends such young people the ability to engage in new and (hopefully) beneficial situations.

As her Formal Operation skills become more complex, Chloe can then do **hypothetical** testing of scenarios. When a new situation presents itself, she comes up with a list of possibilities and compares these imaginary scenarios with potential outcomes.

For example, 14 year old Chloe considers this scenario:

"My bicycle has a flat tire but I want to go to Alistair's house. Can I walk? Yes, but the road is dangerous. Can I go behind the bowling alley? Safer, but longer. That way is still on the table. Can I get a ride? Mom? No, at work. Dad? No, at work. Brother Bailey? His car is working now, but he's at practice. Weird neighbor? NO WAY. Susie's big sister? Maybe, but she would be a pain about it. Maybe fix the flat tire? Do I have a new tube? Yes, in the garage. Do I have tools? Yes. Can I do it quickly? Hmm, yes, I think quick enough to make it worth going. OK, settled, I'll try to fix the bike tire myself. Then I will ride my bike to Alistair's house."

These Formal Operation skills allow us to mull over scenarios that exist only in our imagination and consider their implications in the real world. (If you ever felt deeply worried about something unlikely to come to pass, you experienced a downside of this ability.)

This incredibly useful problem-solving skill helps us create and order the world around us. As a higher level thinking process, Formal Operations help us deal with the chaos in our personal world based on the knowledge (or wisdom) that we have. It also gives us the highly technical and scientific world we see around us.

As Chloe grows in her Formal Operational understanding, it will take her some life experiences and Biblical understanding to have a fully-formed and well-rounded ability in grown-up decision making. Most kids like Chloe will get there. Perhaps there will be a few hiccups but with good parental guidance, she will develop into a wise Christian adult.

Understanding Piaget's Stages of Cognitive Development gives us the ability to understand that children grow massively in the way they think. From his work, we parents can see that we cannot teach children the way adults learn. Knowing what and how children think will make parents more successful in communicating God's truth to your young disciples.

Piaget's work is foundational to Erikson's Psychosocial Development as well as Kohlberg's Moral Development model. We know that you will find these equally useful in understanding your child's development.

APPLICATION

List two or three things that you learned or found interesting:

1

2

3

Reflection and Discussion Questions

1) Find your child's age on the chart on page 121. What specific characteristics of this stage do you see in your child?

2) What other things will you now be looking for as your child develops?

3) How will you intentionally enjoy the current stage your child is in?

4) Before reading this chapter what has been your understanding of the experiences discussed?

5) What is your greatest discovery from this chapter?

Chapter 20 – Psychosocial Development

The hearts of small children are delicate organs. A cruel beginning in this world can twist them into curious shapes. The heart of a hurt child can shrink so that forever afterward it is hard and pitted as the seed of a peach. Or, again, the heart of such a child may fester and swell until it is misery to carry within the body, easily chafed and hurt by the most ordinary things.

Carson McCullers

As we see in Cognitive Development, children are not fully formed mini-adults. Our kids start out with only the tiniest ability to interact with the world around them. And yet, completely dependent babies become fully functioning adults? Consider the infant Lord Jesus, wrapped in swaddling clothes, lying in a manger. Though completely dependent on family for all His physical needs, that little baby grew into the savior of mankind. He started out exactly as we do.

Psychosocial Development describes how we interact with the world around us. It poses the ways in which we answer the question, "Who am I?" Perhaps you don't recall asking it directly. However, we ask this question indirectly numerous times during our lives, "Who am I compared to my parents? Who am I in relation to my physical skills and limitations? Who am I in relationship to the world around me?" What can I do? What should I do?

We ask and answer this question many times, as we move through life. In certain stages of life, we come up with a workable answer about our place in the world. We accept it until we grow up against the next set of boundaries. We then ask and learn to answer again, the same questions, "Who am I? How do I fit into this culture and my world?"

Erik Erikson created the groundbreaking theories of human growth and social adaptation that he called Psychosocial Development. Erikson's interest in identity came out of his own questionable beginnings. He was born in a Jewish family under what-would-then-have-been scandalous circumstances. He later married a Canadian woman and subsequently converted to Christianity. They left Germany for America when the Nazi's came to power.

So well accepted was Erikson's work that, though he never attained even a Bachelor's degree, he became a professor at Harvard and Yale. His contemplations about his upbringing led to a fascination for how we become a particular person, out of a world of possibilities. Not everyone agrees with all of Erikson's assessments but his model makes up the basis for most current understandings of psychosocial development.

Erikson's view suggests every person must make peace with the challenges that arise during certain stages of life. Not until these forces are met, and become balanced and understood, can we make the most of them. In certain stages of life, we will face specific growth challenges. When first going to school, we face new input and new relationships that help us answer the question, "Where do I fit in?" Or when beginning to date we learn, "What kind of man/woman am I?" If we do not find balance in our understanding of the world then we are hindered in our development.

Erikson's view suggests every person must make peace with the challenges that arise during certain stages or times of life. Only when the forces behind these challenges are met, and become balanced, can we make the most of them.

For example, baby Layla first faces an uncertain world. Through interaction with her surroundings, she determines that the world and the people around her can be predictable. Her physical and emotional needs find consolation on a regular basis. Through this life experience, she develops a sense of trust and the feeling the world is predictable and safe.

Another baby, Jeffrey, born into a very unpredictable and chaotic situation will develop a profound sense of randomness. Does he get

134

fed when hungry, changed when wet, comforted when upset? As terrible as it sounds, not all babies do. Maybe yes? Maybe no? It may be completely unpredictable based on the actions of their parents and the support around them. How can a sense of trust be expected to bloom and flourish under such chaotic conditions? Trust and predictability are part of the same vine. Imagine how difficult it will be for Jeffrey to trust others, and even trust God, if he never understands trust.

CHANGE and the pain that comes with it.

Throughout the changes in life we find it painful dealing with new circumstances and growing demands on us. The advance of our personal development shows how change comes about through crisis. Each individual will pass through a number of common yet crucial developmental situations (i.e. potty training, middle school, marriage). Resolution of that crisis of demands must happen before one can find peace and move on to the next challenge.

Change remains absolutely essential for our progression through life. Obviously, we can never get better than we are when we stay the way we are...As Christians, we can accept this because we know that all the suffering of change happens in the context of a greater love.

Everyone must be challenged before growth and change can occur. This general structure of living, challenge and resolution, must be understood and appreciated as we watch our kids grow and experience both joyful and painful times in life. All these times are necessary and common to us. It is important to note that such difficulties do not show God's displeasure with us.

Erikson describes it, the Bible prescribes it, bottom line- change happens. Importantly, whatever age it happens, change hurts. Change means that we leave the old life behind. It means leaving the old ME behind. We will no longer be that same person we were comfortable with. That means pain, suffering and in a sense - death. More powerful than the love of our old self, our love for Jesus allows us to follow Christ when he says, *"If anyone wishes to come after Me, he must deny himself, and take up his cross daily and follow Me."* *(Mark 8:34)*

Change remains absolutely essential for our progression through life. Growth requires change. Obviously, we can never get better than we are when we stay the way we are. But oh how we resist it. Like scorching fire, we avoid the pain of change because it hurts us. We already have our patterns and habits and changing them makes us work, think, reflect. This adjustment unsettles us. Many of us avoid doing the things we know to do, even the things we want to do because it upsets us.

We are creatures of habit because our brains operate with ease when our life is familiar and actions predictable. Like a well lubricated engine, life carries us onward. Then, new demands are suddenly placed on us. When things change, our brain grows and changes in structure (as demonstrated on page 121) because changing causes us to learn new patterns and create new memories. This may profoundly change the way we relate to the world.

Think of the changes in your life that are most upsetting: moving, perhaps losing a job, a death in the family, and many others. These events thrust change upon us that makes us leave the predictable and move into the uncertain. However, it's not just the bad things that happen to us that stress us. The very act of change is so traumatic that Psychologists confirm even positive changes causes stress. Getting a new job stands high on the list of top stressors... right near losing a job. This fact might be surprising until you consider that all change, good and bad, is a time of trial.

We know our lives require change and yet, we still feel compelled to resist it. This makes the predicaments of development unavoidable. However, there is good news about change. Entertaining a willingness to change brings many valuable gifts into our life. In fact, life's best things are born out of pain. Consider your child's birth, consider the cross of salvation. God brings forth joy out of suffering.

Not only so, but we also glory in our sufferings, because we know that suffering produces perseverance, [4]perseverance, character; and character, hope. [5]And hope does not put us to shame, because God's love has been poured out into our hearts through the Holy Spirit, who has been given to us.

(Romans 5:3-5)

Consider it pure joy, my brothers and sisters, whenever you face trials of many kinds, [3]because you know that the testing of your faith produces perseverance. [4]Let perseverance finish its work so that you may be mature and complete, not lacking anything.

(James 1:2-4)

Truth be told; happiness is more pleasurable, but pain can be far more profitable. Rare indeed is the person who grows without some crisis-caused motivation.

How many psychologists does it take to change a light bulb? One, but first the light bulb must really want to change.

Understanding and navigating personal crisis is one of the great skills available to Christians. A disciple of Jesus Christ who understands their place in the kingdom may feel pain in changing but not despair. An oyster responding to an uncomfortable debris lodged in its shell will coat the painful thing with layer upon layer of smooth white material. This is the process of producing a pearl, perhaps even a pearl of great price.

We know we humans grow in response to something uncomfortable. That pain might be the consequences of our current situation. It also may be caused by being thwarted from the enticing rewards of a new life. Nevertheless, we always need a powerful motivator to change. And yet, those in Christ can understand the place of pain in the process and stay the course through their transformation.

One of the great comforts in times of turmoil and change has been a short prayer known as "The Serenity Prayer." It says "God grant me the serenity to accept the things I cannot change, courage to change the things I can, and wisdom to know the difference." This excellent little prayer helps those dealing with the personal turmoil surrounding growth. It has been taught in the Alcoholics Anonymous program since early on, and with great success. Though there may be some, we have never run into a recovering addict who doesn't cherish this insightful prayer. However, you can see the deep meaning underneath that little prayer when you read the longer prayer from which it comes.

God,

Give me grace to accept with serenity
The things that cannot be changed,
Courage to change the things
Which should be changed,
And the Wisdom to distinguish
The one from the other.

Living one day at a time,
Enjoying one moment at a time,
Accepting hardship as a pathway to peace,
Taking, as Jesus did,
This sinful world as it is,
Not as I would have it.

Trusting that You will make all things right,
If I surrender to Your will,
So that I may be reasonably happy in this life,
And supremely happy with You forever in the next.
Amen.
                    Dr. Reinhold Niebuhr

With Christ, we all can accept change and better bear the uncomfortable, painful, even devastating suffering of personal growth. As Christians, we can accept this because we know all the suffering of change happens within the context of a greater love. *"And we know that in all things God works for the good of those who love him, who have been called according to His purposes." (Romans 8:28)* This is the life pattern of a disciple, *"weeping may stay for the night but rejoicing comes in the morning." (Psalm 30:5)*

Helping our children change by pointing them to the greater promise in Christ can certainly lessen the pain our kids feel as they change. They might not fully understand it, but you do, and you have the ability to encourage them.

Psychosocial Development

Erikson understood that psychosocial development comes through choices. People do not simply get bigger individually as we do physically. Their life challenges precede a metamorphosis. When we fail to meet the challenge, we suffer loss. According to Erikson, when we succeed at giving up our less mature ways and accepting the demands of our new challenges, we grow into a new phase of life. Then we attain the virtue inherent in that level (see chart on page 140).

Of course, each new level sets us up for the next crisis of our understanding of identity – or "identity crisis." We learn and we grow, at some point we become ready for the new challenges of living. These basic conflicts are in no way our only challenges. However, they profoundly affect our understanding of who we are.

In each stage of life, we find a new conflict between what we were and who we will become. The challenges faced can only be resolved by the individual, within their heart, mind, and spirit. When our world begins to put new demands on us, we must choose to cope with the crisis by selecting a strategy that is helpful or hurtful (anadaptive or maladaptive).

When each challenge becomes resolved, we have a new self-understanding and begin to gain the strength to meet the next developmental stage. Erikson believed that if we are unable to meet these challenges, they will affect us later in life until we resolve that conflict. God is continuously helping us to overcome weaknesses from our past and He gives us opportunities for renewal and a healthy and God honoring life.

Erikson's Stages of Psychosocial Development

Stage	Event	Conflict
1. Infancy (birth to 18 months)	Feeding	Trust vs Mistrust
2.Early Childhood (2 to 3 years)	Toilet Training	Autonomy vs Shame & Doubt
3. Preschool (3 to 5 years)	Exploration	Initiative vs Guilt
4. School Age (6 to 11 years)	School	Industry vs Inferiority
5. Adolescence (12 to 18 years)	Social Relationships	Identity vs. Role Confusion
6. Young Adulthood (19 to 40 years)	Love Relationships	Intimacy vs Isolation
7. Middle Adulthood (40 to 65 years)	Work and Parenthood	Generativity vs. Stagnation
8. Maturity (65 years to death)	Reflection on Life	Ego Integrity vs Despair

NOTE: Chart continues rows across the page division

Erikson's Stages of Psychosocial Development (cont.)		
Virtue	**Description**	**Examples**
Hope	With a predictable life and attentive caregiver, baby learns to trust.	Feeding, Abandonment
Will	Develops basic physical skills and a sense of personal control.	Toilet Training, Clothing Themselves
Purpose	Learns to be properly assertive and take initiative.	Exploring, Using Tools or Making Art
Competence	Meets demands of new skills to be learned in association with peers.	School, Sports, Band
Fidelity	Achieves a sense of personal identity in social, gender, politics, religion.	Social Relationship
Love	Develops love relationship with safety, commitment and care outside family.	Romantic Relationship
Care	Creates things that will outlast them. Family and work - sense of usefulness	Work, Parenthood
Wisdom	Looks back at life with a feeling of culmination and a sense of fulfillment.	Reflection on Life

NOTE: Rows continued from previous page.

Infancy (0 to 18 months) "Can I Trust the World?"

We will look at Psychosocial (or Personal) Development through the growth of Jack. As Jack comes into the world he experiences real change. The basic challenge of infancy is **trust**. During this time, Jack learns about the world around him and how it feels. Also called the Sensory-Oral Stage, this is a time when he experiences the sensations of his universe.

During this time he learns what things feel like, what they look like, and how these items and experiences act upon him, "Milk tastes warm and sweet and satisfies the pain in my tummy. Blanket feels soft and fuzzy and makes me warm and not cold. Mommy's voice sounds rich and pleasant and makes me feel secure."

As the newborn Jack grows into a toddler, he learns to predict when these sensations will happen and for the reason it happens. Jack finds that when these good feelings happen in a predictable way he learns that people can be trusted. This, in return, makes him feel predictability is good and therefore wants to be equally trustworthy. On the other hand, when the situation feels unpredictable (or abusive), another infant learns to mistrust others and finds no internal reason to be predictable.

The place in his heart little Jack finds his sense of trustworthiness, is the same place we find hope. Hope, cannot exist without that sense of trust. Hope longs for the future with expectation. *"Now faith is the assurance of things hoped for, the conviction of things not seen." (Hebrews 11:1)* The internal sense of trust and the ability for willing hope starts early in us.

As you can see parents, God has entrusted us with an extremely important task. **You are called to provide a secure and consistent environment for your child. In this way, your child learns to trust.** In so many ways, this will be foundational to the rest of your child's life.

Early Childhood (2-3 years) "Is it OK to be me?"

Jack makes it through the Infancy Stage of experiencing and learning his world and now begins to venture out. In this time, he begins to move, to walk well, and to explore his world. A major accomplishment in learning to manage his own body is controlling his toileting. As any parent knows, this significant benchmark signals a new phase of personal autonomy for their child! While gaining greater access to the world, kids find activities they like to do, items they enjoy. Jack likes music so he may be found playing with the radio, his neighbor Janet who enjoys the outdoors might be discovered in the garden.

This particular age can be quite dangerous for Jack because he has not yet learned about the many perils around him. Of course, that means a major parenting challenge. What Jack learns in this stage is the ability to reach out and venture forth. If given a strong base of parental safety and still allowed to explore and learn and grow, he will develop a sense of **autonomy**. Jack will begin to develop a sense of his capability to handle various situations on his own. If his parents are highly over-protective, this can mean that Jack doesn't find out how to explore and learn on his own.

Additionally, parents may set the bar too high and Jack will learn that his attempts to do things himself will end in failure. Similarly, if parents ridicule his attempts at autonomy, he might easily develop **shame** and learn to doubt his ability to handle those problems themselves. *Imagine how good it is for your child to have safety and still be empowered to explore and grow.*

Having the underlying personal sense of safety to venture forth can be terrific for Jack as an adult. This self-assurance opens many doors by allowing him to go outside his comfort zone. When we are close to God we can feel secure in our internal comfort level. *"For You have been a refuge for me, A tower of strength against the enemy."(Psalm 61:3)* **Imagine how good it is for your child to have safety and still be empowered to explore and grow. This underlying** positive sense of resolve can make for positive actions and appropriately confident kids.

Preschool (3-5 years) "Is it OK to act?"

At this age, Jack has sorted out the autonomy question. He understands himself as a unique individual with control over his actions. In this personal development stage, he begin to develop a sense of **initiative**. Jack really begins to explore his world and understand how it works. When he drops something, it falls, when he throws something, it flies. At this stage, Jack learns to zip and tie and pull. He begins to count and speak easily. Jack grows beyond exploring and begins interacting with his world.

Reaching out takes a real sense of courage and independence. Jack learns how to relate to these new things in life. Personal initiative starts with a desire to go beyond the comfort of knowing who he is, to finding out even more about the world. At this age, everything becomes a plaything, something to interact with and relate to. In this stage, Jack may begin to find some risky behaviors tempting. Wandering away or crossing the street alone are examples of this type of behavior.

Preschoolers know their instructions but still might search for their own ways to do it (like finger painting the dog). They can also feel the results of frustration. Jack wishes to do something and cannot accomplish it. Just like grownups, he feels the sense of disappointment and powerlessness of being unable to gain what he covets (whether it be an object, a friend, or a new skill). It is not uncommon to act out his frustration through aggressive or overly assertive, even ruthless behavior. Jack's parents will be aghast to see him begin to yell, hit or throw things.

Interaction with the world can be a real learning experience—by which we mean painful. Protecting Jack from all consequences can be problematic; protecting him from no consequences can be disastrous. It is important to draw a good line, which must allow him to make age appropriate choices. Parental planning around life training should allow him to both succeed and fail. As the old maxim states, "nothing succeeds like success." However, we must remember equally that "Failure is a detour, not a dead end street."– Zig Ziglar.

Possibly the greatest danger in this stage is the parent who so rejects the positive lessons of failure, they discourage the child from even trying. This may be with a word, but also with an attitude or even with the simple roll of an eye. This can be devastating to a growing child. The result of a parent discouraging or mocking these stirrings of independence can lead to feelings of **guilt** and a timidity accompanying initiative or decision-making.

School Age (6 – 11 years, grades 1-6) "Can I succeed in the big wide world?"

At this age, Jack is now beginning his formal education, either in school or at home. This means academics. At school, kids begin to try out their budding social and learning skills and see how well they do. In this life challenge, Jack will be exposed to new situations and information. He will use his mind for things he hardly could have imagined. Jack will struggle to cope with a new larger social world and to make sense of a forest of foreign ideas. Through the task orientation of school, Jack will gradually grow a sense of completion and accomplishment. As this happens, Jack gradually let the whims and wishes of play subside.

Children of this age learn to share and cooperate. Jack begins to want to do things right and do it the "right way." ("Can I make my letters right?") He learns a new, greater sense of autonomy and personal expression. As Jack progresses in school, Jack's thinking ability develops. He leaves Piaget's "Preoperational" Stage of Cognitive Development and enters the "Concrete Operational" phase.

Jack now begins to see the world in a more logical, sequential way. He will begin to use inductive reason (inferring general answers from specific information) with concrete objects and situations. An example of inductive reason (or logic) is this: Jack notices that all the boys on the basketball team are tall, therefore he reasons that all basketball players must be tall. We know that this is generally true, but not universally so.

During this elementary school phase, Jack will have opportunities to be creative and successful. He can earn the attention of peers and teachers. Likewise, he will be able to evaluate his peers work as well as assess and compare his own. Jack demonstrates **industry** and diligence by persevering at tasks and delaying gratification. He might finish his math problems while others hurry out to recess.

As he gains experience and education, Jack will choose to pursue his personal interests. As his world widens, Jack may discover athletic, musical, or artistic talents (or a myriad of other abilities) and develop them further. Jack likes music and joins the school music program. He enjoys beginning to learn to play a simple instrument. Other children will have their own interests like, science or sports and look into them as well.

Another import note is that this stage can also be stifled through ridicule or poor feedback. At this School Age stage of Psychosocial development, when continually ridiculed or punished for the attempts he makes or if he's made to feel incapable of meeting adult approval, Jack may begin to feel **inferior**. He may develop a sense that he is one of the substandard students, or even a lesser person.

Adolescence (12 – 18 years) "Who am I? Who can I become?"

Jack and his parents are noticing he is starting to grow up. The period of **Adolescence** is most often a time of turmoil, a confusing soup of thoughts, interest, drives, impulses, goals and dreams. Puberty goes full swing and hormonal balance with it. Yet, puberty means more than simple, if profound, endocrine changes. A child leaving "school age" comes into adolescence with a glut of questions. The big question of **identity** becomes a more formal one. Jack now asks, "Who am I?" because he can see that people have a place in society and begins to evaluate his own. "Where do I belong? How do others see me? Do I like how they see me? What do I think I have to offer? How can I find my place?" He asks himself, "What gifts and graces do I have?"

As an adolescent, Jack wonders what aspects of his life and personality fits with his aspirations and expectations. He begins to gain the ability to see himself as an adult and consider the question, "Where will I fit in as an adult?" As he teeters on the cusp of adulthood, he will have a lot of personal identity questions to answer.

Kids of this age will have many questions about God. To a Christian, including the faith factor will be a key piece of this identity puzzle. That's because a child of God cannot ask, "Who am I?" without pondering, "Whose am I?" This, in itself, is a huge existential question. Since Jack has been raised within the Christian faith, he will have answers to the questions raised around his relationship with God in Jesus Christ.

To an adolescent, the big question of identity becomes a more formal one, "Who am I?"

At this age, Jack's question answering starts with assessing who he has become. Through his years, he will have spent much time and effort learning about himself and the world around him. From the most basic of sensations, baby Jack determined whether the world is predictable and if people can be trusted.

As a young child, he learned his own autonomy and how to control his body. Upon becoming a preschooler, Jack learned to act independently and interact with the world around him. Following this move toward self-control, Jack learned to be industrious, and complete his tasks and delay personal gratification. In adolescence, Jack wrestled with finding a place in the world.

There will be more decisions to come, but here Jack begins to come up with an idea of who he is. If he does not get a handle on this task, he is at risk of real disorder in life with **role confusion**. He will wonder instead of know where his place is. He may make decisions that are not in keeping with his overall personality. His parents desire for Jack to have a strong sense of self, and a strong sense of belonging to family, to the Kingdom.

There are many forces at work here. Biological, psychological, and social forces influence how youth perceive themselves. Regardless of how people have grown up, at this point they begin to decide about their own personal ideologies. At some point, young people have to accept their values as their own. Yes, my family is religious, but I have chosen to accept Jesus Christ as my savior. This seeking to find their path in values often leads to conflict with adults over religion or politics.

Career choice can also cause conflict because parents often want a large say in that decision. A youth can be made to give up on true self-discovery and accept that role, but it short-circuits the big questions of adolescence. When the young person can answer these two questions appropriately, "What have I got?" and "Where am I going?" then they have established their own personal identity.

God is at work telling a story of restoration and redemption through your family. Never buy into the myth that you need to become the "right" kind of parent before God can use you in your child's lives. Instead, learn to cooperate with whatever God desires to do in your heart today so your children will have a front-row seat to the grace and goodness of God.

Reggie Joiner

NOTE: This discussion of Personal Development of children takes us through the main ages relevant to parenting. For continued description of the challenges that continue into adulthood, descriptions of the Psychosocial Development of adults is continued in Appendix B – Erikson's Adult Stages found on page 273

APPLICATION

List two or three things that you learned or found interesting:

1

2

3

Reflection and Discussion Questions

1) What one thing did you learn to help you become a better parent to your child?

2) What stages is/are your child/children in Erikson's Psychosocial stage of development?

3) How does this information for your stage help you in your life at this time?

4) What can you do to help them develop in this stage? Do you agree with Erikson that a person can continue to grow in stages even at later times in life?

5) Describe an area in your life where you think you need to grow in that was not achieved in your younger years.

Chapter 21 – Moral Development

> *Praise the developing character in your child as it emerges in active, loving, responsible behavior.*   *Henry Cloud*

Human beings are moral beings. Though we once thought our species could be defined by our "tool making," perhaps we should be better known for our "rule making." Obviously, human morality reaches far beyond our need to make and keep rules (we seem to like to make them better than keep them).

The ability to see beyond our own wants and needs leads us to embrace a higher calling for unconditional love, justice, and other transcendent principles. It seems clear this human characteristic shows one of the ways in which, *"God created man in his own image, in the image of God he created him; male and female he created them." (Genesis 1:27)*

We start out as infants being selfish and self-interested, which is necessary to get what we need. When we look at our cognitive development, we find children learn to share only when they become ready for it. As much as we melt over baby innocence, at that age babies really know only one thing, "gimme, gimme, gimme." Fortunately, most of us grow out of that stage into a "sharing, caring, and bearing" morality. First, we learn to share what we have with others. Next, we begin to actually, truly care about the welfare of others. Finally, we give of ourselves to bear their burdens.

People grow morally, though some progress farther than others. Even some adults can be stuck in "What's in it for me?" thinking. However, many grow deeper in faith or at least, community responsibility. When we begin to interact with the world around us, we can begin to develop a deeper, fuller understanding of our moral responsibility. This goes beyond feeling of empathy for another person. These traits lead to acknowledging societal needs and agreeing to live according to universal principles such as those we find in the Scriptures. To a Christian, New Testament **agape love must be considered a universal principle.** Jesus gives a universal principle for his disciples to live by when he says:

"A new commandment I give to you, that you love one another, even as I have loved you, that you also love one another." (John 13:34)

Notice that this principle is given as a commandment but the application to love is not specific but universal. In all things, Christian disciples must practice love the way Jesus did. His ministry to the Centurion (Luke 7:1-10), teaching the parable of Good Samaritan (Luke 10:25-37), and His admonition to be perfect in love as the father is perfect (Matthew 5:43-48), are examples of the expansiveness of His love. He expanded on The Law set forth in the Old Testament giving specific actions to perform in specific circumstances. His morality had no intention of replacing The Law. As he said, *"Do not think that I have come to abolish the Law or the Prophets; I have not come to abolish them but to fulfill them." (Matthew 5:17)*

In this Biblical understanding of moral growth, we gain the ability to see that ethics can have levels of development. For example, in the story of Jesus healing a man on the Sabbath (Matthew 12:8-21) we see that obeying the law against working on the Sabbath was not wrong. However, helping someone in need (healing them) superseded that rule. As our professor, Joseph Wang, at Asbury Theological Seminary used to remind us in New Testament Ethics class, "Unlike the world, Christian ethics aren't situational, they are hierarchical."

In this way, we develop a growing sense of justice and righteousness. Building on Piaget's work, Lawrence Kohlberg (1927-1987) proposed a theory of moral development which illustrates how people begin and grow morally. He begins by defining this as "moral reasoning," or how we approach ethics. In Kohlberg's view, six developmental stages exist which he puts into three levels with two stages each. The levels, Pre-conventional, Conventional and Post-Conventional contain overlap (See Chart on Page 153). This is similar to the other developmental models we've presented. Each stage depends on the previous one to present the perspective and experience needed in acquiring the next stage. In Kohlberg's view, no further moral development can take place until fully integrated in the mind and heart of a person. Stages can never be skipped in moral development.

One of the major disagreements with Kohlberg centers around performance: the idea of knowing what we *ought* to do is different from actually *doing* it. True. However, we find that Kohlberg's model is useful and widely respected but should not be treated as gospel. (We only treat the Gospel as gospel.)

The complexity of moral growth describes a vast wilderness of human actions and reactions. In morality, motivations and intentions will be judged alongside actions. Understanding Kohlberg's Stages of Moral Development can help the parent understand the hierarchy of ethical growth. In this way, we may meet our children where they are challenged and be grace-full in our interactions with them around moral topics.

Understanding Kohlberg's Stages of Moral Development can help the parent understand the hierarchy of ethical growth. In this way, we may meet our children where they are challenged and be grace-full in our interactions with them around moral topics.

We want to make a note here for clarity sake considering the definition of a loaded word. In keeping with the scientific literature on the subject here, we use the word "punish" or "punishment" to merely mean, "giving a negative consequence." In some other manners of use, this word could be defined as anything up to and including abuse. We do not intend that usage, nor should you infer that when we use the word. We trust you to follow your own Christ-centered code of ethics when giving negative consequences. Punishment, or negative consequences, can be an important training tool for a child when intentional, measured, and done out of love and never anger.

KOHLBERG'S STAGES OF MORAL DEVELOPMENT			
STAGE	PRINCIPLE	DRIVE	PRIMARY REFLECTION
Level I – Pre-conventional Morality: From Preschool age to some High Schoolers.			
1	Obedience & Punishment	Avoid Punishment	Will I be punished?
2	Individualism & Exchange	Serving Self	What's in it for me?
Level II – Conventional Morality: From a few older elementary age to many high schoolers and adults.			
3	Accord & Conformity	Good Boy/ Girl	Live up to social expectations
4	Authority & Social Order	Law and Order	Laws hold society together
Level III – Post-conventional Morality: Rare before college, few adults ever operate in Stage 6			
5	Social Contract & Individual Rights	Social Agreement	Pick what's best for the most people.
6	Universal Principle	Moral Reasoning	Regardless, I must do what is right.

Level I – Pre-conventional Morality (from Preschool age to some High Schoolers)

Pre-conventional Morality begins in the earliest stages of thought. We begin as babies seeing the world as pleasurable and painful which we learn to equate with good and bad. From there, we begin to develop a morality based primarily around the question of, "what benefits me?" In some ways, the focus on self-interest shows a lack of "morality," at least in the sense of the good of others as part of the equation. Most kids below the age of nine (and some over that age) fall into this level. **The basic idea of Pre-conventional Morality says simply, "I benefit by staying out of trouble."**

Our moral code developed first as a system shaped by the adults in our lives. Though it might be a stretch to call it a "moral code," we simply responded to adult authority. Parents, teachers, children's ministry leaders and other authorities provide modeling for us. Significantly, we also suffer negative consequences for failing to live by their rules and regulations. Following or breaking adult rules plays an important part in the moral lives of children of this age.

Consequences serve as the primary motivator at this level, especially punishment. From our earliest age, we are programmed to learn from consequences. We learn what hurts and what feels good. We tend to avoid what is unpleasant, that is a no-brainer. We have within us an adaptive trait called **aversion**. Have you ever eaten something that made you sick and then lost your taste for that food? Then you have experienced aversion. Getting sick on bad clams one time might mean that you never again enjoy shellfish, and maybe even feel queasy at their sight- or even the thought of them. This is a food aversion.

We have aversion to punishment when young. We simply learn not to enjoy or desire the behavior that brings on a negative consequence. That makes perfect sense; God has given us this gift for our protection.

We first learn to avoid the unpleasant result. When we become old enough to control our actions, we begin to learn to control our impulses a bit. When a child thinks, "I want that light so I'm going to touch it," consequences should teach him that sometimes it's good to refrain from acting on our impulses. "Ouch that light was hot!" can be a reminder that not everything that catches our eye is good for us. Lack of impulse control can often be found in teens, which may be discovered by examining the driving statistics of teenage male drivers.

There are two stages in Level 1- Pre-conventional Morality and they both deal with how events affect the individual.

Stage 1 – Obedience and Punishment (Avoiding Punishment)

The earliest form of understanding human conduct falls in Stage 1- the Obedience and Punishment Stage. Children come to understand early that behavior matters to the authorities in their life. Parents reward or punish the child to influence them to behave properly. Children learn that a look of disapproval can mean mommy must be "unhappy." Mommy being unhappy may bring about unpleasant events. These little sponges of knowledge soon learn about consequences. This appropriately affects their behavior. They learn that some actions bring pleasure, some bring displeasure and some bring little interest.

From the results of their actions, children learn. From the time children begin to understand their senses and explore the world, they soon discover that actions cause results. Actions become pleasant or painful in varying degrees. Children begin to realize that actions have outcomes. They begin to sort their actions into ones that receive good and bad responses. Learning to act or refrain based on the response of the adults in their life encompasses the moral structure of Stage 1.

Billy, a four year old, wants a cookie from the cookie jar. The cookies sit on the edge of the counter where he can reach them. He knows from sad experience that the family rules prohibit taking sweets off the counter before dinner. He knows he will get punished if he steals the cookie, therefore Billy's "moral code" rests fully on the rules set by his mother and the punishment he knows will come if he breaks them.

Amanda feels in a good mood. Her fourth grade class spent the day working on a group project and they selected her as their team captain. She gets to go to the cafeteria and retrieve the cookies for her class. She becomes tempted to run but remembers that school rules forbid running in the hall. She obeys the school rules and walks to the cafeteria because she doesn't want to get in trouble. Here, the basis of Amanda's moral code comes from the school rules.

In both cases, there are rules that must be obeyed and the entire reason for obeying the rules is the avoidance of punishment. This relationship with rules shows how the first stage's motivation centers on the child's desires and the positive or negative consequences they will receive. In this stage, punishment is everything. The seriousness of the offense will be judged on the harshness of the penalty and if an innocent person receives punishment, they "must have been bad."

Stage 2 – Individualism and Exchange (Serving Self)

In Stage 2, the self-focus continues but expands and includes more than their immediate context. It now includes their broader, social perspective. **The center of the moral code goes from keeping safe from punishment to meeting needs**. A broader definition of good now includes self-interest and personal needs. One becomes more concerned with getting what they want. As the child grows, they become better able to discern what will please them and what they want to avoid. These values then become the hub of their code of morality. These individuals (sadly, in some cases even adults) develop a primary motivation focused on meeting personal wants and needs. Here, reputation and other abstract needs find no consideration (as understood in Stage 5—see table on page 153). This area of desire rests primarily on their personal needs.

An interesting expansion of the self-interest of individualism develops in Stage 2. This is the willingness to help others as a means of getting their own way. A quid pro quo or "you scratch my back, I'll scratch yours," mindset comes along with this expanded definition of self-interest. When this young person wants something they can be induced into working for it through helping someone else. Their ways of getting what they want becomes broader and more social. They may even appear to be helping others. However, make no mistake, in this stage actions appearing selfless have an intrinsic motivation of self-interest.

Jane is a freshman in high school. As part of a small group of friends, she will often gather with them. Study hall and lunch period are times when they gather to talk about their day and reinforce their relationships. This time helps the kids get through the day and feel good about themselves. On one particular day, school has an assembly. Jane's class comes into the large auditorium first. She finds herself uncomfortable thinking about sitting with strangers during the program. So, even though she knows it is against the rules to save seats, Jane places her sweater on the back of a seat and her book-bag on another. People walking by simply assumed that the seats are taken.

When Jane's friends Michelle and Angel walk by, Jane tells them she saved seats for them. They thank her, and happily sit, and enjoy the program together. By breaking the school rule and saving seats for her friends, Jane actually serves her own interests. Because she *Finding out that our children are being nice so they can get something may be disappointing and cynical. However, children develop into and out of this stage of self-centeredness.* anticipates anxiety in the large auditorium she creates a small cocoon of friends. In this way, she would be more comfortable sitting within the larger group. Though her friends were grateful, their comfort was not the primary motivator of Jane's actions.

There might be a temptation for the parent to see this behavior as simple selfishness. Helping someone just to get something appears quite cynical. We want our children to be pure of heart, and this hardly seems to fit the definition. However, we must keep in mind the appropriateness of children developing into and through this stage. The social component of Stage 2 sets the stage for more developed and complex interactions at later stages. Remember, the motivations at work here are premature and still appropriate for moral development.

Level II – Conventional Morality (from a few older Elementary to many High Schoolers and Adults.)

Conventional Morality finds its basis in the norms and conventions of society (or their primary social group). This allows a harmony in society and enables people to get along. Here people receive all the benefits of community. Members accept the group's view as "normal" and receive that as their own individual standard of expectation. Role modeling and peer pressure help define and enforce those expected standards. **As might be expected from the name, most adolescents and adults operate within this conventional standard of morality.**

In this Level II Conventional Morality, the individual has previously passed through the Level 1 Pre-Conventional Morality stages where the self matters most. They next grow into the other-oriented stages. People of respect and group institutions persuade and pressure group members to behave in appropriate ways. With social norms well understood, individuals usually base their moral reasoning on society's views and expectations. The community provides the definition of right and wrong and sets the standard of right and wrong. On the other hand, questioning authority undermines the group and creates a sense of moral confusion. This sense of group morality makes challenging leaders an extremely difficult option. Some of the worst human behavior comes from otherwise good people who could not go against the group.

People find comfort and identity in society and to be a part of it they absorb the group's conventions of good and bad. (It is OK to make fun of people who are different. It is NOT OK to make fun of our leaders.) Usually, this happens without a conscious decision about it. Ideas and norms develop as people interact. Individuals internalize these norms and make them their own. Social beings from the sole of the foot on up, following rules and customs provides people with a sense of stability and a type of harmony.

Those in Level II Conventional Morality tend to follow rules rigidly and without truly questioning their fairness. So deeply internalized are group rules that people will often follow these social customs without the possibility of receiving negative consequences. In this way, the moral authority of the group holds sway over the individual. Therefore, when making a moral decision most people (who live their daily life in the Level II Conventional Morality) will choose to accept the group's evaluation of their options. In other words, when facing a decision MOST people will do what society expects them to do.

Stage 3 –Accord and Conformity…(Good Boy, Good Girl)

Stage 3 concerns the development of interpersonal relationships. This is sometimes called the "Good Boy/ Good Girl stage." People in this stage find comfort in their social place through pleasing others. They get along by conforming to social roles, by being "nice" or appropriate, and living up to their group's social expectations. A teen may enter a social group around a shared interest like sports, music, academics. In some communities, teens might feel pressure to join a gang. Teens learn to be social by finding a place and getting along.

As adults, the "Good Boy/Good Girl" lets their social context guide them to join a certain social club, register with a certain political party, to keep their lawn cut and attractive and many others. Neighbors and friends (their social network) and their common values lead the way in this. As from an early age, we learn about the world's expectations through reading the social context.

Teenagers crave acceptance from authority figures like teachers or pastors and especially from popular peers. Receiving approval from their social group means self-validation and a place of their own in the social order. This comforts the teen and helps make their world predictable and to a certain extent, more safe.

When this feeling of social conformity develops in a young person, it happens because they are learning to care about others and maintain relationships. In doing so they use helpful social values like loyalty, trust, and care. At this time, young people develop cognitively and psychosocially. During this social growth, they develop in their ability to make decisions, which includes considering other people's perspectives and intentions: "Does Bev think what Elayna did is wrong? Will my teacher find my work acceptable? What will Alonzo do if I decide to go to Student Prayer Group?"

This critical social skill develops by degrees as we search for our place in society. Through the development of abstraction and logical reasoning, people begin to judge their actions (and the acts of others) by how those actions affect the group.

A few of the basic, yet critical, skills in the "Good Boy/ Good Girl stage" are respect and gratitude. We learn and practice the "Golden Rule," "*So in everything, do to others what you would have them do to you, for this sums up the Law and the Prophets." (Matthew 7:12)* This attitude held close to the heart builds both respect and gratitude for others as well as oneself. As insight into social interaction grows, young people welcome the approval of others and react aversely to any disapproval they find. It is the rare person who can go against their own primary social group.

It takes a while for teens to begin growing to understand that others have similar emotions about their social roles. They soon understand and empathize with making a social faux pas and find it easier to forgive those with good intentions. "They meant well," becomes an acceptable cause for forgiveness. Through all of the coming of age confusion in this stage, teens strongly desire to earn the good graces of their social group or school.

For example, Ethan goes to Northmore High School during his sophomore year. He comes from a background similar to his peers and does not stand out in any negative way. As with most young men his age, Ethan finds himself deeply concerned with his peers and how they see him. He wants to fit in but still stumbles socially. Classmates think he's nice but a little weird.

Ethan's friend Dakota lives in his neighborhood and knows him better than most. They hang out sometimes and go down to the playground with the other teens. As Ethan, Dakota, and the group stand around talking, an errant ball comes their way. Ethan catches the ball and throws it back. As he launches the orb, Kristin walks into the ball's path. Ethan looks on with horror as he calculates that the flight of the ball and the path of the girl will soon intersect. The ball strikes Kristin and more by surprise than injury, she falls down.

Teens begin to understand about social roles. They understand and empathize with making a social faux pas and find it easier to forgive those with good intentions. They meant well becomes an acceptable excuse.

In this moment Ethan, still aghast, must use his budding social skills to keep in good graces with his group. He desperately wants the approval of his friends. As he looks on, Ethan must immediately weigh the situation and determine the group's expectation of him. His ability to sympathize with the girl comes to mind. It appears he hurt the girl and he doesn't like that. "Should I run over to see how she is?" Ethan wonders, "Can I help her? Should I say I'm sorry?" Always good questions to consider.

In that decisive instant, Ethan looks toward Dakota and sees him dissolve into laughter with the rest of the guys. Ethan has gotten his social clue on how to act and will (and in a real way – must) go along and be a "Good Boy." Ethan breaks up laughing too. They all hoot together about it as Kristin climbs to her feet. As the guys tease Ethan about his poor throwing he feels a part of the group. He feels bad about scaring the girl but has been affirmed by his social group. This, after all, is the powerful motivator of being the "Good Boy" in the stage of Accord and Conformity.

Stage 4 – Maintaining Social Order…(Law and Order)

Sometimes called the Law and Order stage, Stage 4 moves on from the special interests of the immediate group. It stresses society's need for structure and stability. In this next natural stage of morality people accept the need for "give and take" in society.

The mutual reliance and deference required for society to function finds its structure in the force of law. Law codifies or defines and presents the values of society and the nation's social expectations. With the law serving as their guidelines, people can know the group's rules and follow them.

As part of law, an enforcement mechanism holds the members of society accountable. When some people cannot (or choose not) to obey the law, society has organized methods of punishment which can be forcefully employed. The law, via the courts and law enforcement responds to those who break the law. The fear of this helps to mold the behavior of many.

In this stage of maintaining social order, moral reasoning goes beyond the mere individual approval that we see in Stage 3 (Good Boy, Good Girl). Stage 4 morality recognizes the importance of obeying laws and social conventions. People understand the necessity for rules to keep society functioning smoothly and, therefore, submit themselves to the law. They reason that if some people break the law, everybody will break the law and then chaos would follow. People at this level of moral reasoning understand this and see obeying the law as their personal duty and citizens' obligation to each other. Therefore, breaking the law must be considered morally wrong.

Stage 4 morality goes beyond being a Good Boy or Girl and people begin to understand the necessity of rules for the smooth functioning of society.

However, having society's sense of right and wrong anchored in the law can also have a downside. Since laws work as a society's "institution of morality," it is extremely difficult to change them. People perceive these rules to be rigid (moral building blocks) and have a hard time recognizing the need to change laws when society changes. (We note that sometimes society's changes do not form an advancement of morality.) People often find exceptions difficult to handle. When special circumstances require a new look at a situation, some people balk. Consider here the Pharisees dutiful reliance on the law when Jesus presented them with humanitarian exceptions. Most adults live in this state of "Law and Order" morality.

James is a small business owner. He runs a print shop making a number of different types of promotional materials. This includes a large contract with the city's NFL team. James has 27 employees to operate the presses, staff the sales room, keep the books and run the website. He finds true joy in supporting his family and employees by being an entrepreneur. His family means the world to him. The whole family participates in the community church and strongly supports their community outreach. James started this business in his basement and now finds himself an important member of his community and is admired by many.

One day, a local government contract for a massive printing project comes open. James scrupulously costs the project. He presents the city with his bid proposal. After waiting, not so patiently, James celebrates upon learning he won the contract. He hires four new people including two from his church.

It is then his ink supplier, Gerald, approaches James. Gerald suggests a convoluted scheme to funnel a great deal of money into their own accounts without the outlay called for in the city contract. No doubt remained about the issues involved and which side of the law they were on. James had a decision to make. As he talked it over with his wife Carmen, he came to this conclusion.

'I've worked hard, and the Lord has blessed me to get where I am. Now Gerald comes to me with an opportunity to make a lot of money, more money than we've ever seen, which we could surely put to good use. I hate to admit I am tempted. However, this is risky and seems so dangerous to me, to us, and to the business we have. If something goes wrong, I will end up in jail. I will lose my business and my place in the community I love."

"We perform this contract for the good of the city and our community. What if people skimmed money from every city contract? Where would our community be then? I cannot take part in this. It

is against the law and is wrong. I will tell Gerald tomorrow that I will not participate."

By fulfilling his contract and not participating in the illegal scheme, James lost out on a lot of extra money. However, by doing business by the law he guaranteed his integrity and continued respect and good standing in the community.

Level III – Post-conventional Morality (Rare before college, few adults ever operate in stage 6)

In Level III, Post-conventional Morality, the individual goes beyond the social agreement integrated into their thinking in Level II. **Level III thinking bases morality on one's chosen principles.** Such a morality actually finds basis in principles the individual finds appealing and willingly follows. The Level III thinker goes from Level II, where every ideal centers on society as the authority, to looking at their own abstract principles as the authority for their lives. A person who chooses the Bible as their ultimate authority and lives largely according to its principles has stepped into the area of Level III thinking.

A deep change of heart occurs when a person begins to realize that society can be at odds with their own deeply held sense of right and wrong. They begin to realize individual moral agents make up society. They see themselves as followers of a greater way of thinking. A new paradigm becomes apparent to the Level III individual. They grow to understand that wise and courageous individuals must follow their conscience. This means they sometimes may come across a situation where laws and morality come in conflict.

A person who chooses the Bible as their ultimate authority and lives largely according to its principles has stepped into the area of Level III thinking.

An obvious example comes from the outrage following the Nuremberg Trials (This was the tribunal following World War II where Nazi's received judgment for their participation in war crimes.) People naturally asked, "Why?" The most repugnant response to that question was, "I was only following orders." Courts of law and courts of public opinion cried out against this line of thought and together collectively said, "It's not OK to behave immorally because of social convention."

Similar to a person from Stage 4 (Law and Order), Level III individuals recognize the place of society as the source of general social order and the protection of human rights. However, they view laws as useful tools but not absolutes beyond questioning. In Level III laws are seen as flexible and changeable so they may serve people and not master them. These pliable social rules will be seen as requiring to preserve human rights and justice. Therefore, when a law violates these dictates of conscience, adherence to a personal code of ethics may sometimes demand such laws be disobeyed.

Interestingly, Post-Conventional (Level III) people recognize their own moral judgment over society and sometimes might be viewed as self interested or Pre-Conventional. In reality, Level III thinking starts with external guiding principles, such as Scripture. These people will then use their principles to guide them in their moral lives and decision-making. It is interesting to note that according to some sources, Level III thinking only affects 10% – 15% of individuals and rarely before the age of 30.

Stage 5 - Social Contract and Individual Rights(Social Agreement)

In Stage 5, individuals begin to truly appreciate the value of the individual. They gain a respect for others as independent beings. This leads them to a general esteem for the rights and value of every person even when disagreeing with them. To such a person, all people have value and an intrinsic right to hold their own opinions, values and beliefs. For example, "all men are endowed by their creator with certain unalienable rights; among them are life, liberty and the pursuit of happiness." (The American Declaration of Independence.)

To an individual residing in a Stage 5 morality, each person matters and everyone's rights and views have significance. Yet, with society's competing interests there must be some way to maintain the social order. Whatever solution the Stage 5 person may support, in their mind it must primarily ensure the protection of vital human rights. Therefore, society must have rules agreed upon and approved by the members. Citizens must "buy in" to the process that protects everyone. This is true individually and collectively. When viewed in this way, laws must be flexible and changeable to serve society as well as individual people.

When laws serve society they function as agreements between people and not as rigid edicts handed down from on high. Laws promoting the general welfare can be enacted but can be also altered as the needs of society changes. Consider child labor laws that became enacted in the early 20th century. People began to see child labor as exploitation and so they created laws limiting and then prohibiting it. The American Founders' principle of limited government comes from this ideal of a social contract negotiated between the members of society. Voting and compromise underpin democracy at work.

Thomas was a well-educated philosopher and gentleman who served in local government. As his community struggled with economic and political oppression, he received an assignment to write a letter to the leaders of the national government. In it, Thomas was charged to lay out their complaints and explanations. He did so, citing the importance for the government to respect citizen's rights.

Thomas placed citizens at the center of the equation of governing. He said that governments exist solely for and by the good will of the citizenry. In final form, this document presented a plan for an order of society in which the people's needs would be met because of dialogue, compromise and majority vote. He rejected authoritarian rule hands down.

President Thomas Jefferson wrote the *American Declaration of Independence* believing that society should be governed by social agreement and respect for individual rights. This radical form of limited government had at its heart, a belief that laws are contracts people make with each other. However, since sinful human beings make up society, difficulty in implementing the heartbeat of democracy cannot be avoided.

However, respect of the law as a way of binding people together raised the stake in governance. People were no longer seen as subjects of the ruling class but as citizens. Citizens became an integral part of the social contract. Thomas Jefferson became part of the legacy of democracy that America gave the world. Truly and fully living out democratic principles does take a thoroughly Post-conventional view of Morality: that other people are important in their own right.

Stage 6 – Universal Principles (Moral Reasoning)

Stage 6 individuals base their view of morality based on Universal Principles. In this stage, moral values find basis in abstract principles such as the equality of all people, respect for human dignity and commitment to justice or the practice of agape love. Few people operate regularly under these universal ethics. According to Kohlberg, there is little evidence of people living their entire lives under this moral code of Universal Principles. A brave few will strictly follow a moral code, but few (if any) will be able to live their entire lives fully according to the Universal Principles.

When operating according to Universal Principles, one sees certain basic or foundational truths as the highest of values- even above self-preservation. Living in Stage 6 takes a tremendous amount of courage. These individual must have a strong inner compass and follow those principles wherever they lead. They might be called upon to willingly break society's laws that violate their conscience. This is because Stage 6 people reach an absolute commitment to justice and so these principled few individuals will likely suffer for their decision.

The moral development of a Stage 6 individual includes a commitment to the principles they hold as absolute. They understand that following their conscience may lead to legal punishment and social disapproval for their actions. These individuals choose to follow their principles and if necessary, willingly pay the consequences for transcending the law. We are reminded here of the Christian martyrs through the centuries and up to today.

The Universal Principles are not a means to gaining something else. The fulfillment of the principle is the end in itself; doing what is right for righteousness sake. Therefore, this person seeks to act according to their principles in spite of punishment or personal interest, regardless of whether it is legal or contractual. To them, these moral principles

The moral development of a Stage 6 individual includes a commitment to these principles as absolute. They understand they might suffer legal punishment and social disapproval for their actions.

exist on a higher plane than any self-interest and the Stage 6 individual obeys those principles because it is right to do so.

Dietrich, a well-educated Lutheran pastor in Germany, wrote books about how Christians should live in a secular world. His book, "The Cost of Discipleship" often makes the list of contemporary spiritual classics. The rise of his academic and church career took a major detour in 1933 with the election of Adolph Hitler.

Dietrich had opposed the Nazis from the beginning of their rise to power. Two days after the election, he denounced Nazism publicly during a radio address. The radio station mysteriously quit broadcasting in the middle of that speech. During his ministry in Nazi Germany, he worked feverishly against the Nazis as they set out to co-opt the German Protestant Churches. He also fought strongly against the Nazis' Jewish policy.

In 1943, Dietrich Bonheoffer was arrested and imprisoned for his work in religious and human rights. While in prison, he continued his ministry. He wrote a number of works and served as pastor to other inmates. Later, after a failed attempt on Hitler's life, information emerged which linked him to the plotters. In a rage, Hitler ordered the execution of everyone possibly connected. Two weeks before the American Army liberated his prison, Bonheoffer was finishing Sunday worship service in the prison. Guards came to take him for execution. Before leaving, he told a fellow inmate, "This is the end, the beginning of life for me."

Dietrich Bonhoeffer worked to oppose the injustice of the Nazi regime and it cost him his life, as he knew it might. This is an example of a Stage 6 moral code, working for justice for the sake of justice, regardless of the consequences.

For an example of each stage of moral reasoning centered around a common question, see an example of "The Heinz Dilemma" in the Appendix C on page 277)

APPLICATION

List two or three things that you learned or found interesting:

1

2

3

Reflection and Discussion Questions

1) If you could give one gift to your children, what would it be?

2) Growing up, what virtue did you see in your parents that you hope to emulate?

3) What would you do over if you could go back five years? (in regards to parenting)

4) What do you remember about your first day of school or your first teacher? (See Level I on page 153)

5) In what stage do you think you were? (Stage 1 - Will I get punished? Or stage 2 - What's in it for me?)

Chapter 22 – Christ in the Developmental Stages

[I] make myself available in the routine tasks and myriad interruptions of daily life because I believe it is God's will for me to serve my family through them. Sally Clarkson

Together, we have reviewed Piaget's Stages of Cognitive Development, Erikson's Stages of Psychosocial Development and Kohlberg's Stages of Moral Development. These resources will give an idea of how children grow. **Growth is, after all, the point of this book.** We grow in faith and love by submitting ourselves to Christ and allowing the Holy Spirit into our lives and our homes. Having a basic understanding of the God-designed processes of how humans grow, we can give kids what THEY need and when they need it.

As much as we like to think our little bundles of blessing simply ooze genius, we cannot take them into a stage where they are not ready to go. God created us, skill building upon skill, process upon process, as we grow into adulthood. We need to be aware of our children's abilities.

One example of an incorrect application of developmental knowledge occurs when we see parents respond to a young child's indiscretions through abstract reason and long winded explanations. Young children do not and cannot, understand their parents abstract reasoning. They cannot put themselves in another person's place yet. However, we parents may be fooled into thinking they comprehend us because they can learn to give us the response we unwittingly coach them into.

Knowing how our young disciples grow puts us in a position to instruct kids AT THEIR OWN DEVELOPMENTAL LEVEL. When we know that a cross face or stern voice impacts a younger child far better than an explanation, we can help them better grow in grace and truth. **At whatever level, we know the entire family will be blessed with Christ as part of the equation.**

171

Why Bible stories instead of theology? Younger children understand the world of story and imagination. This is why we recommend C.S. Lewis to you, especially the *Chronicles of Narnia*. As they grow into their tweens (age between child and teenage) they will develop the ability to understand stories in a more concrete way.

Physical development can mask a child's real developmental conditions. Did you ever meet a child large for their age? You might ask a question and be surprised by the immaturity of their response. Have you ever watched a TV commercial where you see very young children do amazing things? Many times they are children who appear far younger than their development. The internal development of children usually has little to do with their appearance.

Children go through their developmental stages successfully or unsuccessfully. They succeed fully, partly or not at all and still physical development goes onward. People get older, change, and pass into eternity. All of the major questions in our search for self-identity find answers in Christ. This is not to say we do not wrestle but that our wrestling finds purpose in something greater than ourselves. Let us accept that fact and end our hesitation at bringing the Good News to children early and continually in their lives. This will build, block upon block, as we share it in appropriate ways.

We can jumpstart this process by clearly accepting that children understand God differently than adults do. **Children understand God in the ways He designed them– in their proper season.** Their little hearts accept truth in ways that life has conditioned out of adults. Who has not marveled at this scene from the gospels?

> [13] *People were bringing little children to Jesus to have him touch them, but the disciples rebuked them.* [14] *When Jesus saw this, he was indignant. He said to them, "Let the little children come to me, and do not hinder them, for the kingdom of God belongs to such as these.* [15] *I tell you the truth, anyone who will not receive the kingdom of God like a little child will never enter it."* [16] *And he took the children in his arms, put his hands on them and blessed them. (Mark 10:13-16)*

Many preachers have trod these waters explaining the nature of the child, trusting and loving. Yet, this deserves a fuller understanding since we just explored how people develop. When mentoring children, we must remember they are more than "pre-human beings." Children have a life and an integrity of faithfulness all their own. It is not the faith of an adult but perhaps our own arrogance is the same as the disciples, "What does a child have to offer us?" Well, Jesus told us to look to them as a model for our faith.

Perhaps we need to become more discerning in expecting to give them an adult-looking faith at too early an age. Let's pay attention to their abilities and look to understand the development of their faith in its appropriate season. **Parents need to help our children understand God and experience Jesus IN THEIR WAY.** This may take rethinking some of the things we know and presenting them in a manner tailored for children of various ages. This process takes form in understanding the Cognitive, Psychosocial and Moral developmental stages of our young disciples. Understanding our young disciples and instructing them in the ways of the Lord is the calling of a parent.

With the Lord in the midst of our lives and a commitment to keeping a Christian home, we CAN disciple our children. Familiarity with this growth process can lead us to better communication, better instruction, and most importantly, greater love and empathy. With Christ welcomed into the midst of our lives, our young disciples develop the most important skill they will ever need: the ability to know, love, and follow our Heavenly Father.

APPLICATION

List two or three things that you learned or found interesting:

1

2

3

Reflection and Discussion Questions

1) As parents, we need to help our child understand God and experience Jesus IN THEIR WAY. How has this section prepared you to help your child experience Jesus?

2) In what ways do you see your role as parent more clearly after reading about developmental stages?

3) In what ways does this make parenting become more complex? Does this scare or intimidate you?

Section 4

REASON FOR HOPE

SECTION 4 – REASON FOR HOPE

Chapter 23 – The 7 Pillars of the Christian Family

Wisdom has built her house; she has set up its seven Pillars.

Proverbs 9:1

It's sometimes true that you lose sight of the forest for the trees. That old adage reminds us we may focus so intensely on the details that we lose sight of the big picture. When we focus on the details to the exclusion of the broader view, we may end up making bad decisions. Todd reports receiving a building program proposal exactly opposite of what the group set out to do. The group focused on solving minor problems and lost sight of their major goals. Like traveling cross-country through a forest, when we keep our eyes on the ground we can lose direction. How many times have you, as a parent, felt like you were going around in circles?

The profound confusion in many homes springs from our parental management style. We often deal uncertainly with the non-stop push and tug of parenting. Every new challenge can seem like the end of the world when we can't look at the bigger picture. In business (as well as government, non-profits, etc.), focusing exclusively on emergency following calamity chasing catastrophe has a name. "Management by crisis" keeps us fixated on the urgent problem at hand while we miss the important decision waiting in the background.

With all the demands of modern parenting, the easiest thing in the world may be developing tunnel vision. We can simply slide into a day-to-day "family management by crisis." While focusing so intently on the daily activities of life we can lose our way. Parents can become so tied up with cleaning, clothing, feeding, teaching, and everything else that family life becomes like the fabled Gordian knot–stuck fast.

According to the legend, the ancient Gords had a specialized test for leadership. Before they would submit to the rule of Alexander the Great, they called on him to solve the puzzle of an intricate knot. Despite his efforts, Alexander failed to untangle the hopelessly snarled knot. In frustration he pulled his sword and raised it above his head. He swung the blade forcefully downward and cleaved the knot thereby solving the problem. Like Alexander, sometimes we have to quit working with the problem and move on to solving it.

We propose a solution to help parents caught up in the day-to-day grind to step back and look at the forest instead of the trees. We call it the Seven Pillars of The Christian Family and use it to help organize the thinking about our Christian family. This Seven Pillars Method is an organizational assessment we developed to give a well-rounded view of the various domains or functions of a Christian family (or any Christian organization).

When we look from the middle of life we usually see only the many trees of the forest. However, by stepping back and understanding the patterns of the trees, we can see the path that leads us out of the forest.

It may seem strange to look at your family as an "organization." However, a family operates in much the same way as a small business or ministry. You have a purpose, which may be to provide for the rearing of children and the mutual support of each member. You have policies and procedures usually called "family rules." Expectations exist for every family member, and there is often a division of labor. (Little Susie puts out the utensils for dinner, Mike cuts the grass, Mom cooks while Dad drives home from work.) You have an income and outgo. (With children in the family, the outgo can easily outpace the income.) Daily operations provide the necessities for the family organization. You even have a headquarters which we usually call home.

When we look from the middle of life, we usually see only the many trees in the forest. However, stepping back and understanding the forest helps us see the patterns of the trees. We can see the paths that lead us out of the forest.

With such a strategic approach, you can live intentionally; you can set and make goals. You can cease being a slave to the urgent and become a servant of the important. By gaining an understanding of the big picture, you have a greater ability to get your day-to-day life on track. Armed with this knowledge, you can live the way you wish. The first step requires some attention. It's time to step back and review how your family lives compared to how you want to live.

As has been said, "every organization is perfectly designed for the results it is getting." This pithy little quote on why we are the way we are says a lot. Like many people, you desire something better for your family. However, you probably don't know how or what to change. Change frightens and perplexes us. Fear tempts us to say, "I'm good enough where I am." While you feel things are acceptable, as we stated earlier in this book, "God has more for you than 'good enough.'"

We have developed this method of looking at our family, which we call, "The Seven Pillars of the Christian Family." The purpose to understanding these domains or "pillars" is to help us integrate our family life. As in any group dynamic, different areas of family life affect the others. For example, let us ask you a question, "What is the purpose of your family?" Some of you will likely answer, "We fell in love, kids happened and here we are. I don't know the "purpose" or goals of our family." We actually think this happens far more often than people are willing to admit. Is that bad? Not if it leads you to breaking out of the rut of complacency and developing a desire to understand the soul of your family.

This Seven Pillars method takes a holistic approach to looking at the areas in which an organization operates. It presupposes that every organization has a unique character made of its members and their attitudes. The Seven Pillars method helps you look at your family like you would hold up a mirror. Would you do your hair or makeup without looking in the mirror? How might you look in that mirror if you have no idea about how you want to look? (Admittedly, we have both seen that sight in the morning mirror. Not at all pretty.) The Seven Pillars method is a way of looking at the family (or any Christian organization) that gives perspective to its various parts.

Each pillar represents one domain or area of our family life. They correspond to various aspects of life that Christian families will find important in building their walk of discipleship. Taken together they form a balanced view of the considerations that spiritual families creating young disciples will want. Please understand that we do not intend to tell you how to practice your family's Christian faith. We believe that presumes too much on our part. What we will tell you is this, "Whatever you do, do it wholeheartedly. Practice your faith with conviction."

Purpose
Integrity
Leadership
Lifestyle
Attitude
Relationship
Service

We believe that viewing these Seven Pillars through the eyes of faith will enable your family to bring your spirituality into every facet of your life. Reconciling your faith with each Pillar will build a strong home and a close family. By creating a faithful home structure, you teach your children that faith is more than something we put a few hours into every week. By viewing life in this way, you can now experience family life together in a way uplifting every area of life. We urge you to take full advantage of this method of standing back and evaluating what you're doing so you can go where God leads you.

We developed these Seven Pillars for Christian families, but we quickly noted that these domains can be easily adapted for churches, ministries, and Christian businesses.

7 PILLARS OF THE CHRISTIAN FAMILY				
DOMAIN	PARENTING PATTERN	THEOLOGY	ACTION	COMPONENT
P urpose	Objective of living out Christ's Command to make disciples within the family	Great Commission	Pursue	Directional
I ntegrity	Confidence in the faithfulness of God's character and the dependability of His promises.	God's Provision	Trust	Ethical
L eadership	Practice of parental primacy within a strategic approach to spiritual nurture	Parental Training	Guide	Operational
L ifestyle	Manner of daily Christian living that engages and also encourages children.	Life-style Discipleship	Engage	Functional
A ttitude	Approach of submission in hearing and obedience toward the Creator.	Humility & Adoration	Submit	Emotional
R elationship	Development of a connection built on expectation while avoiding alienation.	Keeping Children's Hearts	Cherish	Relational
S ervice	Participation in opportunities for spiritual growth through family charitable projects.	Family Service	Perform	Ministerial

Section 4 – Reason for Hope

You may look at the list of pillars and be surprised at the lack of pillars called God, faith, or religion. We are very certain that God is not one-among-many pillars holding up the structure. God is far more important than that. Faith is first. Christ is the cornerstone. You practice your faith according to precepts of Scripture and the leading of the Holy Spirit; Christ will provide the solid foundation upon which the pillars find their strength.

> [24] *"Therefore everyone who hears these words of mine and puts them into practice is like a wise man who built his house on the rock.* [25]*The rain came down, the streams rose, and the winds blew and beat against that house; yet it did not fall, because it had its foundation on the rock.* [26]*But everyone who hears these words of mine and does not put them into practice is like a foolish man who built his house on sand.* [27]*The rain came down, the streams rose, and the winds blew and beat against that house, and it fell with a great crash."* (Matthew 7:24-27)
> (Also found in Luke 6:46-49)

Nothing supports and uplifts your family more than faith in God through Jesus Christ. Through the foundation of faith and the ongoing presence of the Holy Spirit, Christian families find the strength and the courage to live a life of blessing. As God blesses us, we bless others. The Seven Pillars of Christian Families helps us see how we firmly build our home on the solid rock of Jesus Christ.

APPLICATION

List two or three things that you learned or found interesting:

1

2

3

Reflection and Discussion Questions

1) As you reflect on the 7 pillars, can you think of ways that parts interact with each other? (One example might be that if your purpose is different, then you might have different daily lifestyle decisions.)

2) How does the parable of the House built on sand relate to our family goals and decision-making?

3) Which of the 7 Pillars surprised you the most and why? How can you use this new information to help your family.

Chapter 24 – Family Discipleship

What it's like to be a parent: It's one of the hardest things you'll ever do but in exchange it teaches you the meaning of unconditional love.   *Nicholas Sparks*

In this section, we are going to do some theology together. We are going to "study God," which is the combination of two Greek words, Theos and Logos. These words mean God science or God study. Just as Biology is the study of life, geology the study of the earth and zoology the study of animals. (Like us, you may be surprised to know that Otorhinolaryngology is the study of the ear, nose and throat. Say that three times fast.) We'll be looking at theology in a variety of ways.

So, what we mean when we say "The Theology of <u>Something</u>" is "How God is at work in <u>Something</u>." For example, we'll be talking about, "Integrity and God's Provision." In this area, we will be looking at the ways in which God provides the necessities for parents to reach beyond their own strength in raising Godly children. Similarly, "Purpose and the Great Commission" looks at God's design for discipleship as seen in Scripture and history. In this theological context, we are seeking to learn how God works in Holy Christian parenting.

Gaining knowledge benefits us tremendously and study gives us a great avenue for learning. Studying the things of God tops the charts in the most important knowledge we can gain. However, we need to remain humble in our study because when we attempt to study the divine Creator we *"look through the glass darkly." (1 Corinthians 13:12)*

We can learn a lot about God by His actions. We have three important ways to know God above our own opinions and understanding. First, we have the Scriptures, God's revealed word to us. Second, we have the inspiration of the Holy Spirit leading us toward truth and away from error. Third, we have the truth of Jesus through whom we know God in a human way. In many situations, we can look to church history for a tradition of great thinkers. We ask you to prayerfully consider these theological implications of God's word. In "studying" God, always invite the Holy Spirit into your end of this discussion and try to discern where Christ leads you.

The three theological contexts concerning us here are **The Great Commission, Discipleship**, and **Parenting**. These three spiritually significant areas find common ground in each other. The Great Commission:

> [18]*Then Jesus came to them and said, "All authority in heaven and on earth has been given to me.* [19]*Therefore go and make disciples of all nations, baptizing them in the name of the Father and of the Son and of the Holy Spirit,* [20]*and teaching them to obey everything I have commanded you. And surely I am with you always, to the very end of the age."* (Matthew 28:18-20)

God calls natural parents to include the role of spiritual parents. We parents should, and are called to, disciple our children into the living image of Christ. We cannot do this alone, this is the work of the Holy Spirit. However, it is hardly the daunting task most of us imagine. One reason stands out, spiritually mentoring our children creates another avenue to love them.

These crucial words, the final message of Jesus in the Gospel of Matthew, specifically calls for believers to "make disciples." Christian faith necessarily includes a component of helping others find Christ, committing themselves to Him, as well as lifelong growth in devotion and understanding. We are "born again" (John 3:3) and grow to maturity into Christlikeness.

We often call those who disciple us our "spiritual parents." We have both had these spiritual mentors and noticed that nearly everybody who grows in faith does. Can we take one further step? Let's acknowledge, God calls natural parents to include the role of spiritual parents. We parents should (and are called to) disciple our children into the living image of Christ. Clearly, we cannot do this alone, this is the work of the Holy Spirit. However, it is hardly the daunting task most of us imagine. One reason stands out, spiritually mentoring our children creates another avenue to love them.

Breaking It Down

Scripture is God's inspired and ever faithful word. Sure, a multitude of versions exist. Some of those versions contain unfamiliar wording. However, you will find the truth of the Bible clear, consistent and certain.

> [16] *All Scripture is God-breathed and is useful for teaching, rebuking, correcting and training in righteousness, [17] so that the servant of God may be thoroughly equipped for every good work.*
> (2 Timothy 3:16-17)

As we search for the truth of living well, we find many principles and concepts God has given us in His Holy Word. We will narrow that searchlight beam down to look at seven principles we think will be helpful. These Godly principles will meet your desire to nurture your children in God's way. Obviously, the following discussion is by no means the end to all that God has for us as mothers and fathers and all spiritual parents.

Scripture Study

In this section, we examine seven key Scripture texts as they deal with the **Great Commission**, **Discipleship** and **Parenting**. As you study these theology discussions, you will find a connection between these Scripture lessons and general parenting. Fear not! It makes good sense that the traits making good spiritual parents will help enhance natural parenting as well. That seems to be the way with Scripture, filling us with all the goodness we can hold. Sometimes this happens in surprising ways.

As we begin our theological exploration, we will continue to use our yardstick of The Great Commission, Discipleship, and Parenting. **Many books on parenting are available, both online and in stores. Churches and Christian circles hardly lack for books on disciple[ing]. However, our task differs from both in that we hone in on Parenting AS Discipleship!**

Here are the Seven Theological inspections (study of God's ways) to set the stage, and to encourage you. What you have been thinking is right. Parenting is critical work, valuable beyond measure and important to God's plan for the evangelism of the future.

The Theologies of the Seven Pillars of the Christian Family

1. **P**urpose & the Theology of the Great Commission

2. **I**ntegrity & the Theology of God's Provision

3. **L**eadership & the Theology of Parental Training of Children

4. **L**ifestyle & the Theology of Life-Style Discipleship

5. **A**ttitude & the Theology of Humility and Admonition

6. **R**elationship & the Theology of Keeping Children's Hearts.

7. **S**ervice & the Theology of Family Service to God

APPLICATION

List two or three things that you learned or found interesting:

1

2

3

Reflection and Discussion Questions

1) If you could give some advice to all parents, what would you say?

2) If you could change anything about your relationship with your parents, what would it be?

3) In learning from the past, what could you (or did you) change about yourself that would help your children be closer to God?

Chapter 25 – Lifestyle Discipleship

> *Acceptance and appreciation tells the child that he or she is of tremendous worth. And I can only express my acceptance and appreciation through being affectionate- and available.*
>
> *Josh McDowell*

Jesus is telling the disciples to do with others what He did with them. Jesus invited these twelve men into His inner circle. They became His close friends, supporters, and students. Jesus lived His life with them as family. Together they met daily challenges while the disciples learned in the classroom of life. School was always in session. As Jesus walked through the towns and countryside, he intentionally taught his disciples in the context of everyday life.

We find one rich example of this in Luke 11. Jesus was with the disciples and they noticed Him praying. Respectfully, they did not interrupt Him. Instead, they waited until He had finished with His prayer time. They were impressed and moved by what they saw in Jesus. One of them asked Him to teach them to pray the way that He prayed. He taught them what we now call the Lord's Prayer:

> *¹One day Jesus was praying in a certain place. When he finished, one of his disciples said to him, "Lord, teach us to pray, just as John taught his disciples." ²He said to them, "When you pray, say: "Father, hallowed be your name, your kingdom come. ³Give us each day our daily bread. ⁴Forgive us our sins, for we also forgive everyone who sins against us. And lead us not into temptation.""*
>
> *(Luke 11:1-4)*

This act of leading by example is called "Lifestyle Discipleship." We share Jesus through the course of living our lives. **In Lifestyle Discipleship, we don't put it on; we put it all out there.** Lifestyle Discipleship allows us to show Jesus through the course of our life; our words, our actions and our attitudes. It reminds us of this lovely old poem.

"He has no hands but your hands, to do His work today.
He has no feet but your feet, to guide folds in His way.
He has no lips but your lips, to tell them how He died.
He has no love but your love, to bring them to His side."

This mentoring through living is the essence of parenting. We teach them so much more through our actions than our words. We disciple them by the way we live in front of them. Through an intentionally focused process, we live our life disciple[ing] our children. **This isn't an added agenda item that you put on your to-do list.** This process consists of living our common, ordinary life. Cooking, cleaning, banking, working, housework, laundry, mowing, trimming, gardening, errands, going out to eat, recreation, grocery shopping, education, sporting events, all create perfect opportunities for sharing the good news that Christ makes life better. This is Life-Style Discipleship.

Oftentimes we parents scurry around and become absorbed in the "busy-ness" of parenting. We can live out our parental responsibilities in 24/7 crisis management mode and miss the opportunity to uplift our children. OR, we can intentionally disciple our children in the context of life.

Mom, Billy and Justin are getting ready to leave for soccer practice. There are a few things that need done before they leave, one of which is feeding the puppy. Mom is tempted to do the chores herself because it will be quicker. However, she decides that it's better to let Justin care for the dog. They will just have to take the chance at being late. This way will take longer but Justin needs work on caring for his responsibility. She takes the time for Justin and encourages him. This was a better life-style discipleship choice in the midst of a busy life.

Too often we are trapped by the common thinking that busier is better, (or more accurately, busier is blessed). We couldn't disagree more. It's good to keep in mind the quote from Alfred Montapert, **"Do not confuse motion with progress. A rocking horse keeps moving but never makes any progress."** Does that describe your life?

Jesus made a personal relationship with God possible. He sat down with His disciples and taught them, but not just abstract, academic lessons. Jesus taught in the context of what they were dealing with at the time. A perfect example occurred when Jesus taught His disciples the Lord's Prayer (Luke 11:1-4). They found Jesus praying and asked Him to teach them to pray. So, Jesus expounded on the passion for prayer they saw in Him.

How often have we had a child ask us, "Whatcha doin'?" What an amazing opportunity to teach them, "Here's how you change a spark plug" or "Here is how to frost a cake." "Watch me, then you try," we may reply. **This practice works doubly well with faith because true faith is not simply a doctrine you obey but a way of life.**

The Great Commission writ large

When we look at the scope of the commission, we see it applies to all nations and all people groups. The ending is clear. Every person needs an invitation to become a disciple of Jesus. However, the beginning is not as clear as the ending. Where does the Great Commission start?

The Greek word for nations is *ethnee* (where we get the word ethnic). According to Thayer's Greek Lexicon, the definition for *ethnee* is a multitude associated or living together: a company, troop, swarm. [27] If we put the word "all" in front of nations, we would have the beginning of verse 19 read something like this: "Therefore, go and make disciples of all multitudes associated or living together." The Great Commission and the call to "all nations" begin with those we live with.

We miss the point and begin the Great Commission in error if we detour around those we live with. Since discipleship, as commonly seen in mentoring, requires ongoing relationship we must first disciple the people to whom we relate. As we will see later in this section, the discipleship process occurs in a day-to-day lifestyle.

The Message, Eugene Peterson's paraphrase of the New Testament, helps clarify the meaning of Matthew 28:19. It illustrates the importance of disciple[ing] those who are in our own homes first. *"Go out and train everyone you meet, far and near, in this way of life..."*[28]

We strongly suggest to you that faithfulness to the Holy Spirit in performing the Great Commission requires we reach those near before we try to tackle those afar. Both of us have close friends in missions. We see that successful missionaries reach their children first. Truly, we highly commend those with a special calling for reaching the nations. It seems to be part of their family calling, too. As we mentioned on page 8, the evidence clearly shows that the single most important social influence on the religious and spiritual lives of adolescents is their parents.

On most days, we will spend some time with the family members living in our homes. This includes our children and spouse. Maybe not as much time as we like but it will happen. We will have a continual and long lasting "association" with our loved ones.

Truth be told, if we are not disciple[ing] our family members we most likely are not disciple[ing] anyone else. Discipleship begins in our own homes. What could be more instructive, productive and profitable than to be in your home sharing and living out expressions of the Good News?

The Great Commission is Jesus' command to all Christians. We believe the context of the passage itself and the family Scriptures we will talk about later, clearly shows that "going to all the nations" begins within our homes with our family. We are called to make disciples of our children. We must start with those within our homes.

"Therefore, go and make disciples of all nations..." It is our calling, as Christ's disciples, to reproduce disciples. When Jesus says, *"Therefore,"* on what is He basing his direction? When looking back, we see the clear authority of Jesus. In essence, Jesus says, "Since I have the authority of God, what I send you to do is... make disciples."

"...baptizing them in the name of the Father and of the Son and of the Holy Spirit, and teaching them to obey everything I have

commanded you. And surely I am with you always, to the very end of the age" (Matthew 28:19-20).

Isn't this a great description of how a parent should raise a child in faith? We should baptize them in the name of the triune God, teach them God's narrow way, and remember we need not overly worry because Christ participates in the entire process. Besides a simple (co)mission statement, these words of Christ also offer all the encouragement we will ever need. We learn that Christ is with us in the entire process of spiritually nurturing our children! We can certainly raise hands of praise to God over that good news.

APPLICATION

List two or three things that you learned or found interesting:

1

2

3

Reflection and Discussion Questions

1) How would you define "Lifestyle Discipleship?" Give an example.

2) Where do you see the connection between The Great Commission and Lifestyle Discipleship?

3) "Together they met daily challenges while the disciples learned in the classroom of life." How is this lifestyle discipleship?

4) Jesus used lifestyle discipleship with his disciples. What can you transfer from the example of Jesus to help you be a better parent?

5) For you, where does the Great Commission start?

Chapter 26 – Purpose & The Great Commission

Children are our second chance to have a great parent-child relationship.   *Laura Schlessinger*

We want to start by exploring the answer to a question. Rather, two questions joined at the seam. What exactly is the Great Commission and why is important to parents? More importantly, what does it mean to … You, as a parent? Let's explore the Great Commission and study what God intended to do with us through the words of Jesus commonly known as "The Great Commission."

The name "Great Commission" is widely known, even to non-Christians. However, Jesus did not coin the term himself, but these Scriptures earned their title through the centuries. It may sound a bit commonplace to call it a nickname, but in some ways it is. Like calling a tall, thin guy "Stretch" or even calling a big guy "Tiny," the nickname is a title that draws attention to a notable characteristic. This nickname brings focus to the core of that message. Jesus gives his followers a commission, and a great one at that!

Great can mean grand; it might be famous or noble, or possibly huge or important. The greatness of Jesus' commission wraps up all these attributes and more. It certainly is grand and noble and famous, huge and significant. A directive to His disciples to bring the message of salvation and righteousness to the entire world could certainly be described as "Great."

As we write this, Facebook founder Mark Zuckerburg is making headlines by seeking to give the entire world internet access. This great plan seems like child's play compared with the challenge of revolutionizing the way that human beings think, interact with each other and connect with God.

So, the commission is great, but what exactly is a commission? Let's look at the word itself first. The Merriam-Webster dictionary shows "Co" used at the beginning of a word means with, together, joint, or jointly. We know many words that start with "co," for example, co-author, co-pay, and co-founder. Of course, these words mean together. **The word "together" appropriately describes the mission Jesus is teaching.**

First and foremost though, we must understand that "the Great Commission" is a mission. It is a task, a goal, a focus, but more. It is an assignment, an undertaking, sometimes even a quest and an adventure. The word "mission" carries the weight of expectation. It is a directive for everyone who wants to follow Jesus. Even more to the point, we may define it as a group calling. Clearly, the Great Commission is much more than a suggestion or option.

For the best possible definition let's look and see how Jesus defined it. After all, He gave this mission to the disciples after His resurrection.

The Four Great Challenges of the Commission

After His resurrection, Jesus spoke with His disciples about their future work. At that point, there remained little doubt their task would continue. When we look closely at Scripture for Jesus' post-resurrection instructions, we find four major or "great" challenges.

To understand the Lord's instruction to us, we need to see that the Scripture context shows those challenges with emphasis in slightly different ways. "The Great Commission" has at least four separate expressions in the Gospels. The best-known Scripture and most widely used articulation of the Great Commission is found in Matthew 28:18-20. There Christ emphasizes discipleship. For the purposes of this book we focus on the Great Commission and the challenge of discipleship.

However, as we look at the other expressions of God's commission in Scripture, we can see other sides to the mission. For a fuller understanding of the heart of God, let's look at these inspired words and descriptions.

(1)The Disciple[ing] Challenge of Matthew

[18] Then Jesus came to them and said, "All authority in heaven and on earth has been given to me. [19] Therefore go and make disciples of

all nations, baptizing them in the name of the Father and of the Son and of the Holy Spirit, [20] *and teaching them to obey everything I have commanded you. And surely I am with you always, to the very end of the age."* *(Matthew 20:18-20)*

As we can see in Matthew's expression, the focus is on the making of disciples. That is, the molding of people into the image of Christ. This verse spotlights the importance of reaching out so that others can find salvation in Christ, walk His path and receive all the positive transformation and blessing God provides. Parents are in a perfect position to do this with their children.

(2) The Evangelistic Challenge of Mark and Luke

He said to them, "Go into all the world and preach the good news to all creation." (Mark 16:15)

…"repentance and forgiveness of sins will be preached in his name to all nations, beginning at Jerusalem." (Luke 24:47)

This aspect of Jesus' commissioning words focuses on taking the message of restoring the relationship with God who is holy and just. God loves His creation but because of God's glory and holiness, sin will never be allowed in His presence. Truly, *"all have sinned and fallen short of the glory of God." (Romans 3:23)* As a work of grace alone, those people who repent and accept the Lordship of Christ can find reconciliation with God. It's that simple and that difficult.

Repentance precedes forgiveness and all humanity must be made aware of that amazing grace of God. The world cannot know without hearing the importance of this prescription for salvation. The same goes for our children, they need us to bring the message of repentance and forgiveness to them as well.

(3) The Missionary challenge of John:

"As you sent me into the world, I have sent them into the world."
- (John 17:18)

Again Jesus said, "Peace be with you! As the Father has sent me, I am sending you." (John 20:21)

In this reflection of the Great Commission, we see the "missionary" challenge of the Gospel. The expectation in this statement is that the Disciples/Apostles will take Jesus message into the world in an incarnational way. That is, as God in Christ appeared in our world so we will go into the world of others. We will meet them on their terms, in their own setting, even their own language. By the presence of the Christian we will make Christ known. How much more clearly can we understand our sending than being "sent" to the family God has given us?

(4) The Global Challenge of Acts:

"But you will receive power when the Holy Spirit comes on you; and you will be my witnesses in Jerusalem, and in all Judea and Samaria, and to the ends of the earth." (Acts 1:8)

The Global portion of Christ's challenge to the Christian believer means, "Go. Take this message and do not stop for man-made boundaries. Go near, go far, go to the very ends of the earth." In this way, the message and the example of Jesus will make an impact throughout the world. This Scripture shows us a universal intent in the Gospel. Every country and every culture must be made aware of the new relationship with their creator. The message of God's love, repentance and forgiveness is for everyone...everywhere.

Taken together, these Scriptural references point even more emphatically to the critical nature of the Great Commission! So let us ask, since the Gospel is so important and intended for the whole world who better to share it with than your own child? Who is more beloved than your child? Who needs the Gospel more?

As you develop the Great Commission with your child, please remember it is a mission with Jesus. You are not on your own! The Great Commission is birthed in the heart of God, passed on to us through His resurrected son, and implemented in the power of the Holy Spirit.

Mission Possible

If you're a grandparent, you may remember Peter Graves in the TV show, "Mission Impossible." Probably, if you're a parent, you remember the Tom Cruise films of the same name. The premise of these shows starts with an extremely difficult, near-impossible task. That's when they sent in the Impossible Mission Squad. A stealth message set the wheels in motion, "Good morning, Mr. Phelps. Your mission, if you choose to accept it, is to solve an unattainable goal in an implausible amount of time." (Stop a terrorist or perhaps, get a finicky toddler to eat Brussels sprouts).

As a parent (or grandparent), your mission, if you choose to accept it, is to save a child and bring him or her into the Joy of the Lord. Not only is your own child at stake but so are all future children. Not only your own family but God's family counts on you too.

The Great Commission is Jesus' command to all Christians. We believe the nations mentioned in this Scripture logically starts within our homes, with our own families. Therefore, we must hear the call to first make disciples of our children. We must begin Christ's mission in our home.

We Christians live in many different dwellings, from mansions to huts. In our homes, we find the most open and receptive being in all creation; a human child. That child, created in the image of God and only a little lower than the angels, holds the power of all God's promises in their little life. This child drips with promise. Every baby made in His image overflows with God-given potential. We have the opportunity to feed that hungry spirit with the nutritious things of God.

> [14]*How, then, can they call on the one they have not believed in? And how can they believe in the one of whom they have not heard? And how can they hear without someone preaching to them?* [15]*And*

how can anyone preach unless they are sent? As it is written: "How beautiful are the feet of those who bring good news!

(Romans 10:14-15)

You as the parent are the one being sent to bring the good news to your child. Not as an expert, not as a specialist, but as a parent just as God designed it. You bring the Gospel. You need only find the love in your heart to share a relationship with God and with your child.

That might sound daunting, though we surely don't parent alone. We disciple those impressionable children through the power of the one who "taught with authority."

*[18]"Then Jesus came to them and said, **"All authority in heaven and on earth has been given to me**. [19]Therefore, go and make disciples of all nations, baptizing them in the name of the Father and of the Son and of the Holy Spirit, [20]and teaching them to obey everything I have commanded you. And surely I am with you always, to the very end of the age." (Matthew 28:18-20)*

Jesus opens the Great Commission with a running start. The Great Commission does not begin with verse 19. "Go." The Great Commission starts with Jesus stating He has "all authority in heaven and earth" given to Him. He received that authority from God, the Father. Jesus came to minister among us and teach us the Way. Through His gruesome death and descent to the dead He atoned for our sins. In fatality, he received resurrection to demonstrate God's mastery of even our greatest fear- death. Oh yes, Jesus has the authority.

How did Jesus expand on His claims of all authority? Clearly, since Jesus has all authority He has the power to tell His disciples what is expected of them! So, He loved them, He showed them, He lived it in their presence.

APPLICATION

List two or three things that you learned or found interesting:

1

2

3

Reflection and Discussion Questions

1) How would you define the Great Commission?

2) Where is the starting point? Ending Point?

3) How do the four great challenges help you with your parenting?

4) "As you develop the Great Commission with your child please remember it is a mission with Jesus." Does this encourage you? Why?

5) The authors write, "We believe the nations mentioned in this Scripture (Matthew 28:18-20) logically starts within our homes, with our own families." Also, "We must begin Christ's mission in our home." Are you willing to accept this (co) mission?

Chapter 27 – Integrity & God's Provision

Your children are the greatest gift God will give to you, and their souls the heaviest responsibility He will place in your hands. Take time with them, teach them to have faith in God. Be a person in whom they can have faith. When you are old, nothing else you've done will have mattered as much."　　　Lisa Wingate

¹Unless the LORD builds the house,
*　its builders labor in vain.*
Unless the LORD watches over the city,
*　the guards stand watch in vain.*
²In vain you rise early and stay up late, toiling for food to eat —
*　for he grants sleep to those he loves.*
³Children are a heritage from the LORD,
*　offspring a reward from him.*
⁴Like arrows in the hands of a warrior
*　are children born in one's youth.*
⁵Blessed is the man whose quiver is full of them.
(Psalms 127:1-5a)

The strength of our faith can be seen on how we view God's integrity. Do we view God as having integrity? We may say, "Certainly, God has integrity. Many people don't but God does." But then we must ask, "Do we act as though God keeps his promises." We do believe in God's integrity when we expect God to be where He says He will be. We do when we expect that God will do what He says He will do. We believe in God's integrity when we trust his promises. Will God keep His parenting promises? Yes.

Integrity is a central character issue of any person or group. Do we consistently express our values in our choices and actions? Do we deliver what we promise? Do we provide what others rightly expect from us? This shows our integrity. We think we would never question God's integrity. Yet, when offered an opportunity to act on God's promises to us we often hesitate. "Can I trust God to keep His promise to me and my family?" becomes our unspoken concern. As parents, our growing edge in parenting may be our willingness to trust Him.

Children bless parents. This Biblical attitude could hardly be clearer from this wonderful Psalm. As arrows provide food, protection and influence so a child goes out to provide blessing for the parent and the family. An arrow overcomes distance; children overcome distance and time, (measured in both yards and years). When we have passed on, our heritage will still be carrying on with our values and promoting God's kingdom.

This passage of Psalms provides a clear teaching that all things come from God. It teaches that children are a heritage from the Lord. This insight means even our children come as a blessing from God. Because our children originate with God, they actually belong to God. As with all gifts of God, they come for our blessing and application but they don't change ownership. As much as we love them and care for them, cry for them and lift prayer for them, God loves them even more than we do.

There comes a radical shift in our parenting when we break through and realize God is the true parent of our children. Our Heavenly Father is their Heavenly Father, not their heavenly Grandfather. God holds more love and concern towards our children than we have within us.

As Jesus taught on the subject:

> *"If you, then, though you are evil, know how to give good gifts to your children, how much more will your Father in heaven give good gifts to those who ask him!"(Matthew 7:11)*

This principle of God giving better than what we expect should teach us this, "We love and care for our children, but God does so much more. Because this is true, we are not alone as we nurture and care for our children."

As parents well know, the responsibility of raising children sometimes daunts us. If we possess Godly wisdom, it humbles us. Peace comes when we look at our children and realize God gave them to us intentionally and will lead us in raising them. (See

Selection in Chapter 15 on page 62.) We can trust God will give us the wisdom and strength along with the responsibility to raise our children according to His ways.

Fear not, for we are not alone in this journey of parenting. God empowers us to live up to the honor and privilege of raising His children.

As with all gifts of God, they come for our blessing and our application, but they don't change ownership. As much as we love them and care for them, cry for them and lift prayer for them, God loves them even more than we do.

Tom remembers, "I experienced God's love and grace, before my wife and I had three boys. However, since becoming an earthly father my understanding and experience of God's love has grown a hundred-fold. Having a child of your own binds you together with a love that cannot be expressed. Then realizing that God, your Heavenly Father, is Heavenly Father of your children as well, becomes an unspeakable joy."

He continues, "An epiphany light bulb went off in me the day Michael, our oldest son passed his driver's test. I took him to get his license and on the way home, he dropped me off at my office. I watched him driving off alone in the car for the very first time. Forlornly, I went back to my office knowing our relationship changed forever. I realized the days of driving him to sporting, music and church events all began to end that day. Soon, I would no longer be in the front seat of the car driving with him. Now, he is able to drive by himself and be at the wheel in all the dangerous situations I could imagine. Here I found my peace; my comfort is in knowing my son is not by himself."

*"I know God loves him far more perfectly than I do. I know God will protect him from becoming lost and alone on these crazy roads of life we all travel. We cannot always be with our children; they grow up, they start driving, and they leave home. However, **my Heavenly Father is my children's Heavenly Father too.** My Heavenly Father never leaves me. So I know He will never leave my beloved children. God's promise holds true for all parents!"*

This critical point comes at the time in parents' lives when the realization hits us that God cares more about our precious child than even we do. That gentle feeling of tenderness along with the yearning to protect them, coupled with the desire for them to blossom and flourish pales in comparison to God's tender mercies. As when we use the delegation technique and allow the children to care for the family pet, it is still our responsibility to see that our animal friend gets food and water when our child forgets. God ultimately works for our children's good even when we fail them.

Seen only through the eyes of the world's love this hard concept cannot be grasped. However, God's love goes far beyond the affection that we have towards our young. This love for our children reaches into the realm of God's own love, a perfect, complete and fully-formed love. In other words, as much greater is the creator than the creation, that's how much greater is God's love for our children than our own simple affections. We need never lose sight of the fact that God gave us this reward and duty in the first place. **You can take heart in that His care for your child means He trusts you with this awesome responsibility called parenting.**

The Psalm below is a reminder that all of life's securities come from God and not as a simple result of hard work and personal abilities. The first two verses of this Psalm reveal the goodness of God regarding our homes and daily living. More specifically, God builds our homes for shelter, protects our community, provides food, and grants us sleep. These items in verses one and two are the basic needs of living.

> *"Unless the LORD builds the house, its builders labor in vain. Unless the LORD watches over the city, the watchmen stand guard in vain. In vain you rise early and stay up late, toiling for food to eat — for he grants sleep to those he loves." (Psalms 127:1-2)*

Living in a world of plenty, like most Americans do, we can easily overlook God's provision. We can assume that the basics arrive for us simply as a result of our own effort. We work, receive a pay check, and buy things. We neglect to consider the economic blessing that makes that little formula possible. Both of us have been in numerous missions and deeply realize how hard many people work for so little reward. This blessing is one reason we encourage Christians to travel on short-term missions, if at all possible. Seeing our faithful Christian brothers and sisters strive to scratch out a living humbles us and flames the fire of gratitude within us.

One example Todd shares, "I was leading a particular mission team and having an evening discussion about the day's events. (A good mission team is a spiritual formation retreat and not just free labor.) One in the group went on at length about how noble and wonderful the local people must be to carry on and actually seem happy in spite of their crushing poverty. I was having the same thought when the Lord laid it on my heart that we were misunderstanding His lesson for us. I told that man, 'Perhaps, we need to rethink the reason for our admiration. What makes us think that affluence is the key to happiness. Isn't that what our culture teaches? But, these people struggle terribly and still have times of great happiness. What does God want us to learn here today?'"

As much greater is the creator than the creation, that's how much greater is God's love for our children than our own simple affections.

Yet, until we realize we receive even our basic needs from God, we will not understand the last part of this Psalm revealing how our children represent a gift from God. As parents ourselves, we certainly understand that moments arise when we would love to return or exchange these gifts. However, (thankfully) these moments are fleeting. Other moments include the times when we watch them sleep and feel the wonder and joy of parenting. When we see their still bodies and hear their soft breath, we gain an inkling of insight into the precious love we have for them. At such times we know and we feel at the core of our being that only God can give such good gifts. (It may be a good practice to intentionally recall this moment when they are teens.)

Parenting fills our lives with mountains and valleys. Parenting often brings the most joy in life. Yet, many of our greatest difficulties and heartaches spring from our parental experiences. When we can shift the paradigm, the scales fall off our eyes. When we begin to lose the responsibility perspective and embrace both the heartache and joy, we can view our children as God's gift. **When we see our children as a gift, it changes our whole perspective on parenting:**

> "Children are a heritage from the LORD, offspring a reward from him. Like arrows in the hands of a warrior are sons born in one's youth. Blessed is the man whose quiver is full of them." (Psalm 127:3-5)

The *Wycliffe Bible Commentary* sums up this same concept of the importance of God's provision and building of a strong healthy family by stating:

> "The concept of the necessity of dependence upon God is carried over into the building of a family. (Genesis 3:20) Recognition that children are God's gift is the basis for building a successful home. Joy and protection are pictured as the results of fruitfulness in the bearing and rearing of children."[29]

In many ways we can build up our children and increase our trust of God's integrity and faithfulness. When we name our children in family prayer and thank God for them, we reinforce their worth in both them and us. When a child accomplishes any milestone and we stop and notice and bring attention to it, we exalt God in both our minds. When we stop dwelling on our frustrations with our children and accept their achievements as gifts and not entitlements, we bring everyone closer to our heavenly Father. So, don't just think about it, name your children in prayer, speak that gratitude aloud, celebrate your child's accomplishment and do all in the name of the one who gives life and love.

How can we fail to see both the promise and reward in our children? Any parent whose parents have wished upon them a "child just like you" can relate. Frustrating though parenting may be, children are a reward from God and a promise for the future. As Henry David Thoreau wrote in his classic American book *Walden*, "Every child begins the world again..."[30] Every new human being experiences the world as new. There are certainly a lot of things to learn- and mistakes to make. But thankfully, God has a family business and He is in the home building trade!

APPLICATION

List two or three things that you learned or found interesting:

1

2

3

Reflection and Discussion Questions

1) What is your most important insight you will implement in this chapter? Why?

2) How are your children a gift from God?

3) How does this statement give you comfort during all of the noise we receive from our culture; "We love and care for our children, but God does so much more."

4) Describe a time when your child reached a monumental stage and you had to trust God during this transition? Or how can you prepare for this stage in the future?

5) Read Psalms 127:1-5 out loud and thank God for all of your God-given gifts.

Chapter 28 – Leadership & the Parental Training of Children

> *Many things we need can wait. The child cannot. Now is the time his bones are being formed; his blood is being made; his mind is being developed. To him we cannot say tomorrow. His name is today.*
> *Gabriela Mistral*

> *"Train a child in the way he should go, and when he is old he will not turn from it." (Proverbs 22:6)*

Children grow from dependent infants into self-sufficient adults. That is the order of creation and the way of the world, but how does that happen? Physically, kids need only shelter and sustenance to grow. Developing to fit into a family and community becomes another matter altogether. Beyond that, becoming a spiritual being in harmony with God and man reaches the pinnacle of humanness. How does a newborn homo sapiens become a fully formed spiritual being? With the power of the Holy Spirit, parents nurture us to enable our relationship with God.

While exceptions clearly exist, the vast majority of people become what we were trained to be as children. Parents teach us and train us to be who we've become. Our parents may not have been intentional; we may not be happy about the results, but they made the biggest impact on our formation.

This truth brings up the old nature versus nurture debate. The old fatalism which said genes determine our future met with hard science. We now understand our DNA influences our destiny but does not determine it. Most today believe that our behavior comes from a combination of genetics, environment, and personal choice. Once we determine who we're going to marry we can't do much about our kid's body and brain. However, parents can greatly affect a child's future, here and hereafter, by influencing their environment and the ways in which they learn to make their personal choices.

The Bible tells us to train our children the way they are to go. The wording clearly shows training of our children is the responsibility of parents. Can we outsource this responsibility? Obviously yes, but should we? This might be another story altogether. We believe the opportunity for family bonding and relational formation clearly outweighs the gains in the number of facts memorized.

Parents bear the responsibility for training up a child. Are we saying that only parents can teach children about God? Obviously not. But as President Harry Truman famously said, "The buck stops here." It is a parent's duty, their responsibility and their honor to captain the education of their own children. A wise parent enlists the help of the family, the faith community and the church in helping children learn how to actualize their faith. The most important family discipleship item remains keeping control of the agenda.

> *"Train a child in the way he should go, and when he is old he will not turn from it"* (Proverbs 22:6)

This verse starts with the command "to"; (train up a child in the way he should go) and follows it with a promise or reward (and when he is old he will not turn from it). This is the nature of God's covenant, "If you" followed by an "I will." God gives love unconditionally! However, His blessings come with a condition sometimes even at a cost. Even salvation comes at the price of repentance.

As child development specialists tell us, parents have a window of opportunity to train their child that closes quickly (remember development in Section 3). Wise parents use every situation to influence their children. If they don't, a willing culture stands eager to train them in the ways of the world… not in the ways of the Lord.

It is interesting to us that the Old Testament Hebrew word (transliterated chanok) which we translate "train up"[31] also means to initiate or dedicate. It is similar to the New Testament use of "sanctify," meaning to set aside for God's purposes. Not only do we teach skills but parents help define a child's place and purpose in life. We instruct them about God and condition them in God so that

God's purposes may be fulfilled in their life. It is through the repetitive and building nature of instruction that we enable them to have the blessings of God throughout their life. (Remember the importance of Demonstration in Section 2.)

Both of us played sports. As we trained and did the same activities over and over again they became second nature. As we write this Todd, recounts a fresh experience. "Recently I walked across a deserted high school football field and had the opportunity to play around with a practice blocking dummy. In my years of playing football, I have smashed into one of those big foam pillars attached to a sled literally thousands of times in my youth."

Todd remembers, "We trained using a specific technique allowing maximum force to be applied to the dummy. We could then use this on an opponent in a game. After years of practice, it became second nature. Now, it has been 30 years since I used this technique. That day I got in my stance and launched toward the sled like I used to do. I found I could still execute this maneuver flawlessly without even thinking about it." We remember what we practice.

Wise parents use every situation to influence their children. If they don't, a willing culture stands eager to train them in the ways of the world...not in the ways of the Lord.

Isn't this second nature recall just what we want for our children? We hope to train them in ways that will encourage and help them for all their life. It is one thing to know something, another to practice it and still another to own it as part of your very nature.

Proverbs 22:6 calls on us to mold our children into Christ followers from their core. Wouldn't it be helpful later in life to have learned God's lessons as a youngster? How great to learn to forgive those who hurt you, to persevere in difficulties through trust, to give our childhood fears over to God. How great would it be to already hold these traits within their character when our children really need them as adults. How awesomely we bless our children by teaching them the things of God when their little minds need filling.

The Parent/Child relationship may be the most critical relationship in the kingdom because of the impact on the future. One of our favorite contemporary theologians, Thomas C. Oden, addresses this relationship in his book, *Pastoral Theology: Essentials of Ministry*.[32] This masterful book has been a constant source of encouragement and insights to all types of theological issues in our years of pastoral ministry. According to Oden, no one is as important to spiritual upbringing as parents:

> *This is doubtless the most far-reaching and significant of all teaching contexts: the primary relation of parents and children. No teacher can quite match the importance of the rich gifts that parents can give children in spiritual foundations.*[33]

We know teachers can instruct children about Jesus. It happens every day and blesses everybody involved. However, teaching the facts about Jesus truly fulfills only part of the commission to parents. Modeling how Jesus lived touches like no other. Demonstrating how those interesting Bible stories impact children best comes from the adults who spend the most time with children. So many personal qualities become immersed into little lives as parents set the standards of normal. Oden lays out Biblical building blocks of Christian character:

> *Parents have both extraordinary influence and extraordinary responsibility in the religious education of their children. Not only may moral virtues be taught early, such as courage, honesty, prudence, compassion, and temperance, but also intellectual virtues, habits of consistency and of looking for good evidence, habits of order and precisions of thought.* **These are basic patterns that can be engendered more effectively by parents than anyone else.**[34] *(emphasis added)*

Is this really a surprise? Have we become so specialized in our approach to parenting that we tend to overlook the importance of character education? Our important role as parent delivers to society and the future a man or woman who walks "*in the training and instruction of the Lord*" (Ephesians 6:4). Each character trait listed by Oden, represents a deep blessing to those who possess it.

These characteristics, long associated with a successful life, ground a person. They prepare kids for real life, a life of struggle and stretching, a life demanding the strength of character needed to be successful in relationships, family, career, philanthropy, as well as in practicing one's religion.

Unfortunately, human nature means we often wait for a crisis before we prepare for it. Sad stories abound from people who waited until their boat accident to think about life vests. Rarely can a seat belt be buckled once we notice an impending crash.

The death of a loved one must not be the time to begin considering life and death. Impulse decisions on sexuality made when the teen's parents are not home from work rarely turn out well. When the critical time comes, when temptation arises, having confidence in your values and goals makes life's calamities easier to navigate.

So many personal qualities become immersed into children's little lives as parents demonstrate the standards of normal.

In the U.S. Army, there exists a type of document called "Commanders Intent." In it, the unit commander spells out the reason for the operation and how a victorious situation should look. Often individual decisions need to be made without the commanders input. Understanding the mindset of the commander leads to making good decisions.

In concrete ways, the training we receive as children ingrains in us the intents and purposes of God. Living life fruitfully requires good decisions based on solid values. Do your children know your "Commander's Intent" based on God's intentions for them? When we make our ideals clear and acknowledge the connection between choices and outcomes, it helps our children understand the "value of values." So, be clear about your values and their importance and you can help them make good decisions.

The window to "train up a child in the way he should go" closes quickly. While this certainly doesn't mean your older kids are lost, they do require a more intensive focus. Researcher George Barna shares:

> *The significance of focusing on the development of children is underscored by findings showing that the moral foundations of children are typically solidified by the age of nine, that lifelong spiritual choices regarding one's faith and one's relationship with Jesus Christ are generally made before they reach age 13, and that a person's religious beliefs are usually worked out prior to becoming a teenager - and that those beliefs rarely change to any meaningful degree after age 13.* [35]

If parents do not take the initiative in disciple[ing] their children, a long line of cults, businesses, tempters, and culture worshippers gladly wait to sway our children's affections. **Manipulation is the name of the cultural game while true freedom is found only in Christ.** We urge parents to receive training at every level in the church. The church will be stronger, the salt and light that God intended. We urge every church to prioritize the equipping of parents!

Christians are called to be change agents to the culture and not the other way around. By parents stepping up to their essential role in the kingdom, God's people will thrive and flourish. When that happens, the world feels blessed, and the future becomes well founded. As the old saying truthfully tells us, "The hand that rocks the cradle rules the world."

APPLICATION

List two or three things that you learned or found interesting:

1

2

3

Reflection and Discussion Questions

1) How much influence has your family heritage had on your ultimate religious beliefs? Explain

2) What is your earliest childhood memory?

3) Re-read Barna's quote on page 214. How does this help you see the importance God has placed on you the parent during these early years?

4) "Wise parents use every situation to influence their children. If they don't, a willing culture stands eager to train them in the ways of the world...not in the ways of the Lord." What are your thoughts about this statement?

5) Discuss the quotes from Thomas Oden beginning on page 212 in this chapter.

Chapter 29 – Life-style and Life-Style Discipleship

Enjoy one another and take the time to enjoy family life together. Quality time is no substitute for quantity time. Quantity time is quality time.   *Billy Graham*

[4]Hear, O Israel: The LORD our God, the LORD is one. [5]Love the LORD your God with all your heart and with all your soul and with all your strength. [6]These commandments that I give you today are to be upon your hearts. [7]Impress them on your children. Talk about them when you sit at home and when you walk along the road, when you lie down and when you get up. [8]Tie them as symbols on your hands and bind them on your foreheads. [9]Write them on the doorframes of your houses and on your gates. (Deuteronomy 6:4-9)

One of the most powerful passages in the Bible is Deuteronomy 6:4-9. This Scripture, described by Jesus as, "The Greatest of the Commandments," paints a clear picture of the nature of life-style discipleship. It shows the critical importance of the parent and child relationship in regards to training in the ways of God. Our Heavenly Father calls us to disciple our children in the context of living life. **It is not an overstatement to say parental life-style discipleship is a clear commandment from God's Word in this passage from Deuteronomy.**

We show here that parental discipleship is not just a New Testament idea, as we viewed it in the Great Commission. This call to fill our hearts and minds with His presence represents a life-style. Often we think about life-style in a commercial way involving related products. That's because every third commercial sells us something based on some "life-style." The most noticeable may be clothes, food or exercise equipment, but there's a product marketed toward every life-style.

The Old Testament also teaches and commands parents about life-style discipleship. How does faith become a life-style? How does a community involve God? How should faith be transferred? **This**

Scripture shows the critical importance of the ways in which the family raises the next generation of God's people.

These verses are known as "The Shema" (Sh'ma). Shema is the Hebrew word for "Hear"[36] as in "*Hear, O Israel...*" The Jewish people now use the Shema as their confession of faith. How important is this portion of Scripture to the teachings of Jesus? Very! In two of the four Gospels, Jesus quotes verse five when asked what was the greatest commandment. Jesus replied to His questioners:

> [37]*"Love the Lord your God with all your heart and with all your soul and with all your mind.* [38]*This is the first and greatest commandment."* (Matthew 22: 37-38)

> [29]*"The most important one, answered Jesus, is this: 'Hear, O Israel, the Lord our God, the Lord is one.* [30]*Love the Lord your God with all your heart and with all your soul and with all your mind and with all your strength'"* (Mark 12:29-30)

In the Gospel of Luke, Jesus tells the parable of the good Samaritan (Luke 10:29-37) in responding to a question from an expert of the law. The specialist asks, "What must I do to inherit eternal life?" Jesus responds in His usual style, "What does the law say?" The expert replies by reciting The Shema, upon which Jesus assures him, "Do this, and you will live."

Jesus obviously validates this Old Testament Scripture when He calls it the most important commandment to live by. In this Gospel of Luke passage, Jesus even makes it a point of eternal life. One of the greatest lessons we learned in Seminary is the extreme importance to all context in the Bible (CIE - Context Is Everything). We see Jesus validating these Scriptures and their importance in three out of the four Gospels.

Deuteronomy 6:6-9, then blueprints a plan to live out verses 4 and 5. We should take these instructions quite seriously. They are from God, confirmed by Jesus, and give us clear teaching of how and what we should teach our children. We evangelize the future by instilling the Gospel into our children for them to teach their children.

As we stated earlier, parents cannot teach what they do not know. Of course, that only makes sense. However, we can also intellectually know the things of God without bringing them into our heart and lives. We can have "*a form of godliness but denying its power.*" *(2 Timothy 3:5)* Remember, sometimes the longest journey you will make is from your head to your heart.

Children will not follow just words from parents; parents must live and breathe their commitment to God. All human beings have a built-in hypocrisy detector. It alerts us when we discover contrasts between what someone says and what they do. Sometimes it whispers, like when we hear the crybaby athlete talk about good sportsmanship. Other times it screams as when we watch the unfaithful politician spout forth about political transparency. Whenever our actions fail to back up our words, we lose credibility.

Mom sees Carol yelling at her younger brother, "Hurry up! Slow poke." Mom scolds her saying, "Carol, don't be mean to your brother just because you are impatient. You aren't the most important person in the world. Other people have needs and feelings that might not be in line with yours."

Later, Mom is driving Carol to the pool for swim lessons. They are running late when a sluggish truck slows them down even more. Carol watches Mom start muttering to herself as she grows visibly agitated. Carol realizes that being annoyed is really how grownups act. She learns Mom was less than honest with her in teaching that she should stay calm when she felt impatient. Little eyes are watching!

Bible Study in Deuteronomy

Let's do a short Bible study. Deuteronomy 6:6 states, "*These commandments that I give you today are to be upon your hearts.*" What commandments should be upon our hearts? They are the commandments of verses 4 and 5. "*Hear, O Israel: The LORD our God, the LORD is one. Love the LORD your God with all your heart and with all your soul and with all your strength." (Deuteronomy 6:4-5)*

Verses 4 and 5 tell us what God's commandments are. After living them out in everyday situations and obeying them and making them a part of our heart and life-style then verse 7 directs us to teach it to our children. Deuteronomy 6:7 NIV uses the word, "impress" as in *"impress them on your children."* All the English translations use words to describe a faithful and effective teaching through repetition and perseverance.

The Hebrew word translated in this passage as diligently (Shinantaam) means to repeat, to do something repeatedly toward achieving a goal.[37] Clearly, teaching our children takes more than presenting a premise and ordering them to accept it. **God is more about promises than premises, anyway**. It's always about building relationship with God.

Like a chef sharpening his favorite knife on a polishing stone, teaching our children about God takes deliberate, painstaking, time and focus. The blade of a quality Chef's knife consists of high quality carbon or stainless steel. Its ability to create neat cuts and slices rests upon angling that flat sheet of steel down to a razor edge.

A well made, finely sharpened Chef's knife is an exacting tool in the hands of a master chef. In like manner, our parental calling hones the tools of our master for lifelong productivity. For the benefit of our children, what better source of lifelong joy exists than to live out their purpose in God's plan?

Sadly, it often goes the other way. As pastors, we have witnessed this following pattern so often that we might consider it almost a stage of young adulthood. Young adults quit going to church; young parents start coming to church. Most often, the same ones who felt so grown and self-assured come to realize how much they need God for their children's sake. The birth of their children gives rise to a return to their faith in Jesus.

With the momentous duty of raising children ahead of them, young parents quickly realized they lacked a solid foundation to lay for their children's lives. We have experienced, when they return to church and start seeking God, they do so in a new and desperate way. For many parents, having children creates a second chance to start again or rebuild their relationship with God. When that little being comes into our lives, we begin to realize that more important things exist than our own wants and desires. Someone else's wants and desires become paramount. In that, we learn God's lesson of self-sacrificial love.

We parents now discover the eternal dimension to life. Despite what the world tells us, we do not exist for ourselves, we exist for others: our children, our family, our community. However, knowing we lack something and passing it on are two different things. When the water starts dripping from our ceiling, we realize the roof leaks. That's a far cry from climbing up on the roof and replacing lost shingles.

Realizing a lack just begins the process of fixing it. **We cannot download these truths into our children if God's commandments are not impressed upon our own hearts and lives**. We like the wording in Peterson's Bible paraphrase "*The Message.*" He highlights the connection between verse 6 and verse 7. **"***Write these commandments that I've given you today on your hearts. Get them inside of you and then get them inside your children.***"** *(Deuteronomy 6:6-7 The Message)*

The last part of verse seven communicates how we can "get them inside your children." This is one of the greatest supports for disciple[ing] our children in the Bible. "*Talk about them (God's commands) when you sit at home and when you walk along the road, when you lie down and when you get up.*" *(Deuteronomy 6:7)*

First, "*talk about them when you sit at home.*" The opportunities we have at home, relaxing and being family, while we "sit" are an important part of the training for our children. Some of the best times when the family comes together at meal time. A blizzard of studies show, and we concur, that solid families eat together. Just one example is a study by Dr. Blake Snowden of Cincinnati Children's Hospital. This study found that children in families that eat supper together 5 times per week are the least likely to use drugs, feel depressed or get into trouble. Eating together builds language and manners in young children and strongly relates to grades and test scores. The evidence is overwhelming; mealtime brings parents and children closer.

Another good time for "*sitting down*" with the family is while resting. Playing games or just being together with your children in the quietness of the moment brings you close. At such times, we find a great opportunity to talk about these commandments and love God. These should be a natural extension of your conversation. We talk about what interests us.

Tom's wife, Beth, often talks about the positive impression of her family meals as she was growing up. It was a family priority to have evening meals together. Her father, a business owner, would often work all day, come home for dinner and then go back to the store. This importance of having family meals together has made a lasting impression on her life. It so impacted her that it is a family priority to this day.

Today, one of the most important parts of the Schwind family day is their evening meal together. It goes way beyond the presence of three (always hungry) teenage boys. It is a family tradition they enjoy and hope their future families will embrace. You have heard it said, "A family that prays together, stays together." A Schwind family motto is, "The family that eats together, meets together!"

We cannot download these truths into our children if God's commandments are not impressed upon our own hearts and lives.

Second, "*when you walk along the road.*" The modern day equivalent would be "when you drive in your car." You can find a great time to teach your children while driving. Tom says, "Sometimes, I cringe when driving with my family at night, and I see four television sets in a mini-van with all family members glued to the sets. Sometimes, even the driver is watching the television. In that case, I pass right by them."

We realize such technology can be useful, especially on very long trips, and we certainly appreciate our technology. However, just like at home, plugging the kids into the TV keeps them from interacting with us (and their siblings). When we spend time largely on individual experiences, we find ourselves, like so many families today, living "alone together." Driving can be an incredible time to communicate with your children. At such times, we will get an open opportunity to connect and share about God.

Lastly, "*when you lie down and when you get up.*" We should begin our day with God and end our day with God, and every minute between the two. We can start the day anticipating what will happen and what we can do, with God's help. A moment of focus prepares everyone with a much better alternative than simply ending up blown about wherever the wind takes us.

A Humorous Morning Prayer

Dear Lord,
So far I've done all right. I haven't gossiped, haven't lost my temper, haven't been greedy, grumpy, nasty, selfish, or overindulgent. I'm really glad about that. But in a few minutes, God, I'm going to get out of bed. And from then on, I'm going to need a lot more help. Amen.

Family nighttime prayers and age-appropriate Bible story reading also helps bring a family close. It also helps children be with their parents while communing with God. Tremendous learning takes place in this environment. This time relaxes children and gets them into a bedtime routine. Routine helps children's little bodies and mind to slow down and go to sleep.

When Todd's children had trouble getting ready to sleep, his wife Ginny gently reminded them, "It's time to give your day back to God. But that's OK, He'll give you another one with new blessings tomorrow." What a powerful reminder in a little mind about where they fit in this big world. Bedtime is a perfect time to focus on God's love through prayer and other acts of remembering God.

In her book *Almost Christian; What The Faith Of Our Teenagers Is Telling The American Church*, Kenda Creasy Dean confirms the importance of life-style discipleship with her comments on Deuteronomy 6:4-9:

> *Note what the Deuteronomist is actually saying here. Parents are not called to make their children godly; teenagers are created in God's image, no matter what we do to them, or what they might do to disguise it. The law called upon Jewish parents to show their children godliness-to teach them, talk to them, embody for them their own delight in the Lord, 24/7. Everything they needed for their children's faith formation, God had already given them. In the end, awakening faith does not depend on how hard we press young people to love God, but on how much we show them that we do.[38]*

To put it plainly, these Bible verses show us life-style discipleship in detail. Family life-style discipleship helps a parent live life together with their children, eating, traveling, playing, and resting with an included focus of teaching about God's love in life's context. Jesus did this when he walked the earth with his disciples. He taught them in the context of life. When an experience called for a teaching, he would teach in the context of the moment. Remember, Context Is Everything.

As parents, we would be truly wise to do the same in the context of our children's lives. May we turn off the world for a while, give pause to the loud urgency of the immediate and communicate the glory of God with our children He has given us.

APPLICATION

List two or three things that you learned or found interesting:

1

2

3

Reflection and Discussion Questions

1) Read Deuteronomy 6:4-9 and list ways you can impress these words on your children's heart. We see three areas to consider: a) when sitting at home b) walking or traveling c) before bedtime or first thing in the morning.

2) What would be the application in your home of writing these commands on "the doorframes of your houses and gates?" If you could hang a motto in every home, what would it say?

3) The authors think that praying with your children and age appropriate Bible reading (see appendix page 263) is a good step to lead your child in Life-Style Discipleship. How could you implement them in your routine? Be creative, one size does not fit all. What was your favorite Bible Story growing up and why?

4) Todd's wife Ginny gave us a wonderful example of Life-Style Discipleship when putting her children down to sleep. What parenting tips have you seen work for others?

5) What does your family meal time look like currently? Are there any changes you need to make at this time?

Chapter 30 – Attitude and Humility & Admonition

I don't remember who said this, but there really are places in the heart you don't even know exist until you love a child."
                                                        Anne Lamott

The word humility may be as misunderstood as any word used. Humility and its adjective humble seems to be used most often to describe a poor condition or diagnose low self esteem. Generally, we think humility describes a person who thinks poorly of himself or herself. Perhaps Eeyore exhibits this misdiagnosis the best. If you have children or grandchildren, you certainly know Eeyore, the melancholy donkey of the Winnie the Pooh stuffed-animal menagerie. Eeyore's catchphrase always causes a grin. "Thanks for noticin' me."

If Pride says, "It's all about me," then humility replies, "There is no 'I' in TEAM."

Humility isn't thinking less of yourself, it's thinking of yourself less."
                                                        C.S. Lewis

Having a humble heart opens the door to improvement. How often has our stinging ego kept us from hearing wise words of admonition and instruction? Even a reprimand or rebuke can serve as good medicine for us when we heed appropriate warnings and correction. How foolish it would have been to ignore our parents warning to look both ways before crossing the street. "I want to cross the street, NOW," doesn't change the physics of a hurtling car. Thanks to our parents for insisting we learn this lesson, even when it stung our pride…or our bottoms. God, too, lovingly admonishes us when we do that which could hurt us or His other beloved children. Humility is absolutely essential before we can hear God's teaching voice.

Humility and Admonition

Jesus welcomes a child into his presence and cautions the disciples that welcoming a child is the same as welcoming Him. Certainly, Jesus is talking about all children. Bringing any child into the presence of Christ blesses us. How many more blessings abound when that child is our own flesh and blood?

On the other side of the coin, Jesus warns about misleading children and leading them into sin. Honestly, this seems to put a tremendous amount of both responsibility and privilege on parents, caregivers and those who influence children.

> *"And whoever welcomes a little child like this in my name welcomes me. But if anyone causes one of these little ones who believe in me to sin, it would be better for him to have a large millstone hung around his neck and to be drowned in the depths of the sea."*
> *(Matthew 18:5-6 ESV)*

Biblical scholar William Barclay, in his commentary on Matthew, makes some powerful observations about the two verses in Matthew above. While we study the importance of parents in spiritual nurture, his words help us properly understand parenting.

> *"Anyone who has changed a diaper or had to clean spit-up off their shirt can testify that providing for basic needs of a child is not glamorous. It reminds us of the old reminder that we want to see neither sausage nor laws being made because we'll never look at them the same way again."* Perhaps this is why *"a prophet has no honor in his own home town."(John 4:44)* [39]

In spite of the messiness of living, these day-to-day events create an atmosphere of relationship; a garden, if you will, where God's kingdom grows and flourishes. In his commentary, Barclay gives us another important word:

> *To satisfy the physical needs of a child, to wash his clothes and bind his cuts and soothe his bruises and cook his meals may often seem a very unromantic task; the cooker and the sink and the work-basket have not much glamour;* **but there is no one in all this world who helps Jesus Christ more than a teacher of the little child and the harassed, hard pressed mother in the home.** *All such will find glory in the grey, if in the child they sometimes glimpse none other than Jesus himself.[40] (emphasis added)*

To this we say, Amen!

As we've mentioned before, one of the most important lessons in Bible study is the concept of CIE (Context Is Everything). A single word or sentence relies on many sentences around it to give full meaning. Even the setting in which it was spoken or the circumstances lend much meaning to those few words. You simply can't just pick a single Bible verse (or even a snippet of ordinary conversation) for clear communication. This humorous headline makes the point,

"When Baking Cookies Include your Children."

(No thank you, I think I'll just have the Girl Scout Cookies.)

So, knowing that context is everything let's take a deeper look at verses 5 and 6 of Jesus' teachings.

> *"And whoever welcomes a little child like this in my name welcomes me. But if anyone causes one of these little ones who believe in me to sin, it would be better for him to have a large millstone hung around his neck and to be drowned in the depths of the sea."*
>
> *(Matthew 18:5-6 ESV)*

The beginning of the immediate context is found in Matthew 18:1 which says,

> *"At that time the disciples came to Jesus and asked, "Who is the greatest in the kingdom of heaven?"*

We should ask, "What might have been going through the minds of the disciples at this moment?" It certainly makes sense that they are trying to figure out the hierarchy of the kingdom. Earthly kingdoms have obvious hierarchies (i.e., king, prince, duke, baron, count, etc or perhaps, Chairman, President, CEO, Vice President, Supervisor, Manager), but what about the kingdom of God? If you want to know about this kingdom, it could make sense to ask, "What kind of person would be the greatest?" They just witnessed Jesus providing for tax payment with money from a fish. This undoubtedly began to open up the disciple's mind about Jesus. With them ready, Jesus began to do life-style discipleship and teach the disciples an important life lesson.

Mentor and Disciple, parent and child, join together in relationship so the secrets of God may pass between them.

What does it mean to be great in God's eyes? The disciples were starting to see the power and authority of Jesus. The disciples, in their human nature, each began to consider their own position as a disciple of Jesus. So, the Master brought a child to himself and used this moment to create understanding about His kingdom. The following quote about the child event comes from Matthew Henry, another noted Biblical Commentator:

> *He set him in the midst of them; not that they might play with him, but that they might learn by him.* **Grown men, and great men, should not disdain the company of little children, or think it below them to take notice of them.** *They may either speak to them, and give instruction to them; or look upon them, and receive instruction from them. Christ himself, when a child, was in the midst of the [learned men]. (Luke 2:46)[41] (emphasis added)*

Discipleship may not be flashy or high profile, but Jesus teaches this way. Mentor and Disciple join together in relationship so the secrets of God may pass between them. In the same way, parent and child bring a mentor-disciple relationship. Being a mentor means to be like Christ: loving, serving, and teaching. As Jesus answered the disciple's question, being a great disciple means being humble, trusting, and open to new ways of thinking- just like a child.

Being humble like Jesus

Part of our concern as pastors over the years has been the rise of the "sports culture." Please do NOT misunderstand us. We both played sports in our youth. Tom played football and baseball in high school. Todd won football honors in high school and college, and was selected MVP of his college team by his teammates. Both have dedicated many hours of our life to sports. We deeply appreciate the lessons and experiences of our youthful sporting ventures.

Sports are one of the great interests of our time. Sports and music have a great impact to reach people for Christ. We think about the Tim Tebow phenomenon. A Heisman trophy winner and pro quarterback who acts humbly and shines in adversity, whether Tebow's challenge is eluding a 250 pound linebacker or being a good teammate while riding the bench.

Sadly, many parents encourage their children to "keep your eye on the ball," while the culture is running over them like a Mack truck.

As pastors, we have seen that sometimes the love of success in sports becomes the most important issue in the family. Honestly, with all the fame and money in sports, we can hardly blame people for being zealous. We follow that statement with a big "however." However, sometimes our tunnel vision for good things keeps us from seeing the best things.

When we miss taking our kids to worship for months at a time because of Sunday morning games, this hurts our children spiritually.

229

When our conversation turns increasingly to winning and overshadows effort, courage and sportsmanship, then we reinforce the bad things about sport instead of the Godly things. Sadly, many parents encourage their children to "keep your eye on the ball" while the culture is running over them like a Mack truck. Keeping our eye on the ball means keeping focus on the most important thing, not the distractions. Moreover, God fits the definition of the highest, most important thing we need to focus on.

Many options for living present themselves to us. We often make choices between good activities that are all God approved. Sometimes God's will appears to us like a basketball court, with many legitimate choices inside the boundaries, all within God's will for us. Whatever choice we make, as we live together and disciple our children, we know ALL things can be used as a source of teaching and demonstration. Even in such a popular realm as sports, we can *"take captive every thought to make it obedient to Christ." (2 Corinthians 10:5)*

The Other Side of the Coin

This passage in Matthew regarding bringing children to Christ also displays a great warning about leading children astray.

> *"But if anyone causes one of these little ones who believe in me to sin, it would be better for him to have a large millstone hung around his neck and to be drowned in the depths of the sea."*
>
> *(Matthew 18-6 ESV)*

Gulp. This appears serious, and we need to look closely here for a little clarity, "If anyone causes these little ones ... to sin." Since sin exists as a condition of the heart, you can't really force anyone to sin. In the same way, you can't force someone to enjoy liver and onions. You can make them eat it, but you can't make them like it. When Todd was growing up, his mother liked and enjoyed cooking liver and onions. He cleaned his plate, but sure didn't like it.

You can force someone to perform an act against God, but if the sense of rebellion isn't there then you haven't caused them to sin. In

2010, in Coral Gables, Florida, three armed and masked men burst through the apartment door of bank teller Diego Uscamayta. They locked bomb vests on Diego and his father. When the bank opened, Diego was ordered to get as much money out of the vault as he could and give it to the robbers outside. The bandits told him that if he failed, both bomb vests would be detonated. Diego complied, and the robbers got away with the loot. After questioning, police declined to file charges against Diego because of the coercion.

In our Matthew text, "causing someone to sin" might include offering temptation or enticement. Life bubbles up with temptations and enticements to sin. Even Jesus received temptation in his wilderness sojourn. But refusing to help a child grow up to love and obey God can only lead them into sin.

What happens if we fail to give our child the most precious gift, a worldview that enables them to choose a relationship with God in Christ? Can this lead to anything other than sin? This puts big responsibility on parents. After raising them in the "*training and instruction of the Lord*" (Ephesians 6:4) the choice is theirs. However, in the mean time we can help them learn to choose God's way and not the highway, so when the rubber meets the road they will be ready.

> *Refusing to help a child grow up to love and obey God can only lead them into sin.*

What would cause a believing child to sin? One sure way would be abandoning children and letting the world raise them. Letting the sinful world have direct access to your child with no checks and balances is a bad idea. For example, Tom counseled a youth pastor to be more Bible focused when teaching the children of the church. Tom recalls, "That youth pastor's comments almost knocked me out of my chair. He said, 'if a child can be talked into something, another person can talk them out of it so we should not teach the Bible to them.'"

It's amazing that otherwise intelligent people spout this nonsense. The whole secular/ non-Christian world feels comfortable telling our children how they should think and how they should live. From revisionist history to kindergarten sex education; from corporate sponsorships in schools to federally dictated curriculum, the world doesn't hesitate trying to indoctrinate kids. In fact, they actively work to undermine parental influence in the lives of children. "He alone, who holds the youth, gains the future," even Hitler knew that controlling the attitudes of children meant controlling the future.

Another notable Bible commentator, Adam Clarke, wrote some useful advice about letting children run unattended in the world without the benefit of solid Biblical discipleship. Over 200 years ago, he found the same destructive attitude we see today. Then (as now) some parents believed that teaching a child common values actually corrupts them. According to that line of thinking, society damages them. Therefore, if left to find their own way unassisted, they will arrive at their own correct pattern of life.

Clark summed up the foolish and dangerous attitude he witnessed, "[they wrongly suggest] Children ought not to be taught religion for fear of having their minds biased to some particular creed, but they should be left to themselves till they are capable of making a choice, and choose to make one."[42]

He further offered that people who profess such things do so because "they are unaffected by the religion they say they profess."[43] After all, if they felt their religion was good for anything they would surely teach it to their children. Why require children to reinvent the wheel? Why make them spend the fleeting hours of their lives learning the lessons previous generation struggled through and yearn to pass on to them?

Clark adds, "parents who have a better faith and equally neglect the instruction of their children in the things of God. They are highly criminal; and if their children perish through neglect, which is very probable, what a dreadful account must they give in the great day! "[44]

Clark's words may sound harsh and "judgmental." However, we think most parents do actually believe what they profess. Unlike the parents of Adam Clark's discussion, parents who care about faith work to pass it on to their children. Since the Christian faith is true and valuable, neglecting to pass it on does a serious injustice to our children- and their children on down the line. You do, indeed, have the privilege to affect the future of your family.

A Parental Reward

What would you do if Jesus showed up at your door? After the initial shock, you'd probably invite Him in. Maybe you would offer Him some sweet tea or lemonade and prepare some of your favorite dessert. You would offer Jesus your best hospitality. In short, you would welcome Him.

The Bible quotes Jesus making a statement on how to welcome him, "*And whoever welcomes a little child like this in my name welcomes me.*" *(Mark 9:37)* When we welcome a child in His name, we welcome Him. That certainly catches the attention.

When Jesus makes such a conditional statement of how to welcome Him into our lives, we all need to pause and consider this wonderful promise!

The Lord's statement includes so much more than "be nice to a kid and say 'Jesus loves you' to them." Jesus welcomed that child into His presence as well as the company of the disciples. In doing that, Jesus welcomed them into the kingdom of God. His example is a clear call for us to include children and, while working at their level, help them become disciples. This certainly includes mentoring our own children in Christ.

When we welcome children, (our own children are clearly included in these words of Jesus) we welcome Jesus. That powerful statement opens up a richer way of connecting and communing with Christ. When Jesus makes such a conditional statement of how to welcome Him into our lives, we all need to pause and consider this wonderful promise!

How should we understand this? How would welcoming a little child welcome Jesus? It really comes down to what Jesus is teaching in this setting; the importance of humility. Children are humble, for the most part. They may be selfish, as people are, but they recognize

233

their position in the world. The things they possess come through their parents. Their self-awareness comes from feedback offered by parents. Utterly dependent, they sense their position of being a child in a grownup world. They know they really have nothing to offer, nothing but affection to trade for your attention.

Jesus tells his disciples to welcome a child, not for what you are going to get out of it, but relishing what you do for the child just because you do it for Jesus.

Welcoming a child is an act of humility in itself. It is giving to a person who cannot give anything back. Of course, we are speaking in terms of physical and material "stuff." Children give love and joy to us without even realizing it. Created by a loving God, we cannot help but to respond to the love of a child. So, Jesus essentially tells his disciples to welcome the children, not for what you are going to get out of it, but relishing what you may give in the name of Jesus. Simply, love them. Forget who will be first and last, best or worst, highest or lowest. Simply welcome children into your presence.

Humility allows us to accept God's sovereignty and, therefore, His admonition and correction. When we can accept God's ways, His straight and narrow path, only then can we effectively understand and teach those ways. Only then can we model Christ. Only then can we truly participate in the faith life of another person, especially our children. If for no other reason, we should bow before God for the sake of our children. The rewards of parenting can be spectacular. Moreover, what could possibly be greater than greeting your children in heaven?

APPLICATION

List two or three things that you learned or found interesting:

1

2

3

Reflection and Discussion Questions

1) Who was your favorite Winnie the Pooh character and why? The authors are big C.S. Lewis fans. What is your reaction to how Lewis defines humility? "Humility isn't thinking less of yourself, it's thinking of yourself less."

2) Read Matthew 18:1-6. What are your first impressions? Note the context!

3) Read Barclay's quote on page 227. Then pray for all mothers you know. Feel free to send them these encouraging words. If you are reading this book with a small group please pray for the mothers in the group.

4) What was the hierarchy in your family growing up? What is it like now?

5) What has been your vantage point in the "sports culture?" What would your reaction be to the youth pastor Tom encountered?

Chapter 31 - Relationship & Keeping Children's Hearts

> *The heart of a child is the most precious of God's creation. Never break it. At all costs, never break it.*   Joseph L. Whitten

> [5] *"See, I will send you the prophet Elijah before that great and dreadful day of the LORD comes.* [6] *He will turn the hearts of the fathers to their children, and the hearts of the children to their fathers; or else I will come and strike the land with a curse."*
> *(Malachi 4:5-6)*

One of the many fascinating things we learned in seminary was Inductive Bible Study. (Thank you, Dr. Bauer.) This technique uses cues from the Bible text itself to draw out rich meaning from the Scriptures. (The technique is laid out in a scholarly book by Dr. David R. Bauer and Dr. Robert A. Traina, "Inductive Bible Study"). One interesting fact is that the relative importance of an item can be determined by where it is located in the text. Terminology, imagery, and ideas located at the beginning, end, or center of a passage should be noted to look for some important connection to the rest of the passage.

We noted that these poignant family relationship verses in Malachi make up the last words of the Old Testament. The Old Testament starts out by saying, *"In the beginning God created the heavens and the earth."* (Genesis 1:1) The concluding words of the Old Testament warn parents to turn their hearts towards their children, and for the children to do likewise. From beginning to end, the Old Testament teaches about the obvious disconnect between God's intentions for living and life's reality. This includes family life.

The joyous news we read regards God's promise to send help for parents and bring our hearts back to our children. This critical relationship of family harmony in God's kingdom holds great importance to God and His people. Noticeably, God lays out a warning to heed His call before disaster strikes; turn toward God and heal your family or the results will be devastating. (One could be forgiven for wondering if this explains a few things about our American society today.) Whatever the case, we certainly think these last words of the Old Testament would be a great warning to all parents today. And we should note these words are a bridge from the Old Testament prophets to the Gospel of Jesus.

These last two verses in the Old Testament point to John the Baptist and his ministry as described in the following verses.

> *"And he will go on before the Lord, in the spirit and power of Elijah, to turn the hearts of the fathers to their children and the disobedient to the wisdom of the righteous — to make ready a people prepared for the Lord." (Luke 1:17)*

Note the agreement between the Malachi passage and this Luke passage. This concept builds a bridge between the Testaments. How important is parenting to God? The Old Testament closes with a parental admonition and a significant part of the New Testament story opens with it. This concept begins with the passage of God sending the Spirit of Elijah to empower John the Baptist. Next, we find the important section of fulfilled prophecy telling how John began to minister and prepare the way for Jesus and His message of Salvation. **Based on the prominent placing in the text, the importance of family relationship can hardly be overstated.** This centrality of home and family assures continuity of God's kingdom and salvation for many.

Christian Educator and Old Testament commentator Joyce G. Baldwin states this concept in these words:

> *The future ministry of the coming prophet is described in terms of bridging the generation gap. The fifth commandment (Honor Father and Mother so you may live long in the land the Lord is giving you) implied that the home was essentially the school of the community. There, in a 'world in miniature', authority and submission, love and loyalty, obedience and trust could be learned as nowhere else and, with the word of God as guide in the home, society could be changed.[45]*

Fathers and mothers, our prayer for all parents is, "May we never lose sight of the importance of having our hearts and our children's heart in unison. May we always be comforted knowing Jesus helps us in this most important task."

The question for our tumultuous times is, "How do we keep our hearts in unison with our children?" How do we hold onto that sense of unity? How do we recreate it when it has been lost? The techniques of restoration will be different with every family, but the principle remains the same. We walk through life together, teaching as we go.

Consider how we teach a child to cross the street. We don't walk up to the curb of a busy highway and yell, "Run!" We first take walks down a quiet street and see the traffic. At a later time we explain what we're doing and we hold their hand while crossing the street. Then we will cross without holding hands. Later we will go first and then watch them cross and help them. After they can cross by themselves while we watch (and correct their errors if needed) we will grant them permission to cross the street on their own. The discipleship process outlined in Section 2 also helps us build relationship.

Todd has been in the habit of using an illustration in pre-marital counseling to explain how couples can achieve greater intimacy in their relationship. He learned this in his own pre-marriage counseling sessions with Pastor Tom Keene. The same principle holds true in the family. It's a law of spiritual relationship as clearly as a mathematical one.

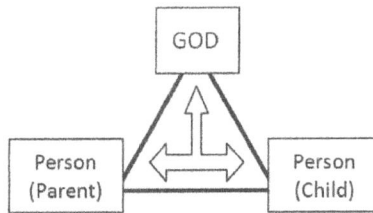

The Geometry of Relationship

Looking at this relationship pyramid, we see God at the top with parent and child at the lower corners. When parent and child move toward God, they become closer together. The further up the pyramid parent and child climb closer to God, the closer they become with one another. (This principle actually goes for anyone in a relationship that includes God. The closer you come to God the closer you will come together.)

The Bible teaches the critical importance of keeping the affection and trust of our children. This is clearly not a call to let children do whatever they want and avoid upsetting them by correcting them. Long history has shown that leaders, teachers, bosses, and even drill sergeants can hold the respect of their students while being highly demanding of them.

We both have had coaches that were highly demanding and whom we deeply respected. Others were very demanding and created no love in us. The difference comes from the perceived motivation of the mentor. We believe some people challenge us because they want what's best for us, and others because of what's best for them.

Todd says, "During football at BGSU, my position coach, Jim Heacock, worked us to death and held sky-high expectations of us. He always caught us when we fell short. This could have caused some players to hate him. However, that wasn't the case, far from it. Coach Heacock showed in many ways that he loved football (the thing we loved), loved his players and wanted the best for us in everything, not just football. He was demanding but fair, asked nothing greater of his players than he would give and would let his affection for us "slip out" on occasion. Besides his football expertise, I think Coach has had a great college coaching career because of those character traits."

Parents too, can call for high expectations and not lose the heart of their children. When we continually show and tell them we want the very best for them we give them love. When we "lead by example" we reinforce both the value of the lesson and our own integrity. When we show them we are pleased with them just because God created them, we strengthen the emotional bond between us.

There is more to Christian parenting than performance, there is love. When we lose that perspective, we can lose their hearts.

By diligently seeking God and teaching our children to love and respect God, parents fulfill God's admonition to *"turn the hearts of the fathers to their children, and the hearts of the children to their fathers."* *(Malachi 4:6)* By doing this, we put our loved ones on the path to avoiding the tragedy of fractured families and the terrible connected consequences.

There is more to Christian parenting than performance. There is love. When we lose that perspective, we can lose their hearts.

God's plan is beautiful in design and powerful in implementation. He admonishes us to keep family unison, explaining that we want to avoid the consequences. We know that you want to both reap the reward of a close family and avoid the outcomes of failing to have that. Following God's advice has never steered anyone wrong, and we can safely say, you will not be the first.

APPLICATION

List two or three things that you learned or found interesting:

1

2

3

Reflection and Discussion Questions

1) Did your parents keep your heart? Why or why not?

2) Discuss: Did your parents keep your heart? Why or why not? If not, have you forgiven them? Will you forgive them?

3) Discuss your thoughts on the placement of Malachi 4:5-6. Do you see the connection between these verses and Luke 1:17? What is God telling us in these Scriptures?

4) Using the Geometry of Relationship illustration on page 238, where would you put your dot on the line that represents you and your relationship to God. How close do you think God wants you to be. How will the place you place your dot affect your children?

Chapter 32 – Service & Family Service to God

Training a child to follow Christ is easy for parents, all they have to do is lead the way.   *Author unknown*

[14]Now fear the LORD and serve him with all faithfulness. Throw away the gods your forefathers worshiped beyond the River and in Egypt, and serve the LORD. [15]But if serving the LORD seems undesirable to you, then choose for yourselves this day whom you will serve, whether the gods your forefathers served beyond the River, or the gods of the Amorites, in whose land you are living. **But as for me and my household, we will serve the LORD.**
(Joshua 24:14-15)

Families of believers reinforce each other. Parents who follow God pass on their faith as a living gift to their children. That faith multiplies when serving God together as a family. Faith becomes a family inheritance and a family identity shared between parents and children. An even greater sense of belonging and identity comes when Grandpa, Grandma, aunts, uncles and cousins serve God. While contrary to our radically individualistic culture, God created us to live, love and serve in community. The central place we learn that begins in our immediate family.

Parents first must fear (Holy Reverence) the Lord and serve Him in faithfulness. Joshua demonstrates the importance of fear and faithfulness, as families serve the Lord together.

This passage from the book of Joshua stands near the end of Joshua's story. Joshua learned his leadership from his mentor, Moses. Joshua offers his farewell speech after having led the Israelite nation through the trials of the Conquest of Canaan. He reminds people where they came from and counsels them to give up other ways of living and worshipping other gods. He admonishes the Israelites to serve The Lord faithfully, then points out the inevitable choice that must be made. Knowing that a servant cannot serve two masters (Luke 16:13, Matthew 6:24), Joshua sets before them a choice: serve the gods of the past, serve the gods of your neighbors, or serve The Lord.

Famously, Joshua speaks, "*As for me and my house, we will serve the Lord.*" *(Joshua 24:15)* This powerful declaration shows Joshua's conviction that his family will also be part of that inheritance. There is no hesitancy or waffling. He straightforwardly states, "I will serve the Lord, my wife will serve the Lord, my children will serve the Lord, my possessions will serve the Lord, all I control will be put to the Lord's service."

Note how Joshua's household connects to his personal choice of serving the Lord. These mighty words lose their luster if Joshua says to the assembled, "As for me, I will serve the Lord." This statement does not have the depth and challenge as his real words. Parents need to be followers of God in order to have a God centered family. There is simply no way around that.

We have participated in and witnessed many great family opportunities to serve. From raking an elderly neighbor's leaves to a Saturday morning shift at the food pantry, from church workday to short-term missions, serving God together builds faith and cohesiveness. Tom writes, "I personally know no greater joy than when I am serving God with my family. Going to work camp, a short-term mission to Costa Rica and Guatemala, stocking the "Clothes Closet" or playing in the Praise Band, we draw close to God and each other. Serving God together truly blesses us."

Parents set the tone for the entire family. Families serving God together not only build strong Christians but strong families.

Parents set the tone for the entire family. Families serving God together not only build strong Christians but strong families. As a parent, serving God with your family models Jesus' discipleship process discussed in Section 2.

Joshua made a statement by including his family in his decision. As people remembered Joshua's words, he gained the opportunity to witness every day by showing the faithful acts of the Household of

Joshua. Similarly, our entire community watches to see us, to see how our family is serving the Lord. When a family is faithful, it encourages other families to do the same. What a terrific "two for one." We can serve God as well as witness by example about grace. As a bonus, surprised people will sometimes ask, "Why do you do that?" When they do, you have the privilege of giving them the reason.

APPLICATION

List two or three things that you learned or found interesting:

1

2

3

Reflection and Discussion Questions

1) What negative behavioral pattern has been passed down from generation to generation within your family? (the gods of your forefathers from Joshua 24:14-15 on page 242)

2) In what way, if any, do you accommodate the gods of the "Amorites" i.e. the people in whose land you are living?

3) If you were to fast-forward your by life five years, where would you be and what would you be doing? How old would your children be?

4) Looking back at Section 3, what stages of development will your children be in five years? What changes would people see in you?

5) How important is it to set personal goal for your family? List several you have for serving the Lord together.

Chapter 33 – We Are Not Alone

What it is children become, that will the community become.
Suzanne LaFollette

To round this out, let's be clear that there exists a special place for families in God's plan. The Bible teaches that God loves families and created them as a "life lab" to train children in God's love and to walk in His ways. A parent's love is the first model of God's love. As we learn to obey our parents we learn about God's ways. Teaching a child to submit to God crafts them into an adult who can listen to God and find the power and comfort offered in the freedom of the Gospel. A child trained to see grace as guidance and not license will find both success and happiness in their life.

This fully formed child of God can be delivered to the next generation as a spouse, parent, boss, employee, leader, follower. The world will be a better place, truer, more just, more peaceful, more holy.

Faithful families training up God-centered children helps God evangelize the future. Children trained up in a Godly family will make a profound impact on their communities and the world. A child taught how to love and follow God will be open to the Holy Spirit and likely display the Fruits of The Spirit: love, joy, peace, patience, kindness, goodness, faithfulness, gentleness and self-control. Truly, what better gift could a parent give? What greater legacy could you leave?

Imagine a person with these spiritual characteristics and the effects on their own family, their workplace, church, social circles and community. This fully formed child of God can be delivered to the next generation as a spouse, parent, boss, employee, leader, follower. The world will be a better place, truer, more just, more peaceful, and more holy. We can have great expectations for the future when it includes adults raised from childhood to worship God and model Christ. What an encouraging thought!

Strong families and Godly young people don't come from some new or special program. They don't come from a book, movie or social media (though all those things can be tools). Godly children come from Godly families because they have God at the center of their family.

Parents need not be fully formed, wholly sanctified, and perfect in saintliness to lead a God-centered family. Loving God and seeking His will for your family lays the foundation for all growth within yourself and your family. Just as the strong, sturdy oak begins with the tiny acorn, a growing love for God eventually transforms a biological family into a spiritual family.

We must keep in mind, God has also given us very specific warnings about not having our hearts connected to our children. We see its importance in the fact that these words of warning close out the Old Testament and open the New Testament. This word of caution was the first idea that John the Baptist preached to the people when preparing the way for Jesus.

Just as the strong sturdy oak begins with the tiny acorn, a growing love for God eventually transforms a biological family into a spiritual family.

Lastly, and perhaps most importantly, we have not been left alone to disciple our children. Scripture clearly teaches our children are not ours alone. They are primarily God's children. We can know that, because while we love them with the greatest love we have, we can't love them with the greatest possible love of all. God can love them far more than we think or imagine. He has blessed us by allowing parents the privilege of helping raise His children.

We should be encouraged. We are not alone; we have all the resources of Heaven itself! Within our parenting assets, we have both the command and the resources of God to assist us. With such a treasure in hand, we can concentrate on simply helping our children know, love, and obey God. Rest assured, God will take care of His part.

Remember, you need not fear the difficulties of parenting. God will give you what you need. As has been said innumerable times, "God doesn't call the qualified, He qualifies the called." This principle has been proven in many different circumstances, and is equally true in the ministry of Christian parenting. As Paul said so beautifully:

> *"That is why, for Christ's sake, I delight in weakness, in insults, in hardships, in persecutions, in difficulties. For when I am weak, then I am strong." (2 Corinthians 12:10)*

Afterward

Parenting is an integral part of God's plan. Christian families that seek to grow in faith enrich the lives of their children, bring salt and light to their communities, and raise up God's disciples to evangelize the future. Parents truly do the Lord's work every day when they raise children in a family of faith. Nothing is more important than the day-to-day disciple[ing] of children in a Christian home. We salute you.

Much of our culture knows little about the practice of Biblical faith, but how could they? It makes sense that they seem increasingly at odds with the faithful practice of the Christian faith. However, the really troubling fact is that an astoundingly large number of Christians are ignorant of all but the barest basics of their faith. They cannot defend the beauty, majesty and power of their faith against the dominate worldview because they don't truly understand the basis of faith. They cannot receive the fullness of their blessings when they don't know their faith and how it works.

This must change. For our families, for our communities, for the sake of the kingdom, this complacent unawareness needs to end. Too much joy is being wasted, too much peace is slipping away, too much power is evaporating into the air. God blesses us in so many ways and yet we still look to the world for guidance.

We call on parents to receive the empowering knowledge of this book and to make a decision to grow in faith for your children's sake. You will find grace and peace uncountable when you see God. Most of the perceived needs and wants we struggle and strive for are but illusions. God will provide our needs when we stop pursuing those things and follow Him. "No one can serve two masters," therefore, "Seek first the kingdom of God."

We call upon all churches to prioritize making disciples above collecting memberships. We call upon pastors and church leaders throughout the Kingdom. To you we say, "You must work diligently to provide and create every opportunity for parents to grow in the understanding of the principles of the Christian faith and the wisdom that permeates the Scriptures. In this way, the next generation of Christians will fill your pews. We call on congregations to truly and continually uplift the parents in their midst through providing parenting programming as well as services like "Parents Night Out," meals, and excellent childcare during worship, among many others.

We call on Christian Universities and Seminaries, Christian publishers, producers and content providers to create even greater works to support the front line work of parents in a Christian home. You have the greatest minds and the greatest talents in the world as well as the empowerment of the Holy Spirit; uplift families by providing books, resources, films and internet content that will enrich them and strengthen their faith.

Also, we call on Christian artists everywhere to affirm you. Art is powerful. Art speaks directly to the soul. If you can write, write for God, if you can paint or sculpt or dance or play or sing, if you can create websites or video or film, by all means, honor God with your gifts. Parents and children will be blessed and edified in so many ways. The Kingdom will be uplifted and the King will be glorified. Further, God will be pleased you used the gift He has given to you.

Christians are fond of saying, "The children are the future of the church." We call on every Christian in the kingdom to realize that the future begins right now. The next generation of the church is being formed today. Do you want to leave the world a heritage? Today, empower and encourage parents to raise children in the faith. That gift to the future will reap a harvest of blessing for generations to come.

APPENDIX

"Independence isn't doing your own thing; it's doing the right thing on your own."

Kim John Payne

Appendix A – Small Group & Application Manual

Disciple[ing]

Our

Children

A Study for Parents and Christians

who nurture God's children

Disciple[ing] our Children

Contents:

Overview and Small Group Guidelines

Below are eight sessions designed for you to do alone or with a small group of parents. We recommend doing one session per week after you finish reading the book. These sessions are the application of Section 2 of this book. (The Discipleship Process)

Our hope is you will develop some **Life-style Discipleship** aspects to your life. For the next eight sessions you can cultivate these principles in your group time. These principles are teaching the lifestyle of discipleship.

Eight session do not make a life but can help to **form goals and habits**. Enjoy these days with your children. Intentionality and accountability are important as you move through these sessions.

1: Selection   *He chose from them twelve (Luke 6:13)*

2: Association   *Lo, I am with you always (Matthew 28:20)*

3: Consecration   *Take my yoke upon you (Matthew 11:29)*

4: Impartation   *Receive the Holy Spirit (John 20:22)*

5: Demonstration   *I have given you an example (John 13:15)*

6: Delegation   *I will make you fishers of men (Matthew 4:19)*

7: Supervision   *Do ye not yet perceive? (Mark 8:17)*

8: Reproduction   *Go and bring forth fruit (John 15:16)*

I'm Praying for You

Session 1: Selection

"When morning came, he called his disciples to him and chose twelve of them..."   *Luke 6:13*

Prayer is powerful. The best single thing you can do is to pray for your child(ren) and do so diligently!

1) Thank God for the gift of your children and the children in your life.

2) Pray over them tonight when they are sleeping.

3) Bless them as they sleep.

4) Hug them and tell them you love them daily.

5) Thank God that he has placed your child/children in your life.

6) If your children have moved out of the house continue to pray for them. Tell them you have done so, and do any of the steps above which you are able. If they are out of the house, make a phone call or send a card. Continue to make efforts to communicate with them regularly.

God has chosen to put them in my life:

Write down the names of your children, grandchildren, nephews, nieces, friend's children, neighbor children, and any other children involved in your life.

_____

_____

_____

_____

_____

_____

_____

_____

_____

_____

_____

_____

_____

_____

_____

_____

Keep this list to regularly pray over them, remember them to the Lord, or just to remind yourself of how blessed you are to have this child in your life.

Let's do this together!

Session 2: Association

"...and teaching them to obey everything I have commanded you. And surely I am with you always, to the very end of the age." Matthew 28:20

While parenting can sometimes be a daunting business, Jesus has promised He will be with us. This is also a terrific model of being together, mentor and disciple. Normally parents spend only a small amount of time per week with their child. One way to increase that time is to include your child in things you normally do alone.

What can you do with your child that you normally do by yourself? Make an effort to intentionally include your child(ren) in one activity this week. For example, take a walk or fold laundry together. One-on-one time is important to you, your child, and your relationship. Perhaps you could commit to a monthly breakfast, lunch or dinner out with your child.

Ways to increase relational time together.

Things I normally do alone   **Ways to Include my child**

_____

_____

_____

_____

_____

_____

I commit to:

_____

_____

_____

_____

Let's get our roles straight

Session 3: Consecration

"Take my yoke upon you and learn from me, for I am gentle and humble in heart, and you will find rest for your souls."   *Matthew 11:29*

You are the parent and the God-given authority for your child. The Bible teaches that the parents set the agenda for the family and that Godly parents disciple their children. Examine your interactions with your child/children. Do you fully understand that saying, "No is NOT the same as saying, I don't love you." It's not when you say it...and it's not when THEY say it.

1) Do you find that role easy or difficult?

2) Do your children obey?

3) Do your children set the family agenda? Why or not?

4) Are you happy with the direction of your family?

5) Are you happy with the level of harmony in your home?

Ways to feel confident in our parental role

In what ways does fear govern my acting as the Biblical leader of my family?

_____

_____

_____

_____

_____

Knowing how you are addressing the 7 Pillars (page 180) of a Christian Family helps you develop confidence. Which ones are most meaningful to you right now?

_____

Purpose
_____

Integrity
_____

Leadership
_____

Lifestyle
_____

Attitude
_____

Relationship
_____

Service
_____

Let's read the Bible together

Session 4: Impartation

"And with that he breathed on them and said, 'Receive the Holy Spirit.'" *John 20:22*

Many faith traditions emphasize different aspects of the coming of the Spirit and the work of the indwelling Spirit. However, all Biblical Christians agree that the Holy Spirit is God operating within our hearts and lives. Letting the Spirit come into our lives is a most powerful thing. The act of preparing ourselves for God through devotions or other spiritual disciplines greatly assists us in opening ourselves up to the leading of the Holy Spirit.

1) Do you agree with the following statement? Why or why not? "We cannot teach what we do not know or live."

2) Can you say you are filled with the presence of God's Holy Spirit?

3) In what ways are you seeking God in your life?

4) Do you have a consistent devotional life? How does it help you?

Developing a deeper Spiritual life

Family Prayer and Bible reading are two great ways to get started on developing a regular and consistent connection with God. Perhaps you do other activities that help you connect with God. What are some of these you do and some you may have heard of?

_____

_____

_____

_____

For younger children, bedtime becomes a quiet time when they let the day go and can settle down from all the stimulation of their day. Bedtime is usually a great time to read the Bible and it is no exception for children. They love to drag out bedtime and you can use this time to give your child a sense of peace before they go to sleep. When you read Bible stories to them, you may decide to reinforce the notion that these are more than simple stories, they are the written record of God's activity in the lives of the Bible Hero. You may want to consider these.

The Toddler's Bible by V. Gilbert Beers
Gold and Honey Bible by Melody Carlson
Leading Little Ones to God by Marion Schoolland

Consistency is the key to any spiritual and devotional life. What realistic commitments are you willing to make to bringing that to yourself and your family?

My Commitment:

_____

_____

_____

_____

Let me show you how!

Session #5: Demonstration

"I have set you an example that you should do as I have done for you."　　　　　　　　　　*John 13:15*

Plan an activity this week with your child demonstrating a needed life skill or lesson. It can be simple or complex depending on the needs of the child. In the coming weeks, this activity will be done with you and then completed by themselves. You will evaluate and then have your child teach a younger child how to do it. In this exercise, please select carefully because success is important here (but not absolute).

For example: Household chores are a great opportunity to teach an attitude of serving others in love. Be sure the activity is age-appropriate. Slice a banana with a butter knife for fruit salad for a younger child. Picking up sticks in the yard maybe for a little older child.

Do you have older children? How about mowing the lawn, washing/waxing the car. (wax on, wax off.) At this stage real life activities work well. The serving aspect will come later. Be sure it is age appropriate.

 If the child is ready you can teach them. The object is not to pick something that simply needs done, but to focus on the lesson.

Come up with a particular task. Record some ideas about it beforehand. You can then make notes on a plan and commit yourself to doing it. Then, record some thoughts on how it went.

The lesson is to intentionally plan and execute teaching something to your child or children. Remember to include your demonstration and participation as part of the lesson.

Brainstorm Ideas with the group:

_____

_____

_____

_____

_____

_____

My Plan and Commitment:

_____

_____

_____

_____

How it went:

_____

_____

_____

_____

_____

Now you give it a try!

Session #6: Delegation

"Come follow me," Jesus said, "and I will make you fishers of men."   *Matthew 4:19*

Now, have your child repeat the assignment you recently did together and do on their own. It would be best (not required) to give them the activity you practiced in Session 5 -Demonstration. And have them do it independently.

Check and be certain that the activity is safe, age appropriate and simple enough to be done completely on their own. Allow them to complete the task or chore on their own. Certainly give plenty of encouragement and direction beforehand.

After the work is completed, you need to evaluate what was done to prepare for the next exercise – Supervision. It is important to be positive and encouraging but being accurate is also important. Real self respect comes from successfully learning and performing difficult (to them) activities.

Let them do it on their own and avoid helping. You are setting them up for success on their own. Sometimes that comes at the price of failure. Remember to treat failure like a scientist. A failed experiment is simply a demonstration of what does not work. Cross it off the list. Allow them to "fail" if need be. Be supportive and encouraging.

My idea and commitment:

_____

_____

_____

_____

How it went:

_____

_____

_____

_____

_____

What I would do differently next time:

_____

_____

_____

_____

_____

How are you doing?

Session #7: Supervision

"Aware of their discussion, Jesus asked them: 'Why are you talking about having no bread? Do you still not see or understand?'"   *Mark 8:17*

In this session we are helping learners grow. The parent plays a vital role in this stage. It is the role of mentor. This role focuses on the teaching and progressing of the skill in question. In Supervision, the parent or mentor must evaluate the disciple's progress. After doing this, they must then give proper instruction and appropriate critiques of their work (both positive and negative).

Another important aspect of this process is dealing with your unique individual. Children respond differently to positive and negative responses. It is entirely appropriate to critique the mistakes made by the child. However, even though it may not be your specific spiritual gift, encouragement must be part of the process.

As the supervisor, you will need to look at the parts of the task that your child did well. There is always something even when having a poor result. You need to then consider what your student has done inadequately.

At this point you need to look at the other major factor in this process. You must ask yourself the question that all good teachers, mentors, and parents must ask. It is, "What could I have done better in instructing and modeling the behaviors?" You don't need to be hard on yourself but realistic and fair. You <u>can</u> be a great teacher for God!

What my child did well:

_____

_____

_____

_____

_____

_____

What my child needs help on:

_____

_____

_____

_____

_____

What I could have modeled better:

_____

_____

_____

_____

_____

Show your little sister how!

(Or brother, or cousin or friend.)

TOOL TIME #8: Reproduction

"You did not choose me, but I chose you and appointed you to go and bear fruit-fruit that will last. Then the Father will give you whatever you ask in my name."

John 15:16

If you have several children, it may work very well to have your oldest child teach a younger child the activities demonstrated and delegated by you starting in session 5. If not, another relative or friend will be fine. At this (or any point) you might find it helpful to select another activity that you can start from scratch using your newly improved skill set.

Now you play the role that this group and this group study have done for you. Help them determine which skills are most important to teach and gain an idea of how to present those skills to their student. Also, remember to encourage your student to remember they are more skilled than their student and they shouldn't expect her to know everything they do. This will help them keep from getting frustrated. Remember to make it fun!

Just as a reminder, use the same caution for this exercise as you did in lesson 6. Make sure the activity is safe, age appropriate and simple enough to be done completely on their own.

This exercise can be a lot of fun, so feel free to enjoy it.

What I did to set up the older child to succeed:

_____

_____

_____

_____

_____

_____

How the young child responded:

_____

_____

_____

_____

_____

How it went:

_____

_____

_____

_____

_____

_____

What did you learn?

You might want to take a little time to jot down some of your feelings or thoughts as you went through the process. You might also want to note some great ideas that you got from others as you participated.

_____

_____

_____

_____

_____

_____

_____

_____

_____

_____

_____

_____

_____

_____

_____

_____

Appendix B – Erikson's Adult Stages

From the chapter on Erikson's Psychosocial Development we have here included his adult stages of development. While interesting, it isn't fully relevant to understanding your young children directly. It may help you better understand yourself though. That will help you bring self-awareness and enhance your communication. You may review the chart on page 140 to refresh your memory of this interesting topic.

Young Adulthood (19 – 40 years) "Can I love?"

This stage may not begin at exactly age 19 for many people. Because marriage (or the need or desire for it) may begin early for some and late for others, this stage blurs the line between Adolescence and Young Adulthood. **In Young Adulthood, Jack's connection (or identity blending) with peers begins to be replaced by personal intimacy with a potential spouse.** We hope it is obvious to all, that sexual intimacy should not be confused with personal intimacy. Sadly, popular culture encourages becoming sexually active without personal intimacy. Moreover, divorce statistics show that sexual intimacy makes no guarantee of personal intimacy. Such closeness must be based on far deeper love than mutual satisfaction, though such physical closeness may be a component of a deep abiding intimacy.

As is usual with people in this age group, Jack begins to assert a sense of individual identity that leads him to identification with a potential spouse. However, Jack still wants to be part of a group and fit in. As he becomes clearer about his own identity, he becomes more willing to trade that group identity for a long-term reciprocal relationship. This might be with a close friend or in marriage. This growth will see him become capable of intimate relationships– along with the sacrifices and compromises required in such relationships.

273

Interestingly, some studies have shown that individuals with a poor sense of self tend to have less committed relationships. Some young adults may not be able to form a committed relationship for personal reasons or the fear of getting hurt. When they cannot form such relationships, they may develop a sense of **isolation** or **loneliness**.

Middle Adulthood (40 – 65 years) "Can I make my life count?"

Jack is now married and with his wife, raising 3 children. While this is going on, Jack is now in the Middle Adulthood stage, and he finds a new sense of turmoil. Sometimes, we humorously refer to it as "mid-life crisis" and joke about the middle aged men who buy sports cars. Middle age is often the time we can finally afford to buy that sports car we always wanted. However, as pastors (and middle aged men) we have noticed that the effects of this stage's crisis touch us deeply.

Life's current questions and challenges arise and Jack begins to reflect and evaluate them in a more global way. He asks himself, "Does my life count for something?" This self-evaluation, as much as any other crisis question, asks, "Who am I?" Beginning to look back as well as forward, Jack begins to search for the meaning of his life as it unfolds.

For Jack and other people of this age, most frequent answers to these questions of significance center around two subjects: family and work. During the stage of Middle Adulthood Jack settles down, gets steady in his career, has a family and begins to feel the connection to a bigger picture. This leads him to a desire to be part of society through raising children, being productive at work and involved in church and community. When Jack contributes in these areas, he feels productive and accomplished. If he were to fall short in this part of life, he will feel stagnant– unproductive and uninvolved.

It is in Middle Adulthood that major challenges around work and family present themselves. Jack hopes to feel a sense of accomplishment around raising children, helping them grow and releasing them to their own lives. Jack will begin to truly understand that love finds expression in more ways than sex, and he will be seeking a more profound sense of unity with his wife. In this time, Jack should adjust himself to mature responsibilities to his church and community and begin to care for his aging parents. Jack will also concentrate on health and leisure issues. It is in this season of life, Jack goes beyond asking, "Who am I to myself" and begins ponder the question anew, "Who am I to others?"

Maturity (65 – Death) "Is it OK to have been me?"

This stage of life, Jack looks back at life asking the question, "Did I have a meaningful life?" Remember, in each stage of life we ask the question, "Who am I?" As Jack reaches retirement age, he begins to be aware that the largest part of life has been lived and wants to evaluate it. In Erikson's view, Jack's ability to look at his life history, including both accomplishments and missteps, and make peace with his decisions results in **integrity**. However, if that review leads to dissatisfaction with life, then Jack could develop **despair**. Despair can often leads to depression and hopelessness.

A final developmental task exists for Jack, and that is retrospection. He asks himself, "Did I meet my goals? Did I positively impact my world? Do people appreciate me or my work? If they don't appreciate it, have they been improved by it? Do I understand? Have I become wise? Have I been loved? Have I loved? What have I created or been part of that which will go on after I am gone?" Jack will wrestle with the answer to these and many other tough questions. The resulting answers (hopefully viewed through the lens of grace) determine the personal meaning of his life.

This stage can also occur out of sequence when people experience a terminal disease. Reflecting on their life can be a step of preparation for an early death. Whenever the time occurs, we trust that at the end of his life, Jack will look back and say, "Jesus, I hope I have done my best for you. I'm glad I walked with you during my life and I gladly trust you with the future."

And our desire for all the little growing Jacks and Jills is for them to hear Jesus say, "Well done, good and faithful servant."

Appendix C – The Heinz Dilemma

The Heinz's dilemma is a frequently used example in many ethics and morality classes. One well-known version of the dilemma, used in Lawrence Kohlberg's stages of moral development, is stated as follows:

A woman was near death from a special kind of cancer. There was one drug that the doctors thought might save her. It was a form of radium that a druggist in the same town had recently discovered. The drug was expensive to make, but the druggist was charging ten times what the drug cost him to produce. He paid $200 for the radium and charged $2,000 for a small dose of the drug.

Heinz, the sick woman's husband, went to everyone he knew to borrow the money, but he could only raise half of what it cost. He told the druggist that his wife was dying and asked him to sell it cheaper or let him pay later. But the druggist said, "No, I discovered the drug and I'm going to make money from it." So Heinz got desperate and broke into the man's store to steal the drug for his wife. Should Heinz have broken into the laboratory to steal the drug for his wife? Why or why not?

From a theoretical point of view, it is not important what the participant thinks that Heinz should *do*. Kohlberg's theory holds that the justification the participant offers is what is significant, the *form* of their response. Below are some of many examples of possible arguments that belong to the six stages:

Stage 1 (obedience): Heinz should not steal the medicine because he will consequently be put in prison which will mean he is a bad person. Or: Heinz should steal the medicine because it is only worth $200 and not how much the druggist wanted for it; Heinz had even offered to pay for it and was not stealing anything else.

Stage 2 (self-interest): Heinz should steal the medicine because he will be much happier if he saves his wife, even if he will have to serve a prison sentence. Or: Heinz should not steal the medicine because prison is an awful place, and he would more likely languish in a jail cell than over his wife's death.

Stage 3 (conformity): Heinz should steal the medicine because his wife expects it; he wants to be a good husband. Or: Heinz should not steal the drug because stealing is bad and he is not a criminal; he has tried to do everything he can without breaking the law, you cannot blame him.

Stage 4 (law-and-order): Heinz should not steal the medicine because the law prohibits stealing, making it illegal. Or: actions have consequences.

Stage 5 (human rights): Heinz should steal the medicine because everyone has a right to choose life, regardless of the law. Or: Heinz should not steal the medicine because the scientist has a right to fair compensation. Even if his wife is sick, it does not make stealing acceptable.

Stage 6 (universal human ethics): Heinz should steal the medicine, because saving a human life is a more fundamental value than the property rights of another person. Or: Heinz should not steal the medicine, because others also may need the medicine, and their lives are equally significant. [46]

Teaching morals and the biblical principles of living is one of the critical ways we disciple our children. Understanding and applying how our children learn moral values and grow in wisdom seems to be a fundamental role of Christian parenting. This part of parenting stands on par with nutrition and health care in making sure children grow into adult human beings who live for God.

Appendix D – Scripture Reading List

These Scripture readings were gathered by the recommendations of parents who raised mature Christian Disciples.

The Creation account	Genesis 1-2
The seduction of Adam and Eve	Genesis 3
Moses, the burning bush and Promised Land	Exodus 3
Moses and the plagues	Exodus 5-12
Moses and the Exodus	Exodus 12-14
The Ten Commandments	Exodus 19-20
David and Goliath	1 Samuel 16-17
Solomon's rise and fall	I Kings 9-11
Job's testing	Job
The meaning of life	Ecclesiastes 3, 12
Surviving the furnace	Daniel 3
Surviving the lions' den	Daniel 6
Jonah and the great fish	Jonah
The temptations of Christ	Matthew 4:1-11
Prayer	Matthew 6:5-15
Judging people	Matthew 7:1-6
The "Golden Rule"	Matthew 7:12
Wealth and salvation	Matthew 19:16-30
Servanthood	Matthew 20:20-28
Chasing out the money changers	Matthew 21:12-13
The Greatest Commandment	Matthew 22:34-40

The Last Supper	Matthew 26:17-30
Jesus' crucifixion	Matthew 27:57-28:15
Jesus' resurrection	Matthew 27:57-28:15
The Great Commission	Matthew 28:16-20
The birth of Christ	Luke 1-2
The Good Samaritan	Luke 10:25-37
Nicodemus and salvation	John 3:1-21
The ascension of Christ	Acts 1:6-11
The coming of the Holy Spirit	Acts 2:1-13
The early church	Acts 2
Saul's conversion	Acts 9:1-30
Falling short	Romans 3:9-31
The wages of sin	Romans 6:23
Spiritual gifts	1 Corinthians 12
Love	1 Corinthians 13
The fruit of the Spirit	Galatians 5:22-23
Faith in God	Hebrews 11

Reprinted with permission from the Barna Group, Revolutionary Parenting (2010), pages 122-124. www.barna.org.

Appendix E – Christian Parenting from Proverbs

Positive Attributes from the book of Proverbs

diligence (6:6-11; 11:27; 12:24; 13:4; 15:19; 18:9; 19:24; 20:4,13; 21:5; 22:13; 26:13-16)

justice (11:1; 16:11; 17:23; 20:10,23; 31:8-9)

kindness (11:17)

generosity (11:24; 19:6)

self-control, particularly of speech (12:18; 13:3; 21:23) and temper (14:17,29; 15:18; 16:32; 19:11; 25:28)

righteousness (12:21,28; 14:34)

truthfulness and honesty (12:22; 16:13; 24:26)

discretion in choosing friends (13:20; 18:24)

      particularly a spouse (18:22; 31:10-31)

caution and prudence (14:16; 27:12)

gentleness (15:1,4)

contentment (15:16-17; 16:8; 17:1)

integrity of character (15:27; 28:18)

humility (16:19; 18:12; 22:4)

graciousness (16:24)

forthrightness (rather than duplicity) 16:30; 17:20)

restraint (17:14, 27-28; 18:6-7; 29:20)

faithfulness in friendship (17:17) and otherwise (28:20)

purity (20:9; 22:11)

vigorous pursuit of what is good and right (20:29)

skillfulness in work (22:29)

patience (25:15)

Taken from *God, Marriage, and Family: Rebuilding the Biblical Foundation* by Andreas J. Kostenberger, 2nd. ed. © 2004, 2010, pp. 95. Used by permission of Crossway, a publishing ministry of Good News Publishers, Wheaton, IL 60187, www.crossway.org.

Appendix F – Christian Parent's Resources

What resources are there for parents who want to disciple their children according to biblical principles?

This Appendix shares some resources on Discipleship, the Great Commission and Parenting. Included are brief description of some of books we found most helpful. Parents will all be at different stages in life and Christian depth, so a brief survey will be discussed in this Appendix.

I. Discipleship Resources

Disciplemaking: A Self-Study Course on Follow-up and Discipleship by Robert E. Coleman, with Timothy Beougher and Tim Phillips, eds., (Billy Graham Center, 1994). Tom used this book for leadership development with a discipleship group and a sermon series, and can say from a first-hand experience it is very effective to disciple other people. The book gives a step by step approach to disciple[ing] that is easily transferred to parents.

The Master Plan of Discipleship by Robert Coleman is the follow-up to the book *The Master Plan of Evangelism*. The book takes a look at the book of Acts and how discipleship was done by the early church.

The Master Plan of Evangelism by Robert Coleman. This book goes into more specific detail about the concepts that we discussed in Section 2 of this book.

II. The Great Commission Resources

Prayer Evangelism: How to Change the Spiritual Climate over your Home, Neighborhood and City by Ed Silvoso. The premise of the book is "talking to God about our neighbors before we talk to our neighbors about God."[47] The main Scriptures the author uses are Luke 10:5, 6, 8, 9. *"When you enter a house, first say, 'Peace to this house.' If a man of peace is there, your peace will rest on him; if not, it will return to you... When you enter a town and are welcomed, eat what is set before you. Heal the sick who are there and tell them, 'The kingdom of God is near you."*

The four points he takes from this text are:

1. Speak peace to them
2. Fellowship with them
3. Take care of their needs
4. Proclaim the good news[48]

The author then tells of the importance of Matthew 28:18, "All authority has been given to Me in heaven and on earth." The author states, "A text without its context becomes a pretext. When we look at this verse (Matthew 28:19) isolated from its context, the weight of fulfilling the Great Commission comes to rest exclusively on our shoulders."[49]

The Great Commission Lifestyle by Robert Coleman takes the Great Commission from Matthew 28:18-20 and breaks it into three major areas. First, is the affirmation that all authority in heaven and earth is Jesus'. Second is the mandate of making disciples in all nations. Lastly, is the promise of the Holy Spirit. This book would be a good start to get an overview of the Great Commission.

The Mind of the Master by Robert Coleman. The following quote sets the context for the entire book, "Genuine witness is but the reflection of Christian experience. It can neither be worked up through emotional appeals nor engineered through clever organization. Hence, to the degree that we share the mind of Christ, and feel His passion for the Kingdom-to that degree His ministry comes alive."[50]

We know it is important in life to understand what is important to another person. This book describes the inner life and thoughts of Jesus by looking at what He said and did during his short life on this earth. This book was written within the context of His Great Commission.

Focusing on what Jesus focused on is the obvious starting point for the Great Commission. As follower, we too are called to be heavenly focused.

Out of the Saltshaker and into the World by Rebecca Pippert is a book about lifestyle evangelism. On several occasions, the author contrasts what a project is versus the lifestyle approach. The project approach to evangelism is what most people think of when they hear the word. It can be described as turning on and off your Christian witness when the timing is right. The lifestyle approach is the natural way of evangelism using the way Jesus evangelized. Obviously, the lifestyle approach would be best for disciple[ing] our children. Our children are way beyond just a project!

Authenticity and obedience is far more valuable than thinking you need to have all the answers.

III. Parenting and Discipleship Resources

God, Marriage and Family: Rebuilding the Biblical Foundation by Andreas Kostenberger, is one of the standard books on God, marriage and family. The book details God's design for families from a Biblical perspective. We would highly recommend a reading of this entire book. For our discussion on discipleship and parenting here are four areas to focus on.

1. Family worship, devotions, Bible Study
2. Maintaining family traditions
3. Engage in wholesome activities
4. Spiritual Warfare, there is an enemy

The Power of a Praying Parent by Stormie Omartian is a good resource for all parents. The author writes about the importance of spiritual warfare and being aware there is an enemy who wants to attack the God-given institution of marriage and parenting. This book goes on to discuss many culturally relevant issues and goes in great detail on marriage and the family. It is saturated with Scripture.

One of Omartian's key attributes of discipleship is prayer. Jesus constantly prayed for His disciples. (John 17) This book stresses the importance of praying for our children. The author details about 30 areas of prayer in regards to children. She stresses that no matter how old your children are it is important to be praying for your children.

After being convinced of the importance of praying for her children she did not have peace about the constant need for daily prayer for her children. She knew God wanted to have her constantly put her children in God's hands. "This didn't mean that we would now abdicate all responsibility as parents. Rather, we would declare ourselves to be in full partnership with God. He would shoulder the heaviness of the burden and provide wisdom, power, protection and ability far beyond ourselves."[51]

Omartian goes on to say that there is still the responsibility to teach and nurture their children. However, there was a release of stress knowing God was now involved in parenting. "An important part of our job was to keep the details or our child's life covered in prayer."[52]

She also stressed the importance of not praying for her will to be done but the importance of God's will in all prayers for her children. She writes, "I have found it's better to pray more along the lines of "Lord, show me how to pray for this child. Help me to raise him Your way, and may Your will be done in his life."[53]

Here is a good definition of prayer that is useful in the context of parenting and discipleship; "Prayer is acknowledging and experiencing the presence of God and inviting His presence into our lives and circumstances. It's seeking the presence of God and releasing the power of God which gives us the means to overcome any problem."[54]

Revolutionary Parenting: What the Research Shows Really Works by George Barna is based on research of parents who raised strong Christian children and the children who Barna considered revolutionary. He also came to the conclusion that the Biblical principles are the best advice on how to disciple a child.

Barna describes three types of parenting. The first type of parenting is parenting by default. Second, is the experimental (trial and error). Last, is the Revolutionary Parenting which is the model that would be the opposite of the first parenting model. Revolutionary Parenting is using God's Word as the basis of parenting, which would be disciple[ing] your child with the Christian worldview and the purpose of being obedient to God.

He calls these children spiritual champions who have a Biblical worldview, moral absolutes and believe God has created them. They also are service-oriented wanting to impact their world. Barna writes,

"By spiritual champions, I mean individuals who have embraced Jesus Christ as their Savior and Lord; accept the Bible as truth and as the guide for life; and to seek to live in obedience to its principles and in search of ways to continually deepen their relationship with God. Spiritual champions live in ways that are noticeably different from the norm-even when compared to the average churchgoer."[55]

What was very clear from the research is there were no set rules or predetermined formula for successful discipleship of our children. The research was clear that there was a consistency in the parents' spiritual life to Jesus and this was caught by their children.

Barna used the analogy of the coach to help describe Biblical parenting. Aspects such as clear goals, strong relationships, and a complete investment of time are good examples of coaching.

The surveys from the grown children who were considered spiritual champions stressed a common mistake their parents made was not spending enough time with them and the number one failure was not providing appropriate discipline.

4 proven methods for bringing your family close to God

Bible Reading and Application

Praying for Your Children

Family Worship

Life-style Discipleship

END NOTES

1 F. Philip Rice, Morality and Youth, (Westminster Press, Philadelphia, 1980) p15.

2 George Barna, "Barna Finds Four Mega-Themes in Recent Research," http://www.barna.org/culture-articles/89 [accessed February 8, 2010].

3 Christian Smith, with Melinda Lundquist Denton, Soul Searching The Religious and Spiritual Lives of American Teenagers (New York: Oxford University Press, 2005).

4 Smith, Soul Searching, 260.

5 Smith, Soul Searching, 260.

6 Smith, Soul Searching, 261.

7 Kenda Creasy Dean, Almost Christian: What The Faith Of Our Teenagers Is Telling The American Church (New York: Oxford University Press, 2010).

8 Dean, Almost Christian, 18.

9 Dean, Almost Christian, 18.

10 Dean, Almost Christian, 109.

11 Voddie T. Baucham, Jr., Family Driven Faith: Doing What it Takes to Raise Sons and Daughters Who Walk with God (Wheaton, IL: Crossway Books, 2007).

12 George Barna, "Parents Accept Responsibility For Their Childs Development But Struggle With Effectiveness," http://www.barna.org/barna-update/article/5-barna-update/120 [accessed February 8, 2010].

13 George Barna, "Parents Accept Responsibility For Their Childs Development But Struggle With Effectiveness," http://www.barna.org/barna-update/article/5-barna-update/120 [accessed February 8, 2010].

14 George Barna, "Research Shows That Spiritual Maturity Process Should Start At A young Age," http://www.barna.org/barna-update/article/5-barna-update/130 [accessed February 8, 2010].

15 George Barna, "Teens Evaluate The Church Based Ministry They Received As Children," http://www.barna.org/barna-update/article/5-barna-update/124 [accessed February 8, 2010].

16 George Barna, "Parents Describe How They Raise Their Children," http://www.barna.org/barna-update/article/5-barna-update/184 [accessed February 8, 2010].

17 Robert E. Coleman, The Master Plan of Evangelism (Westwood, NJ: Revell, 1978), 36.

18 Coleman, The Master Plan of Evangelism, 53.

19 Coleman, The Master Plan of Evangelism, 95.

[20]Coleman, The Master Plan of Evangelism, 29-30.

[21]Coleman, The Master Plan of Evangelism, 43.

[22]Coleman, The Master Plan of Evangelism, 46.

[23]Coleman, The Master Plan of Evangelism, 69.

[24]Coleman, The Master Plan of Evangelism, 76.

[25]Coleman, The Master Plan of Evangelism, 76.

[26] C.S. Lewis, Mere Christianity (Book IV Beyond Personality, Section 1 "The Good Infection.")

[27] *Thayer's Greek Lexicon*, Electronic Database (Biblesoft, Inc. 2003).

[28] Eugene Peterson, *The Message: The Bible in Contemporary Language* Electronic Database (Biblesoft, Inc. 2003).

[29] Pfeiffer and Harrison, ed. *The Wycliffe Bible Commentary*, 543.

[30] Henry David Thoreau. *Walden.* http://classiclit.about.com/library/bl-etexts/hdthoreau/bl-hdtho-wald-1.htm

[31] *Brown-Driver-Briggs Hebrew and English Lexicon, Unabridged*, Electronic Database (Biblesoft, Inc. 2003).

[32] Thomas C. Oden, *Pastoral Theology: Essentials of Ministry* (New York: HarperCollins, 1983.

[33] Thomas C. Oden, *Pastoral Theology*, 145.

[34] Thomas C. Oden, *Pastoral Theology*, 146.

[35]George Barna, "Spiritual Progress Hard Find In 2003," http://www.barna.org/barna-update/article/5-barna-update/132 [accessed February 8, 2010].

[36] *Brown-Driver-Briggs Hebrew and English Lexicon, Unabridged*, Electronic Database (Biblesoft, Inc. 2003).

[37] *Brown-Driver-Briggs Hebrew and English Lexicon, Unabridged*, Electronic Database (Biblesoft, Inc. 2003).

[38] Kenda Creasy Dean , Almost Christian: What The Faith Of Our Teenagers Is Telling The American Church (New York: Oxford University Press, 2010) 119-120.

[39] William Barclay, *The Gospel Of Matthew Vol. 2, 2nd ed.* (Philadelphia, PA: The Westminster Press 1958) Chapters 11-28.

[40] William Barclay, *The Gospel Of Mathew*, 178.

[41] Matthew Henry's Commentary on the Whole Bible: New Modern Edition, Electronic Database. (Hendrickson Publishers, Inc., 1991).

[42] *Adam Clarke's Commentary*, Electronic Database (Biblesoft, Inc. 2003).

[43] *Adam Clarke's Commentary*, Electronic Database (Biblesoft, Inc. 2003).

[44] *Adam Clarke's Commentary*, Electronic Database (Biblesoft, Inc. 2003).

[45] Joyce G. Baldwin. *Haggai, Zechariah, Malachi: An Introduction and Commentary*. Tyndale Old Testament Commentaries (Downers Grove, IL: InterVarsity, 1972.) 252.

[46] Wikipedia contributors. "Heinz dilemma." *Wikipedia, The Free Encyclopedia.*

Wikipedia, The Free Encyclopedia, 11 Feb. 2014. Web. 26 Feb. 2014.

[47]Ed Silvoso, *Prayer Evangelism* (Ventura, CA: Regal, 2000), 33.

[48]Ed Silvoso, *Prayer Evangelism*, 37.

[49]Ed Silvoso, *Prayer Evangelism*, 59.

[50]Robert E. Coleman, *The Mind of the Master* (Colorado Springs, CO: Waterbrook Press, 2000), 15.

[51]Stormie Omartian, *The Power of a Praying Parent* (Eugene, OR: Harvest House Publishers, 1995), 16.

[52]Stormie Omartian, The Power of a Praying Parent, 16.

[53]Stormie Omartian, The Power of a Praying Parent, 17.

[54]Stormie Omartian, The Power of a Praying Parent, 18.

[55]George Barna, Revolutionary Parenting: What the Research Shows Really Works, xvi.

www.ingramcontent.com/pod-product-compliance
Lightning Source LLC
Chambersburg PA
CBHW071302110426
42743CB00042B/1141